D0207136

INTEGRATING STUDY ABROAD
INTO THE CURRICULUM

INTEGRATING STUDY ABROAD INTO THE CURRICULUM

Theory and Practice Across the Disciplines

Edited by

Elizabeth Brewer
and Kiran Cunningham

Foreword by Madeleine F. Green

STERLING, VIRGINIA

COPYRIGHT © 2009 BY STYLUS PUBLISHING, LLC.

Published by Stylus Publishing, LLC
22883 Quicksilver Drive
Sterling, Virginia 20166-2102

All rights reserved. No part of this book may be reprinted or reproduced in any form or by any electronic, mechanical or other means, now known or hereafter invented, including photocopying, recording and information storage and retrieval, without permission in writing from the publisher.

Library of Congress Cataloging-in-Publication-Data
Integrating study abroad into the curriculum / edited by Elizabeth Brewer and Kiran Cunningham.
   p.   cm.
Includes bibliographical references and index.
ISBN 978-1-57922-348-9 (hardcover : alk. paper)—
ISBN 978-1-57922-349-6 (pbk. : alk. paper)
1. Foreign study—United States.   2. Foreign study—Administration—Handbooks, manuals, etc.   3. Universities and colleges—Curricula—United States.   I. Brewer, Elizabeth.   II. Cunningham, Kiran.
LB2376.I56   2010
370.116′2—dc22   2009010226

13-digit ISBN: 978-1-57922-348-9 (cloth)
13-digit ISBN: 978-1-57922-349-6 (paper)

Printed in the United States of America

All first editions printed on acid free paper
that meets the American National Standards Institute
Z39-48 Standard.

Bulk Purchases

Quantity discounts are available for use in workshops and for staff development.
Call 1-800-232-0223

First Edition, 2009

10 9 8 7 6 5 4 3 2 1

CONTENTS

FOREWORD

For much of higher education's history, many unexamined assumptions formed the foundation of its practices. Some of these assumptions shaped teaching and learning. For example, conventional wisdom held that students bore the sole responsibility for their success in learning, and that lectures and discussions were effective pedagogies for all students. It was assumed that students would make the connections among the various courses they took, either in a "cafeteria style" general education, or in the major. Additionally, there was little discussion of whether the completion of 120 credits equated to the mastery of a specified set of intellectual skills or body of knowledge. Other assumptions governed institutional behaviors. The recruitment of administrators rested on the belief that the most important qualification for an academic administrator is excellence in research. Many inside of higher education, and beyond, assumed that the quality of an institution is commensurate with the quality of its students or its wealth.

Like the larger higher education enterprise, international education had its own set of unexamined assumptions. Articles of faith in the field included that study abroad and language study, by definition, teach students cultural competence, or that the mere presence of international students internationalizes the campus and that more is always better. Another assumption about international education was that it consisted of a series of activities that were sufficient unto themselves, and that required no particular strategy for integration with each other or with the larger academic enterprise.

The era of the unexamined life in higher education—if it ever existed —is certainly over. The press for evidence of student learning by policy makers, accreditors, and the public has led to a series of national initiatives and transformed the conversation as well as practice on most campuses. The growing complexity of higher education institutions and the pressures of intensified competition and limited resources require every college and university to be intentional in its choices and strategic in its behaviors.

So, too, have educators engaged in a great deal of fresh thinking about internationalization in general and study abroad in particular. Globalization and the geopolitical realities of the post-9/11 world have driven home the need for U.S. graduates to be "globally competent," however an institution chooses to define that term. Most institutions cannot rely on study abroad as the major source of international learning for their students, since so few have a significant proportion of their student body going abroad. Thus, institutions that are serious about producing globally competent graduates must think beyond a course requirement here or an international student festival there to a broader and deeper institutional approach, centered on the campus and in the curriculum.

Similarly, faculty and administrators working on study abroad have recognized the need to become much more deliberate about the objectives for these experiences, about the connection of study abroad to the curriculum, and about the assessment of student learning through study abroad. This work takes on even greater importance at institutions like Kalamazoo and Beloit, where 85 and 50 percent, respectively, of their students study abroad. Thus, the editors and authors of this book are in a unique position to distill the lessons from their experiences for a wider audience.

This book provides both useful theoretical frameworks to apply in designing pre- and post-study abroad programs and helping students be reflective about their learning. It also provides many descriptive examples of how these frameworks are applied in very different courses and disciplines. It situates study abroad in the wider context of student learning and development theory and campus internationalization and provides rich detail that will help readers adapt these approaches to their own courses and institutions.

As U.S. colleges and universities seek to incorporate internationalization throughout the institution, study abroad will need to be a prominent and well-crafted strategy. Making study and work abroad accessible to more students is imperative; there is no better route to global learning than real-life experience in another culture. The old model of a junior year abroad in Europe for affluent students in search of an interesting experience clearly no longer serves American higher education. The task at hand is to accelerate the rate of change, bringing more students of color, more science majors, more part-time students into study and work abroad programs and ensuring that there are opportunities that fit their interests and needs. The growth of short-term study abroad requires even more careful design and intentional integration into the curriculum to avoid the risk of providing a superficial touristic experience.

The challenges of internationalization are clear. Elizabeth Brewer and Kiran Cunningham and their colleagues combine sound research and the lessons of experience in the classroom to help advance good practice in study abroad.

Madeleine F. Green
Vice President for International Initiatives
American Council on Education

INTRODUCTION

Elizabeth Brewer and Kiran Cunningham

"Improve the academic quality." "Reduce costs." "Increase enrollments." "Be more selective." "Find the best program for our students." Such divergent comments are not uncommon when administrators and faculty talk about study abroad. Further, they debate such topics as the purpose of study abroad (is it intercultural learning? maturation? being exposed to other parts of the world? serious academic study?) and who has responsibility for which aspects of study abroad (faculty—content; logistics, adaptation, and intercultural learning—the student and/or program staff). Students who have studied abroad also provide seemingly contradictory responses to their experiences: "Academically, I didn't learn a lot," but "I learned more than in all the rest of my time in college." "It was the best thing I ever did." "I wish I'd taken better advantage of what there was to do and learn."

Interest in study abroad is increasing in the United States among members of government, educators, parents, and students. Employers seek to hire staff with the intercultural competencies and flexibility often engendered by study abroad. Yet these interests sometimes are at odds with the realities of institutional and student resources and capacities, just as the quotes cited previously reveal some of the tensions surrounding the purpose, function, and administration of study abroad.

This book is born of a number of convictions:

- Study abroad can be enormously educational.
- There is no perfect program, nor can any one program or program type meet the needs of all students and institutions.
- Study abroad provides the opportunity to bridge the (artificial) separation of academic learning from experiential and intercultural learning.

- Resource limitations (institutional, personal) are real, are likely to become of greater concern in higher education in the coming decades, and will affect the shape of study abroad.
- It is our responsibility as educators to help prepare students for the particular kind of learning that takes place abroad and help them connect that learning to other aspects of their education.
- The more we do to integrate study abroad with the home campus curriculum, the more study abroad will benefit both our students and our campuses.

An emerging literature is addressing what makes study abroad effective on-site as well as mechanisms that facilitate the awarding of credit for study abroad toward the undergraduate degree. This volume looks at study abroad from a somewhat different angle, namely how our teaching and advising on the home campus can integrate study abroad with the curriculum. As the chapters in this volume attest, the integration of study abroad into the curriculum through teaching and advising requires faculty to modify their behaviors and learn new ways of teaching. Institutional change is also required. It is hoped, however, that the examples in this volume of teaching and advising as well as institutional supports for this work can be helpful to others seeking to similarly better connect students' experiences abroad with the work of the home campus.

What Is Curriculum Integration?

Curriculum integration is variously defined as a teaching philosophy drawing "from several subject areas to focus on a particular topic or theme" (McBrien & Brandt, 1997); an approach to education that "views learning and teaching in a holistic way and reflects the real world" (Innovative Teaching Concepts, n.d.), and pedagogies focusing on issues or concerns, teaching students to bring facts to bear on these, applying knowledge from other areas to them, and reflecting on the learning process (Beane, 1997). When applied to study abroad, curriculum integration "refers to a variety of institutional approaches designed to fully integrate study abroad options into the college experience and academic curricula for students in all majors" (NAFSA: Association of International Educators, 2008). In its most narrow sense, study abroad curriculum integration involves making sure that students can receive credit toward their degree programs for courses taken abroad. Given the great variations in instructional design and delivery in educational systems around the world, this is no easy thing, as students, study abroad advisors, faculty, and registrars can attest. Especially with the expansion or democratization of study abroad to include subject areas beyond its "traditional" domains of foreign language, humanities, and area/international studies, considerable work has and continues to be devoted at individual institutions and in disciplinary and international education associations to finding ways for students to earn credit toward their majors. When the task is too daunting, students may be encouraged to earn credit toward general education and elective courses instead.

Modern study abroad in the United States came into being in 1923, when the University of Delaware, then Delaware College, sent a group of eight students to France for their junior year. As argued by Gore (2005), study abroad from the start was meant to be academically rigorous and an activity that would contribute to the preparation of students for professional life and citizenship. In short, it was meant to enhance and be part of a student's academic studies. Nevertheless, the mechanics of integrating study abroad could not be taken for granted. A 1992 handbook entitled *Internationalizing the Undergraduate Curriculum,* published by the American Council on Education (ACE), for example, lauds Kalamazoo College for making it possible for a very large percentage of its students to study abroad through a campus calendar permitting study abroad regardless of major; offering a variety of programs meeting different linguistic, academic, and personal interests; and allowing financial aid to apply (Pickert & Turlington, 1992). At the time, few such examples of study abroad across an institution existed.

Although arguments to integrate study abroad into U.S. undergraduate studies have been persistent for some time (see, for example, Carlson, Burn, Useem, & Yachimowicz, 1990), the University of Minnesota undertook a major initiative in the late 1990s to encourage academic units not traditionally associated with study abroad to both identify ways in which study abroad could fit within a 4-year undergraduate course of study and make these known to faculty, advisors, and students. The project grew to encompass all of the university's schools and departments, and in 2004 led to a national conference on study abroad curriculum integration. The goals of Minnesota's curriculum integration efforts include the following:

1. increase integration of study abroad into all undergraduate majors and minors;
2. provide additional scholarships for study abroad;
3. enhance faculty/advisor awareness of the contributions that study abroad makes toward creating global citizens and well-educated students;
4. develop innovative practices, materials, partnerships and professional alliances;
5. [ensure that] 50% of each graduating class will have studied abroad; and
6. create long-term institutional change: a more "internationalized undergraduate experience. (University of Minnesota Learning Abroad Center, May 13, 2008.)

Other institutions have followed suit, tailoring curriculum integration to their particular philosophies and contexts. Villanova University, for example, emphasizes students' roles in the integration process through thoughtful preparation and program selection and follow-up upon return home (Villanova University Office of International Studies, n.d.). Augsburg College urges departments to take ownership of study abroad integration as well as to promote institutional change toward more internationalized experiences (Augsburg College Center for Global Studies, 2007). Michigan State University's curriculum integration project ultimately aims to help returned study abroad students integrate their experiences into their ongoing learning, but first the university is prioritizing greater access to study abroad across disciplines and the awarding of credit toward degree requirements (Michigan State University, n.d.).

The Forum on Education Abroad each year invites member institutions to nominate students for awards honoring research undertaken abroad, publishing the best examples in *Frontiers: The Interdisciplinary Journal of Study Abroad*. Introducing the award-winning research of Middlebury College student Brian Hoyer, David Macey (2005) argues that Hoyer is an example of the highest form of curriculum integration, a form that moves far beyond making sure a student can receive credit for study abroad courses and reentry programming. Rather, the best curriculum integration takes "academic experience to new levels" (Macey, 2005, p. 57), which is, in other words, transformational. It is to this kind of curriculum integration that the authors of the chapters in this volume aspire.

Common Institutional Barriers to Curricular Integration

Integrating study abroad education into the "home" curriculum is not without its challenges. Curricular change in general is difficult to create in the world of academia, but asking faculty to rethink or think differently about the content of courses is often met with significant resistance—and often for good reason. Faculty are charged with the responsibility of maintaining the integrity of the curriculum generally and the major more specifically, and this must be done in the face of seemingly endless requests to do things differently to keep up with pedagogical "best practices" and requests from across the campus to better integrate the curriculum with the co-curriculum.

Moreover, asking faculty to connect courses to study abroad is often perceived as asking them to teach in areas outside their expertise. Many assume, for example, that to connect their courses to study abroad would mean teaching about intercultural dynamics, for which they may lack training. Similarly, faculty whose expertise is U.S.-focused often assume that to connect their courses with study abroad means adding content about other countries, which they are unprepared to do.

At some institutions there may also be historical barriers to curriculum integration. At Kalamazoo College, for example, when in the late 1950s the faculty voted on the "K-Plan," which embedded study abroad and other off-campus experiences into the 4-year Kalamazoo College education, support for the then-radical change hinged on the assurance that the on-campus curriculum would not be affected. Although the faculty has completely turned over since then, and experiential education is now embraced as part of the Kalamazoo education, study abroad continues in some ways to be disconnected from faculty members' responsibilities. Indeed, in the college's most recent strategic planning process, "curricular integration" emerged as a central theme underlying many of the action items.

At Beloit College, study abroad began as a faculty-led initiative, and for many years, students traveled with faculty abroad and were supervised by them for the entire semester. This close involvement changed, however, as student demand for study abroad outpaced the number of faculty available to direct programs, and cost-of-living increases abroad made it financially difficult to continue to support this kind of faculty involvement. The addition of exchange programs and direct enrollment to the mix of study abroad offerings in the 1980s further eroded faculty involvement in their students' educational experiences abroad. Although the college could boast increasing study abroad enrollments, it no longer knew as much as desired about the study abroad experience, and thus shortly after 2000, Beloit College joined the trend toward campus internationalization described in chapter 1. This in turn led to greater attention to study abroad's integration with the curriculum, something that will need ongoing attention as the curriculum continues to change and new faculty join the college.

The awareness of barriers to study abroad's integration with the curriculum and a desire to increase the benefit of study abroad to individual students and the institutions led both Beloit College and Kalamazoo College to join ACE's Internationalization Collaborative, whose work is described in the following section.

Origins of the Collaboration Between Beloit College and Kalamazoo College

In January 2004, both Beloit College and Kalamazoo College sent small teams to the annual meeting of ACE's Internationalization Collaborative. Established in 2002, the Collaborative is described as a "learning community" of institutions across the United States, providing a "forum for faculty and administrators to share ideas and help each other in furthering their international agendas" with a focus on "institutional strategies and outcomes and key issues that need further research and advocacy" (ACE, 2008). At its annual meetings, member institutions assemble to learn from each other's best practices, pose questions for further investigation, and reflect on challenges and opportunities for institutional internationalization. Some sessions involve discussions across a variety of institutional types, whereas others bring together institutions of similar size and nature.

At the 2004 meeting, Kiran Cunningham facilitated a preconference workshop session at the meeting attended by Elizabeth Brewer, and the two realized that although both their colleges enjoyed long involvement with several aspects of internationalization and study abroad in particular, they also differed in their approaches and their stage of development along the internationalization continuum. Most obviously, Kalamazoo sends greater numbers of students abroad each year (some 85% of its students study abroad) than Beloit (50% of students). However, Kalamazoo's study abroad program is also structured differently, with its Center for International Programs (CIP) assuming responsibility for most of the programs in which Kalamazoo students study abroad. The average number of Kalamazoo students in any one study abroad site is roughly 8 to 10. Historically, Kalamazoo faculty members have had little to do with study abroad itself and the curriculum is designed with the assumption that students mostly will fill general education requirements while off campus. As CIP director Joe Brockington often says, Kalamazoo outsources its study abroad to in-country faculty and staff, albeit under the CIP's direction. Further, while Kalamazoo College does enroll some exchange students through its partnerships abroad, even with these the percentage of international students in the student body is just 4%. At the same time, the curriculum in Kalamazoo emphasizes experiential and inter-cultural learning, which, many scholars agree, are essential components of study abroad.

Beloit College's Office of International Education, on the other hand, is charged with facilitating campus internationalization more broadly. The average number of its students in any one study abroad site is two to three. Its students mostly study abroad as exchange students, direct-enrollment students in universities abroad, and students enrolled in third-party-provided programs. Of Beloit students, 50% spend one semester abroad, with roughly 10% of these staying abroad for a second Semester. Historically 10% of Beloit's student body has consisted of international students, both exchange (25%) and degree-seeking (75%). Since 2002, Beloit College has emphasized the integration of study abroad into the curriculum, focusing on faculty development activities and curriculum development. These efforts have led to widespread ownership of international education and study abroad across the college.

Cunningham came to Beloit College in 2005 as a member of an international education external review team. The 2-day visit offered opportunities for more extended discussion with faculty, students, and administrators. Like Beloit, Kalamazoo also had recently assessed its program of international education and study abroad. Data from both assessments indicated that although study abroad was generally accepted at both institutions as the most robust vehicle for international education, its connection to the curriculum was not evident to many faculty and students. It thus became a natural step at a subsequent ACE Collaborative meeting attended by teams from both institutions to discuss how they might work together to further their internationalization efforts. This led to an application for a mini-grant from the Collaborative.

The proposal the two colleges submitted would draw on each other's strengths and help each advance their work by learning from each other in a project that would bring faculty from both institutions together in two curriculum development workshops. In the first workshop, held in the fall, the faculty would use a set of common texts as a basis for discussing strategies to integrate study abroad into the curriculum. In the second, held in the spring, they would share class assignments and course syllabi developed in the intervening period, with those already teaching the courses they had modified or developed discussing their experiences. By collaborating in this way, Beloit College faculty members hoped to learn from Kalamazoo's greater experience with using intercultural and community-based learning methods, whereas Kalamazoo faculty members hoped to learn from Beloit faculty members' greater engagement with study abroad through teaching and advising. Many of the chapters in this volume followed directly from these workshops.

Applicability of This Volume to Other Institutions and Institutional Types

Beloit College and Kalamazoo College are liberal arts colleges with relatively high (Beloit) and quite high (Kalamazoo) study abroad enrollments. Both institutions identify themselves as international, include international learning goals in their mission statements, and emphasize international education in their promotional materials. How relevant are their experiences integrating study abroad into the curriculum to other institutions and institutional types?

The editors and authors of this volume believe their experiences can be relevant to other institutions and institutional types. First, integrating study abroad into the curriculum depends on intention, not material resources. Neither Beloit nor Kalamazoo can be said to be wealthy institutions; their endowments are relatively modest and most of their students receive substantial financial aid. Further, although both institutions' efforts benefited from the receipt of external resources to support faculty development activities leading to curricular innovations, as seen in the final chapter of this volume, much work was accomplished with no additional funding. Instead, the work began with listening (to students and colleagues), assessment (of study abroad experiences in particular), and conversation (about what the institutions, faculty, and students were trying to accomplish; why they were trying to accomplish it; and how they were trying to accomplish it). It continued with bringing faculty together to explore different curricular models, to experiment with assignments in development for their students, and to share that work.

As noted previously, a small grant from the ACE led to a curricular collaboration between Beloit College and Kalamazoo College. To disseminate the findings from that collaboration, several participants conducted a workshop in conjunction with the ACE Internationalization Collaborative's February 2008 meeting. Readings distributed in advance of the meeting served to begin a discussion of challenges and ways to integrate study abroad into the undergraduate curriculum, after which examples of curriculum development from the Beloit/Kalamazoo collaboration were presented. The remainder of the workshop was devoted to the development of ideas for curriculum development in the 18 participants' diverse disciplines (from modern languages to nursing) at their different institutions (from community colleges to research universities, with just one liberal arts institution represented) and the institutions' different stages of development along the internationalization continuum. Although the 3-hour workshop could not be expected to produce immediate results, it did serve as a stimulus for thinking about ways to integrate study abroad with the on-campus curriculum, no matter the discipline or institutional type. The participants reported the workshop was quite productive for their thinking about their own work and institutions; curricular examples can, it seems, provide fruitful models for others. It is hoped that the chapters in this volume will serve a similar purpose.

As readers turn to the various chapters that follow this introduction, they will want to look for ideas and practices for adaptation and/or use these to identify and assess similar work being undertaken at their own campuses. They also will want to reflect on how the work of integrating study abroad into the curriculum on the home campus can align with institutional mission and resources, and how conversations within and across academic and administrative units can help advance an institution developmentally.

Overview of the Chapters

This volume begins with two chapters presenting different theoretical perspectives relevant to the integration of study abroad into the curriculum. These are followed by nine chapters providing examples from different disciplines of study abroad integration through teaching and advising. The concluding chapter discusses faculty development activities, and institutional structures and policies supporting curriculum integration.

Chapter 1, "Capturing Study Abroad's Transformative Potential," begins with a discussion of factors that make it difficult for study abroad students to succeed (spending too much time with fellow Americans, lacking language and intercultural skills, ignorance about the host country, difficulties navigating a different educational model, failure to want to learn and engage, weak connection to home campus teaching and learning). Chapter 1 also discusses factors that contribute to study abroad's success, including attention to curriculum; teaching students to learn experientially and interculturally; encouraging reflection; and providing interventions before, during, and after study abroad. As the focus of the volume is on what takes place at the home campus, Elizabeth Brewer and Kiran Cunningham then turn the discussion to the move in higher education toward campus internationalization, which calls for an integrative approach to international education across the institution, as opposed to a set of discrete activities confined to a few administrative units and academic departments. It also looks at structural and historical challenges to study abroad, including falling enrollments in foreign language courses, and competing goals for study abroad, such as skills acquisition for the global marketplace versus personal maturation. The chapter then addresses the dissonance essential to transformative learning, students' readiness developmentally to take advantage of study abroad's learning potential, and the elements of the intercultural toolkit that can support that learning (place-specific knowledge; intercultural theory and skills; and self-knowledge, both positional and attitudinal).

Chapter 2, "Lessons From Geography: Mental Maps and Spacial Narratives," demonstrates how different disciplinary methods can make students more conscious of their sense of place and space, cultural norms, spatial narratives, and stereotypes. This in turn can help them break through the comfort zones increasingly found in study abroad sites. Darren Kelly argues as well that an acquaintanceship with urban theory and practice in observation, mental and other forms of mapping, and physical navigation of host sites will not only help students grow more confident as observers and actors in their new environments, but help themselves better understand both them and their home environments and societies, and contribute to the quality of their reflection about their study abroad.

In chapter 3, "Preparatory Courses for Students Going to Divergent Sites," Elizabeth Brewer and Jan Solberg provide examples of study abroad preparatory courses taught at Beloit College and Kalamazoo College. Assessment data at both institutions led to the conclusion that additional preparation in the form of a course might strengthen the learning outcomes of study abroad for at least some students. The courses developed at the two institutions differ somewhat: Beloit's course puts more emphasis on the acquisition of country-specific knowledge and the development of skills useful in study abroad such as documentation, whereas Kalamazoo's helps students prepare for an integrative cultural research project undertaken abroad. However, both include materials from different disciplines, teach students observation skills, help them develop habits of inquiry and reflection, and draw on intercultural learning theory and practices. The authors discuss not only the challenges of staffing and scheduling such courses, but also how the courses have helped other faculty members develop curricular units within their courses to better prepare students for study abroad. Appendices to the chapter contain examples of assignments and student writing.

In chapter 4, "Culture, Religion, and Nationality: Developing Ethnographic Skills and Reflective Practices Connected to Study Abroad," Carol Anderson and Kiran Cunningham describe and assess their team-taught course originally designed for both departing sophomores and returning juniors. The course draws on a combination of anthropology and religious studies to create a focus on the connections and disjunctures among culture, religion, and nationality. Students are asked to explore these connections in their fieldwork with faith communities in Kalamazoo, reflect on the way they have played out in their own lives, and either anticipate (for sophomores) or think back on (for juniors) the nature of these dynamics in their study abroad site. Developed with the premise that students studying abroad must be equipped with an intercultural toolkit of essential knowledge, attitudes, and skills, the course focuses on training students in ethnographic methods, helping them become adept at understanding and applying theory, developing the skills of structured reflection, and increasing their ability to learn experientially. In addition to describing the way the course works, the authors analyze a sample of work to determine the degree to which this kind of learning is occurring.

Preparing students for study abroad is also a key focus of discussion in chapter 5, "Embedding Preparation in Language Courses: Bonn and Erlangen." Jennifer Redmann argues that conventional ways of teaching language courses may not be preparing students sufficiently for the study abroad experience. Rather than focusing solely on linguistic competence and mastering grammatical structures in controlled classroom settings, foreign language faculty need to rethink the language curriculum so that it is attentive to cultural competence more generally. After discussing the revamped German curriculum at Kalamazoo College, which she and her colleague designed to be more fully integrated with study abroad, Redmann describes a predeparture course she teaches at Kalamazoo College that combines intermediate-level language learning with a focus on Bonn and Erlangen, the two German cities where Kalamazoo College students study. In this course, students develop their linguistic abilities in the context of learning about the city, university, and dorm in which they will be living.

This focus on cities is continued in chapters 6, 7, and 8. Chapter 6, "Semiotics and the City: Putting Theories of Everyday Life, Literature, and Culture Into Practice," is based on a course taught in Ireland to study abroad students. Darren Kelly provides examples of classroom activities, reading assignments, and experiential learning activities in the city of Dublin. These in turn show how connections can be made between the classroom and the street, as well as between high and low culture. Semiotics, *flânerie,* and lessons from French philosophy and the theory of everyday life provide students with the tools to negotiate the city and to unpack its meaning, and novels in which the city also serves as a text provide students with examples of how others have learned to "read" urban settings.

Chapter 7 adds the dimensions of historical comparison and service learning to understanding cities. In "Cool Cities: Kalamazoo and Carthage—The Intersection of Service Learning and Intercultural Learning," classics professors Anne Haeckl and Elizabeth Manwell describe a course designed with multiple goals in mind. First, the course is designed to help students see the relevance of studying antiquity to living their lives today. Through a comparison of Carthage and Kalamazoo, students come to understand some of the similar structural and historical contexts for the urban problems of poverty and cultural marginality. Participation in service-learning projects fosters a sense of immediacy of these issues for students as they work with others in the broader community to address these problems through projects involving, for example, urban planning and public art. Finally, the comparative dimension of the course invites students to examine their own experiences in foreign cities, either while studying abroad or while traveling more generally. These discussions are valuable for students returning from study abroad as they make sense of their experiences. For those soon to be leaving for study abroad, the discussions provide them with a conceptual framework they can use to interpret the urban contexts in which they will be living.

The courses discussed in chapters 8 and 9 represent creative curricular solutions to challenges to successful learning connected to study abroad. In both cases, faculty at the home campus are involved in learning taking place abroad, but are only on-site for short periods. Chapter 8, "Chinese Cities in Transition: The City as Classroom," incorporates distance learning to address challenges connected to a study abroad program in China. Beloit College has sent students to partner universities in China since the mid-1980s, where their curriculum consists of Chinese language instruction. The results, however, in terms of both gains in language competency and understanding China, were uneven. Living and studying with other international students presented one set of obstacles, along with the absence of on-site staff to facilitate intercultural and experiential learning. The course Daniel Youd discusses in the chapter was thus developed to provide students with strategies to learn more effectively through assignments engaging them with local people and environments. Taught largely as a distance-learning course, "Chinese Cities in Transition" enables the instructor to fulfill other teaching obligations at the college, with only a 10-day period on site with the students immediately before the start of the semester and a week on site in the middle of the semester when Beloit has a mid-semester break. Youd uses assignments and student work to illustrate the chapter.

In chapter 9, "Health and Microcredit: Beloit as a Laboratory for Understanding Nicaragua," Nancy Krusko offers an example of how a course with an embedded travel segment can help prepare students for citizenship by studying issues locally, traveling elsewhere for comparative field study, then returning to campus to synthesize the students' learning. In this case, the city of Beloit and several locations in Nicaragua become the laboratories for examining connections between poverty and health. Fieldwork, other activities, and interdisciplinary studies of Nicaragua help the students in the first half of the course gain the knowledge and skills they will need to learn experientially and interculturally in the week they spend abroad. Other readings and assignments teach them about health, poverty, and microcredit programs. Upon return from Nicaragua, reflection helps them unpack their observations and experience, connect them to their studies from the first half of the semester, and select and organize these for presentation to the campus community. Born of faculty–student collaboration and nurtured by the instructor's participation in various faculty development activities, the course offers lessons for others seeking relatively inexpensive ways to increase their students' understanding of the world.

The intersections of science study with study abroad are the subject of chapter 10, "Building Global Awareness Through Biology, Public Health, and Study Abroad." Marion Fass and Ann Fraser take as the chapter's premise that scientific methods of developing and testing ideas through observation and measurement can be transferred effectively to study abroad, both when the study abroad involves science study and when it does not. Examples from faculty development activities and students' study abroad experiences illustrate how the study of science can open up questions for students as they navigate and make sense of their study abroad sites. The chapter also illustrates how science courses taught on the home campus can prepare both science and nonscience majors for their study abroad experiences. Finally, the chapter provides examples of how courses, advising, other experiential learning activities, and synthesizing activities following study abroad can enable students to put their experiences abroad in the context of larger scientific inquiry, expand their knowledge, and help them develop their postgraduation plans.

The senior thesis in international relations, discussed in chapter 11, "Synthesis and Career Preparation: The International Relations Senior Thesis," is an example of how study abroad can be synthesized with students' academic programs on the home campus as well as with their pathways after graduation. Pablo Toral uses three students' experiences to argue that a senior thesis building on research and other activities undertaken during study abroad can bridge the gap between study abroad as a means to acquire knowledge and skills useful in the marketplace and study abroad as a means for personal growth and confidence building. Further, the chapter demonstrates how course selection and advising can position students to select study abroad opportunities to supplement and complement their prior studies. The combination of these, in turn, will prepare them for their senior year, in which further academic studies and the senior thesis will enable them to both add to the prior knowledge they have gained, and help them shape their postgraduation plans. The senior thesis also can help them put their personal and emotional experiences abroad into a productive dialogue with academic theory and practice.

In the final chapter "Capacity Building for Study Abroad Integration," Elizabeth Brewer and Kiran Cunningham discuss the importance of building institutional and faculty capacity to support the integration of study abroad into the undergraduate curriculum. Drawing on the discussion in chapter 1 as well as on research on institutional transformation within higher education, the authors argue that a focus on campus internationalization, rather than discrete sets of activities, allows faculty members to identify study abroad integration as part of their responsibilities. Further, paying attention to the process of internationalization can help institutions deploy resources strategically and intentionally to support study abroad integration. The chapter then provides a number of examples of faculty development activities. These begin with supports to help faculty members advise more effectively about study abroad and culminate with workshops, seminars, and individual activities resulting in curricular transformation. The chapter concludes with examples of how faculty development activities led to the examples of curriculum integration presented throughout the volume. It is the authors' hope that these examples will provide both individual faculty members and institutions with pedagogical strategies useful to their own efforts to integrate study abroad into the undergraduate curriculum.

References

American Council on Education. (n.d.). The internationalization collaborative. Retrieved September 10, 2008, from http://www.acenet.edu/Content/Navigation Menu/ProgramsServices/cii/current/networks/Collaborative.htm.

Augsburg College Center for Global Studies. (2007). Office of International Programs AQIP project study abroad curriculum integration survey: Faculty and staff results summary. Retrieved August 2, 2008, from http://www.augsburg.edu/augsburgabroad/FacStaffAdv%20Results%20Summary.pdf.

Beane, J. (1997). *Curriculum integration.* New York: Teachers College.

Carlson, J. S., Burn, B. B., Useem, J., & Yachimowicz, D. (1990). *Study abroad: The experience of American undergraduates.* Westport, CT: Greenwood.

Gore, J. E. (2005). *Dominant beliefs and alternative voices: Discourse, belief, and gender in American study abroad.* New York: Routledge.

Innovative Teaching Concepts (n.d.). What are thematic teaching and curriculum integration? Retrieved July 1, 2008, from http://www.todaysteacher.com/TheematicTeaching.htm

Macey, D. (2005, November). Intellectual growth and the integration of study abroad experience. *Frontiers: The Interdisciplinary Journal of Study Abroad, 12,* 56–58.

McBrien, J. L., & Brandt, R. S. (1997). *The language of learning: A guide to education terms.* Alexandria, VA: Association for Supervision and Curriculum Development.

Michigan State University. (n.d.). MSU study abroad curriculum integration project. Retrieved August 2, 2008 from http://studyabroad.msu.edu/currintegration/project.html.

NAFSA: Association of International Educators. (2008). Internationalization at home. Retrieved July 21, 2008, from http://www.nafsa.org/knowledge_community_network.sec/teaching_learningand/pfwinternationalizing_the_3/practice_resources_24/iahbest_practices.

Pickert, S., & Turlington, B. (1992). *Internationalizing the undergraduate curriculum: A handbook for campus leaders.* Washington DC: American Council on Education.

University of Minnesota Learning Abroad Center. (May 13, 2008). University of Minnesota model of curriculum integration. Retrieved August 2, 2008, from http://www.umabroad.umn.edu/ci/whatisCI/model.html.

Villanova University Office of International Studies. (n.d.). Curriculum integration. Retrieved July 21, 2008, from http://www.villanova.edu/vpaa/intlstudies/faculty/.

CAPTURING STUDY ABROAD'S TRANSFORMATIVE POTENTIAL

Elizabeth Brewer and Kiran Cunningham

S tudents know when and why study abroad fails or succeeds. In evaluations of their experiences they report failure—or less than optimal
results—when they spend too much time with other Americans, when
they take part in "silly" group field trips resembling tourism more than
engaged exploration, and when lack of language skills and/or outsider status
makes communication difficult or impossible. They also may report that the
academics of the program bring little benefit, because the local educational
system is difficult to navigate, courses are pitched too low, or graded assignments are too few and far between. In these cases, students may feel that
academically they achieved very little, but nevertheless gained new insight
into their studies at home through their out-of-classroom experiences. When
study abroad "fails," students also acknowledge their own shortcomings,
such as an inability or unwillingness to take the risks required to move
beyond their familiar comfort zones to engage with the host community and
culture. They also may report that they saw a study abroad semester as a way
to take a semester off, but still get credit, and thus never really meant to learn
very much. Frequently they also acknowledge that their ignorance of country-specific knowledge made it very difficult to put their experiences and
observations into anything other than a personal explanation. Despite the
sharp rise in short-term study abroad, they also know that length matters.
Students who spend two weeks in Germany in a short "Maymester" and

nine weeks the next summer know they learned more during the latter. And virtually all semester sojourners report just beginning to "get" it when it is time to return home.

Conversely, when study abroad works, students understand why. To quote from a student evaluation, "Taking history courses for the first time, one of my worst subjects until now, I learned so much. I didn't just do well on the test, I absorbed so much I could share it with other people. I actually got to see the sights we were talking about, and could use all my senses to really learn something." Another student writes that study abroad enriched her education "by showing me yet another way to think in the interdisciplinary vein. It gave me more to draw on and rounded out lessons I'd already learned by forcing me to put my education into practice." And, "at home my classmates and I discussed how important experience was to learning something. How much could you learn from a book? How valuable was experience? After studying abroad, I realize how important experience is to education. It teaches you about yourself, your culture, your host culture, and, most importantly, it helps you to connect concepts you have studied in the classroom with real life" (Beloit College, 2007–2008).

Those who *study* study abroad arrive at similar conclusions, albeit through less personal analytic frames. As a starting point, most professionals working in study abroad and international education today embrace the notion that study abroad can enable students "to learn things and learn in ways that aren't possible on the home campus" (Vande Berg, 2007, p. 392). Selby (2008) argues that, whereas students see study abroad's rewards as life-changing, faculty continue to set goals for study abroad that largely mirror the goals for the classes they teach on campus. Similarly, Mestenhauser (1998) argues that the home campus curriculum in which study abroad rightly should be embedded neglects cultural considerations when infusing international content into courses. Goode (2008), in a study of the role of faculty study abroad directors, finds that faculty directors are least comfortable with the intercultural aspects of student learning. Because they are unfamiliar with definitions of intercultural competency and intercultural learning pedagogy, they therefore neglect intercultural learning when designing their programs and study abroad syllabi. To counter or correct the curricular flaws of study abroad, Paige, Cohen, Kappler, Chi, and Lassegard (2002) argue that curricular interventions may positively influence the nonacademic outcomes of study abroad, such as cultural learning. Edwards (2000), writing about American students studying in Britain, likens study abroad to anthropological fieldwork, and suggests that learning outcomes will be enhanced if students are taught such research methods as ethnography and participant observation. Pusch and Merrill (2008), writing specifically about international service learning but with implications for other forms of study abroad, agree with Edwards that to be successful, study abroad/service-learning students need to understand how to learn experientially, and with Mestenhauser (1998), Paige (1993), and others, that they need as well to understand how to learn interculturally. To these they would add country- or culture-specific knowledge such as "history, politics, social institutions, artistic heritage, etc.," as well as language as prerequisites for deep learning and effective action (Pusch & Merrill, 2008, p. 298). Brustein (2007) would point us to curricular innovations needed on the home campus to integrate study abroad into degree programs, to encourage the development of critical thinking skills, establish and assess global competence as a learning outcome, and join disciplinary studies with international and area studies.

A number of authors insist the time has passed when it could be assumed that mere study and presence in another country could produce meaningful results. Instead, preparation and interventions are needed while the student is abroad, not just at the beginning but throughout a study abroad program, if study abroad's potential is to be realized (Engle & Engle, 2002; Vande Berg, 2007). This argument, along with arguments about the importance of reflection and that intercultural skills and behaviors must be taught if students' experiences are to have meaning, are echoed throughout the chapters in a 2008 volume largely devoted to the intercultural and transformative aspects of study abroad (Savicki, 2008a).

This volume builds on that work and the work of others, by focusing the conversation back on the home campus, where the work of readying students before they leave and capturing the learning when they return takes place. Unless students are ready for the experience, the tremendous potential for intercultural development and transformative learning embedded in the study abroad experience is not likely to be realized.

The Shift to Campus Internationalization/ Internationalization at Home

In the 1990s, particularly in the United States and the European Union, a move toward internationalization took place in higher education, replacing a conception of international education as largely consisting of the movement of individuals across borders (study abroad students, international students, faculty) and a focus on a narrow set of disciplines (area and international studies, foreign languages). Critiques of international education to date in the United States included the failure to apply lessons from study abroad and international student experiences to the curriculum (Mestenhauser & Ellingboe, 1998); the danger of excluding from international education students studying subjects other than language and area studies, thereby retaining their "parochial and provincial" outlooks (ACE, 1995); and the fallacy of substituting the infusion of international content into courses for immersion in another culture, only the latter of which can, through "polyphasic learning," teach one how to function in another culture (Dobbert, 1998). Others argued that, despite significant increases in study abroad enrollments since the 1980s and the professionalization of study abroad and international education offices, in general American students' factual knowledge of the world and their intercultural skills had scarcely grown, largely because faculty had failed to believe that their scholarship and teaching would benefit from their own engagement with internationalization (Stohl, 2007).

Data from studies of American higher education institutions reveal relatively little effect from international education activities on the majority of U.S. students. A 2002 report issued by ACE, for example, showed that only 8% of students studied a foreign language, 3% studied abroad before graduation, and in the 1980s only 14% of students took four or more credits of coursework with significant international content (Engberg & Green, 2002). ACE's more recent report on the status of the internationalization of U.S. higher education indicates that the percentage of colleges and universities requiring a course with international or global content for graduation actually dropped to 37% in 2006 from 41% in 2001, although more were referring to international or global education in their mission statements (40% in 2006, 28% in 2001) and more were offering some kind of study or education abroad opportunities (91% in 2006, 65% in 2001). Further, more were providing opportunities for their faculty to gain international experiences as well (ACE, 2008).

Concern about relatively low rates of student and faculty mobility in Europe and the failure of universities to educate students to participate in increasingly multicultural societies led to a call in 1998 at a meeting of the

European Association of International Educators (EAIE) for a shift from a focus on mobility to "Internationalization at Home" (IaH). The idea was to develop "a conceptually integrated systems approach to international education that encompasses the entire university" enabling all students, faculty, and staff to be internationally engaged at one or more points (NAFSA, 2008). By 2003, enough work had been done to further define and implement IaH for the *Journal of Studies in International Education* to publish a special issue on the subject (Nilsson & Otten, 2003). During the next 4 years, 27% of the articles published in 31 issues of the same journal focused on IaH, and IaH could be argued to have become both mainstream and central to higher education (Kehm & Teichler, 2007). Further, the EAIE today has a special interest group devoted to IaH, its annual conference has an IaH track, and other meetings are regularly held on the topic (http://www.eaie.org).

Similar to the EAIE's role in promoting IaH, several organizations in the United States also have taken up the task. NAFSA: The Association of International Educators, by far the largest international education member organization, promotes "the exchange of students and scholars to and from the United States" (NAFSA, n.d.). Its most recent 2008 meeting in Washington, D.C., for example, attracted more than 9,000 participants, more than one third of whom came from outside the United States. Despite its focus on mobility, NAFSA is also concerned with campus internationalization, and its members may elect to join a knowledge community, Internationalizing the Curriculum and Campus Network. Since 2003, NAFSA also has encouraged internationalization efforts by holding a competition each year to recognize best practices in internationalization at colleges and universities.

Whereas NAFSA's definition of internationalization in some ways appears to replicate the list of traditional international education activities (international linkages, study abroad and international student enrollments, foreign language training, curriculum initiatives, and so on), ACE draws on Knight's 2003 updated definition of internationalization "as the process of integrating an international, intercultural or global dimension into the purpose, functions, or delivery of postsecondary education" (p. 2). Knight's original definition did not include reference to global dimensions, and she and Altbach caution against confusing "globalization" with "internationalization," arguing that in internationalizing themselves, institutions of higher education can help their students navigate globalization (Altbach & Knight, 2007). As in the case of European IaH, work is currently being undertaken to better understand and more closely link education initiatives around domestic diversity with internationalization. ACE thus sees parallels between the processes of internationalization and those of multicultural education as promoting institutional transformation, and finds that these intersect in a number of areas, including the development of intercultural skills; helping students understand issues of social justice at home and elsewhere; examining values, attitudes, and responsibilities for local and global citizenship; and preparing students for a multicultural and global workplace (Olson, Evans, & Shoenberg, 2007).

For the purposes of this volume, internationalization has enabled faculty at the editors' home institutions, Beloit College and Kalamazoo College, to bring study abroad into their daily practice as educators, rather than leaving responsibility for the learning that takes place in study abroad solely in the hands of its participants, program providers, and host universities. The shift in thinking about study abroad as part of the process of campus internationalization and having a direct relationship to teaching and advising is not only positively influencing individual study abroad students' experiences, but is also influencing the education of other students and the quality and character of the institutions.

Structural and Historical Challenges to Realizing Study Abroad's Potential

Into the 1980s, study abroad's value was seen in allowing students to increase fluency in another language and extend their disciplinary knowledge through study at a university or in a program in another country. Anything taking place outside the classroom was considered "unacademic" and unmeasurable, and program providers offering "field" and other experiential learning opportunities were automatically suspect in many colleges and universities. Indeed, to receive credit, a course taken abroad had to closely resemble a course on the home campus. At the semiannual meetings of the informal network of study abroad advisors commonly referred to by its members as the "New England Mafia," only one or two outlier institutions could imagine a more expansive definition of curriculum and program intention. By 1988, however, an urgency to increase study abroad participation rates, include students and majors traditionally excluded from it, and expand to locations beyond western Europe had arisen, as set down in a report from the Advisory Council for International Educational Exchange (1988). Under the title "Educating for Global Competence," the report saw undergraduate study abroad as particularly important to furthering the international dimension of higher education and made four primary recommendations: (a) increase undergraduate study abroad participation to 10% by 1995, matching the European Union goal for its member nations; (b) expand study abroad participation to include students from underrepresented majors and social groups, as well as to include more potential leaders; (c) extend study abroad to countries outside "Anglo-European" settings; and (d) place responsibility for college and university internationalization at the highest administrative and leadership levels. A primary driver behind the report was the recognition that in an increasingly interdependent world, the United States would fall behind unless more Americans were globally competent. Study abroad would be a particularly robust vehicle for delivering this competence, *if* it could transform itself from its traditional junior-year abroad focus on European cultural heritage, embedded in liberal arts and humanities, to include majors in the social and natural sciences and the professions.

Writing two years later in an occasional paper, Barbara B. Burn, an early and strong proponent of international educational exchange, described the role of study abroad as increasing language competency and, hopefully, fulfilling requirements toward the major:

> To expand the role of study abroad in international education, more American students should be encouraged to study abroad, especially in immersion situations that require or facilitate gaining a knowledge of the host country language, and, to the extent possible, as part of their studies toward requirements of the major. (1990, p. 41)

By 1995, the American Council on Education (ACE) was advocating adding intercultural competence to the internationalization agenda (ACE, 1995).

Eight years later, NAFSA: The Association of International Educators (which is still known by the acronym of its former name, the National Association of Foreign Student Advisors) issued a report describing the purposes of study abroad. Completing work toward the major was no longer mentioned; however, to foreign language learning were added "understanding others" and "understanding ourselves." Quoting Joyce Bylander, then Dean of Students at Dickinson College, the report promotes study abroad as helping make the country more "secure and economically competitive" by increasing students' capacity to tolerate, in Bylander's words, "dissonance and discomfort" while functioning in another culture. This capacity would enable them to go anywhere in the world following graduation (NAFSA, 2003, p. 5).

Despite the continued call for more Americans to learn foreign languages, the number of U.S. undergraduates studying a foreign language remains quite low (ACE, 2008) and the number of study abroad programs requiring no prior language study and minimum levels of language study during the program is rather high. Nevertheless, foreign language study and the acquisition of skills useful in the global workforce remain central goals for study abroad among policy advocates, as do the democratization of study abroad through inclusion of nontraditional students and subject areas, and a substantial increase in participation rates. Indeed, the 2005 Lincoln Commission, which gave rise to the 2007 Senator Paul Simon Study Abroad Foundation Act of 2007 (H.R. 1469 and S. 991), recommends increasing study abroad participation to one million American undergraduates by 2016–2017 (Commission on the Abraham Lincoln Study Abroad Fellowship Program, 2005).

Whereas policy makers thus now see study abroad's role as increasing foreign language competency among Americans and teaching skills useful for the global marketplace, students and their parents often identify the desired outcomes of study abroad quite differently, namely as personal maturation and the attainment of greater self-confidence. In turn, many advocates of study abroad now describe its strongest outcomes, as discussed in the following text, as increased intercultural competency and affective learning and argue that for these to be realized, students must know how to learn experientially. Our hope with this volume is to provide examples of how intercultural and transformative learning can contribute to disciplinary and interdisciplinary learning, and how these in turn can contribute to intercultural and transformative learning, as the most robust form of study abroad.

Readying Students for Transformative Learning

According to Mezirow, *transformative* learning involves a change in one's frame of reference. He defines *frame of reference* as "the structures of assumptions through which we understand our experiences" (1997, p. 5). These structures of assumptions both shape and constrain our expectations, perceptions, cognition, and feelings. They provide our "taken-for-granteds," set our lines of action, and comprise our habits of mind and points of view.

Transformative learning is often triggered by a disorienting dilemma, the experience of which can lead to a process whereby these taken-for-granted assumptions are questioned, assessed, and even radically transformed (Mezirow, 1997, p. 7). Kiely (2005) builds on Mezirow's concept of disorienting dilemmas in his discussion of the place of dissonance in transformative learning. Disorienting dilemmas create dissonance when what students are seeing, hearing, and feeling is unfamiliar and incongruent with their present frame of reference. In his research with several cohorts of students who accompanied him on service-learning trips to Nicaragua, Kiely found that distinguishing between low-intensity and high-intensity dissonance was important for identifying situations that led to transformative change. Low-intensity dissonance results in adaptation but not in transformative learning. Adjustment to low-intensity dissonance, according to Kiely, "tends to be short-term and manageable by acquiring additional information or drawing from existing knowledge" (2005, p. 11). This kind of dissonance is not likely to lead to transformative learning because the latter is unlikely to occur as long as new information fits comfortably into one's existing frames of reference (Mezirow, 1997).

It is high-intensity dissonance that under the right conditions leads to transformative learning. When encountering high-intensity dissonance, one's existing knowledge is not sufficient to make sense of the contradictions one is experiencing. As Kiely says, "High-intensity dissonance often causes powerful emotions and confusions and leads [students] to reexamine their existing knowledge and assumptions regarding the causes and solutions to ambiguous and ill-structured problems such as extreme forms of persistent poverty" (2005, p. 11). The emotional component of the dissonance is critical. Taylor's work in this area also demonstrates the critical role that the emotional disequilibrium plays in transformative learning. He says that it is the emotions that ensue from the dissonance that provide the driving force for pushing students to search for ways to reestablish balance in their lives (1994, p. 170; see also Erickson, 2007; Joyce, 1984; Paige, 1993). Thus, whereas the effects of low-intensity dissonance fade or are resolved, effects of high-intensity dissonance do not go away; they "create permanent markers in students' frame of reference" (Kiely, 2005, p. 11).

As numerous scholars have demonstrated, and as most of us working with students who study abroad know through experience, study abroad has tremendous potential for transformative learning. Not only are the experiences of dissonance limitless, but intercultural development and transformative learning are closely intertwined. Those working in the area of intercultural education describe the process of developing intercultural competency (e.g., M. Bennett, 1993; Paige, 1993) using language similar to that of Mezirow and others whose focus is transformative learning (e.g., Erickson, 2007; Featherston & Kelly, 2007). Moreover, as Taylor suggests, the two frameworks have analogous understandings of the catalysts for development, the process of development, and the outcome of development (1994, p. 158). In both frameworks, the catalyst for change is disequilibrium or disorientation: the change process involves moving from alienation or disequilibrium through a time of questioning assumptions and testing new habits to a stage characterized by integration of new and old assumptions, and the outcome is a change in frame of reference or worldview. Although much of the literature on student growth through study abroad has been framed in terms of intercultural development, the dissonance-filled, cross-cultural experiences students encounter while abroad are ripe with potential for transformative learning more generally.

However, not all encounters with high-intensity dissonance result in transformative learning. Indeed, the ethnocentrism embedded in our structures of assumptions is a strong inhibitor of this process. Mezirow points out that we have a "strong tendency to reject ideas that fail to fit our preconceptions, labeling those ideas as unworthy of consideration—aberrations, nonsense, irrelevant, weird, or mistaken" (1997, p. 5). This response to dissonance is familiar to any of us working in international education; experiences of high-intensity dissonance on study abroad can result in a hardening of stereotypes when students hold tight to their original frames of reference. Ensuring that this does not happen requires educators to prepare students for their experiences in two ways: Students must be developmentally ready, and they must be equipped with the tools they will need to make their way through the cognitive and emotional dissonance they will encounter.

Developmental Readiness

If students are not developmentally ready to receive and process the experiences productively, transformative learning simply cannot occur. Although there are several rich and useful schemes for understanding the developmental progressions in knowledge construction and ways of knowing (e.g., Baxter Magolda, 1992; Belenky, Clinchy, Goldberger, & Tarule, 1986; King & Kitchener, 1994; Perry, 1968), Kegan's theory of self-authorship (1994, 2000) and other scholars' subsequent work with that concept (e.g., Baxter Magolda, 1992; Erickson, 2007; Pizzolato, 2007) are especially helpful in this context.

Kegan (1994) examines how individuals construct meaning, and his focus is on relationship between the self and the social environment. He argues that there are three developmental phases or systems that are particularly relevant to college-age students: the socialized self, the self-authored self, and the self-transformed self. For the socialized self, meaning is constructed and shaped by the values and expectations of others in one's social environment; it is received and accepted. The self-authored self, by contrast, is capable of generating and authoring meaning that is informed by one's own values and beliefs. Finally, the self-transformed self is capable of understanding the structural systems that underlie meaning making and is capable of seeing "our relationships and connections as prior to and constitutive of the individual self" (Kegan, 1994, p. 351). Students generally begin their college careers in the socialized-self stage, and ideally move into the stage of self-authorship over the course of their college experience (Baxter Magolda, 2001; Pizzolato, 2007).

Erickson (2007) has brought the literature on intellectual development together with that on transformative learning, linking intellectual development stages to the transformative learning process. Drawing on Kegan's work, she argues that the ability to move through the process of transformative learning is constrained by one's meaning-making capacity. For example, in the stage of the socialized self, high-intensity dissonance is perceived to be caused only by factors external to the self. In this context, there is little chance of doing the kind of self-reflection necessary to move through the dissonance in a way that leads to transformative learning. In the stage of the self-authored self, however, dimensions of the dissonance will be framed as connected to the self, and students may even perceive the dissonance as an opportunity for growth (Erickson, 2007, p. 78).

Self-authorship, then, is a prerequisite for transformative learning. To be ready to productively encounter the high-intensity dissonance associated with studying abroad, students need to have achieved this stage because the learning that we want them to do while abroad requires the meaning-making capacity of the self-authored mind. Thus opportunities for students to attain that stage of development must be part of the curriculum and co-curriculum that students receive *before* they go abroad.

Equipped With the Intercultural Toolkit

In addition to developmental readiness, students need to be equipped with the intercultural knowledge, skills, and attitudes they will need to capture the learning from the study abroad experience. Much research and writing has focused on the elements of this "intercultural toolkit" (e.g., ACE, 2008; J. Bennett, 2008; M. Bennett, 1993; Deardorff, 2008; Kim, 1988; Ogden, 2006, 2007–2008; Paige, 1993; Savicki, 2008b), and a general consensus seems to have emerged among intercultural scholars. The key components of the "knowledge compartment" of the intercultural toolkit are place-specific knowledge, knowledge of intercultural theory, and knowledge about self. Clearly, students need to have at least a basic understanding of the cultural, social, political, historical, and environmental dynamics of the place where they will be studying. Knowledge of the language spoken is also critical. In addition, students need to have a handle on intercultural theory. Understanding the nature of intercultural dynamics and the cognitive, behavioral, and affective dimensions of the experience of cross-cultural dissonance provide the conceptual scaffolding that students need to make their way into and through these experiences productively. Finally, students need to understand positionality.

Positionality theory developed in the work of, among others, feminist scholars, anthropologists, sociologists, and geographers to argue that knowledges are situated and produced by actors, who themselves are positioned in particular ways related to many factors, including citizenship, gender, wealth, skin color, age, ethnicity, experience, education, and language. Further, in acknowledging that we look at issues, texts, situations, and people from particular positions and locations, we also admit that knowledge is not objective. "To acknowledge particular and personal locations is to admit the limits of one's purview from these positions. It is also to undermine the notion of objectivity, because from particular locations all understanding becomes subjectively based and forged through interactions within fields of power relations" (Narayan, 1993, p. 679). Often applied within social research, positionality references knowledge production (how is knowledge created and by whom?), power dynamics between researcher and researched, the limitations of particular visions and understandings of knowledge, and the possibility that multiple truths exist at the same time (Mohammed, 2001). Further, "interactions in the field . . . are influenced by the attributes of the participants" (McDowell, 2001, p. 204). Positionality also reveals that in research and other settings there are insiders and outsiders. However, these categories themselves are always shifting such that, depending on the context of the place and time, one can be at once both "insider" and "outsider" (Mohammed, 2001). Equipping students with knowledge of positionality provides them the conceptual scaffolding they need to not only understand these shifts and why they are happening, but to navigate through them.

The main tools in the "attitude compartment" of the toolkit are suspension of judgment, tolerance of ambiguity, curiosity, and confidence. Deardorff (2008) argues that the process of attaining intercultural competence begins with attitudes. Without the curiosity and openness to learn about and from other cultures and the confidence to actually encounter the dissonance that is necessarily a part of this process, the tools in the skills and knowledge compartments cannot be put to use. In interviews with students at Kalamazoo College, students described the point at which their attitudes shifted and began to allow them to really engage in the cross-cultural learning process as "letting go" or "giving up control." They were, in essence, letting go of the resistance to new frames of reference that is so tightly embedded in their own structures of assumptions. At this point, they were able to "go with the flow," and begin the process of using their knowledge and skills to productively encounter and work their way through the dissonance.

The "skills compartment" of the toolkit is composed of tools related to listening, observing, describing, interpreting, and reflecting. These skills are essentially those necessary to proceed through the experiential learning cycle described by Kolb (1984; see also Montrose, 2002; Savicki, 2008b). This cycle begins with concrete experience, which is followed by observation and reflection, which is then followed by the forming of abstract concepts, which are then tested in new concrete experiences, and the cycle continues. For the cycle of experiential learning to produce real learning, students need to be taught how to observe, listen, describe, interpret, and reflect. In short, they need to be taught how to learn experientially.

Fundamental to acquiring the skills of close observation and active listening, to the attitude of suspending judgment, and to experiential learning generally is understanding the difference among description, interpretation, and evaluation. Some international educators use the Description–Interpretation–Evaluation (DIE) model to help students learn this difference (Bennett, Bennett, & Stillings, 1977). We prefer the Description–Interpretation–Validation–Explanation (DIVE) model, which not only has a much nicer acronym, but includes two important differences. First, validation is included in the process of learning cross-culturally. Once students describe what they are seeing and hearing and then develop interpretations of what their descriptions imply about the culture with which they are interacting, they need to validate those interpretations. In Kolb's model, this is the part of the cycle that involves testing newly formed abstract concepts. Without this step of validation, not only can interpretations easily slip into evaluation, they will likely occur only within the students' existing frame of reference. It is through this ongoing cycle of description–interpretation–validation that students are pushed further into another frame of reference. Second, the DIVE model replaces the "evaluation" in the DIE model with "explanation." Because evaluation and judgment are so closely connected, and we are trying to get students to suspend judgment, suggesting that evaluation is an important part of the intercultural development process is counterproductive. Explanation, however, involves connecting their validated interpretations with the theories and concepts in the knowledge compartment of their toolkit, producing deeper learning.

Every year Beloit College holds an international symposium at which returned study abroad students report on their learning abroad. Presentations focus on research findings, reflections on intercultural explorations, educational philosophies and systems, and political and other issues of particular importance in the host countries. The most compelling presentations are those that weave together students' "academic" learning with their insights from living in another cultural milieu, and show as well how the students' out-of-classroom or experiential learning took place. Similarly, an analysis of interviews conducted with students at Kalamazoo College suggests that students who chose to connect their senior theses with their study abroad experiences gained a much deeper and more nuanced level of understanding of the cultures they were studying and their places within those cultures (Cunningham, Grossman, & Udow, 2008). These observations at both institutions point to the importance of connecting theoretical and conceptual knowledge with experience. Real transformative learning entails reflexively making connections among oneself, one's experience, and wider institutional, social, and political structures (Featherston & Kelly, 2007). Being equipped with the knowledge, attitudes, and skills in this toolkit is key to readying students for this kind of learning.

There is an obvious connection between developmental readiness and the acquisition of this intercultural toolkit. Indeed, the relationship between the two is a dialectical one. Helping students develop pieces of their intercultural toolkit, for example, can be a strategy for pushing them along the developmental continuum. Then, as they move along that continuum, they are able to develop additional elements of their toolkit. As subsequent chapters in this volume demonstrate, there are innovative pedagogical strategies that can be used to take advantage of this dialectic and help students acquire both the toolkit and the developmental readiness they need to take full advantage of the transformative learning potential of study abroad.

References

Advisory Council for International Educational Exchange. (1988). *Educating for global competence.* New York: Council on International Educational Exchange.

Altbach, P. G., & Knight, J. (2007). The internationalization of higher education: Motivations and realities. *Journal of Studies in International Education, 11*(3/4), 290–305.

American Council on Education. (1995). *Educating Americans for a world in flux: Ten ground rules for internationalizing American higher education.* Washington, DC: Author.

American Council on Education. (2008). *Mapping internationalization on U.S. campuses: 2008 edition.* Washington, DC: Author.

Baxter Magolda, M. B. (1992). *Knowing and reasoning in college: Gender-related patterns in students' intellectual development.* San Francisco: Jossey-Bass.

Baxter Magolda, M. B. (2001). *Making their own way: Narratives for transforming higher education to promote self-development.* Sterling, VA: Stylus.

Belenky, M. F., Clinchy, B. M., Goldberger, N. R., & Tarule, J. M. (1986). *Women's ways of knowing: The development of self, voice, and mind.* New York: Basic Books.

Beloit College. (2007–2008). Study abroad evaluations. Unpublished. Office of International Education files, Beloit College, Beloit, WI.

Bennett, J. (2008). On becoming a global soul: A path to engagement during study abroad. In V. Savicki (Ed.), *Developing intercultural competence and transformation: Theory, research, and application in international education* (pp. 13–31). Sterling, VA: Stylus.

Bennett, M. (1993). Towards ethnorelativism: A developmental model of intercultural sensitivity. In M. E. Paige (Ed.), *Education for the intercultural experience* (pp. 21–72). Yarmouth, ME: Intercultural Press.

Bennett, J., Bennett, M., & Stillings, K. (1977). *Intercultural communication workshop facilitator's manual*. Portland, OR: Portland State University.

Brustein, W. I. (2007). The global campus: Challenges and opportunities for higher education in North America. *Journal of Studies in International Education, 11*(3/4), 382–391.

Burn, B. B. (1990). *The contribution of international educational exchange to the international education of Americans: Projections for the year 2000*. Occasional Papers on International Educational Exchange 26. New York: Council on International Educational Exchange.

Commission on the Abraham Lincoln Study Abroad Fellowship Program. (2005). *Global competence and national needs: One million Americans studying abroad*. Washington, DC: NAFSA.

Cunningham, K., Grossman, R., & Udow, R. (2008, June). *Emerging insights about transformative learning at Kalamazoo College*. Symposium on Teaching and Learning, Kalamazoo College, Kalamazoo, MI.

Deardorff, D. (2008). Intercultural competence: A definition, model, and implications for education abroad. In V. Savicki (Ed.), *Developing intercultural competence and transformation: Theory, research, and application in international education* (pp. 32–52). Sterling, VA: Stylus.

Dobbert, M. L. (1998). The impossibility of internationalizing students by adding materials to courses. In J. A. Mestenhauser & B. S. Ellingboe (Eds.), *Reforming the higher education curriculum: Internationalizing the campus* (pp. 53–68). Phoenix, AZ: American Council on Education and Oryx Press.

Edwards, J. (2000, Winter). The "Other Eden": Thoughts on American study abroad in Britain. *Frontiers: The Interdisciplinary Journal of Study Abroad, 6*, 83–98.

Engberg, D., & Green, M. F. (2002). *Promising practices: Spotlighting excellence in comprehensive internationalization*. Washington, DC: American Council on Education.

Engle, J., & Engle, L. (2002). Neither international nor educative: Study abroad in the time of globalization. In W. Grünzweig & N. Rinehard (Eds.), *Rockin' in Red Square: Critical approaches to international education in the age of cyberculture* (pp. 25–39). Münster: Lit Verlag.

Erickson, D. (2007). A developmental re-forming of the phases of meaning in transformational learning. *Adult Education Quarterly, 58*(1), 61–80.

Featherston, B., & Kelly, R. (2007). Conflict resolution and transformative pedagogy: A grounded theory research project on learning in higher education. *Journal of Transformative Education, 5*(3), 262–285.

Goode, M. L. (2008, Winter). The role of faculty study abroad directors: A case study. *Frontiers: The Interdisciplinary Journal of Study Abroad, 15,* 149–172.

Joyce, B. R. (1984). Dynamic disequilibrium: The intelligence of growth. *Theory into Practice, 23,* 26–34.

Kehm, B. M., & Teichler, U. (2007). Research on internationalisation in higher education. *Journal of Studies in International Education, 11*(3/4), 260–273.

Kegan, R. (1994). *In over our heads: The mental demands of modern life.* Cambridge, MA: Harvard University Press.

Kegan, R. (2000). What "form" transforms? A constructive-developmental approach to transformative learning. In J. Mezirow (Ed.), *Learning in transformation: Critical perspectives on a theory in progress* (pp. 35–69). San Francisco: Jossey-Bass.

Kiely, R. (2005). A transformative learning model for service-learning: A longitudinal case study. *Michigan Journal of Community Service Learning, 12,* 5–22.

Kim, Y. Y. (1988). *Communication and cross-cultural adaptation: An integrative theory.* Philadelphia: Multilingual Matters.

King, P. M., & Kitchener, K. S. (1994). *Developing reflective judgment.* San Francisco: Jossey-Bass.

Knight, J. (2003, Fall). Updating the definition of internationalisation. *International Higher Education, 33,* 2–3.

Kolb, D. (1984). *Experiential learning as the science of learning and development.* Englewood Cliffs, NJ: Prentice Hall.

McDowell, L. (2001). Working with young men. *Geographical Review, 91*(1/2), 201–214.

Mestenhauser, J. (1998). Portraits of an international curriculum: An uncommon multidimensional perspective. In J. A. Mestenhauser & B. S. Ellingboe (Eds.), *Reforming the higher education curriculum: Internationalizing the campus* (pp. 3–39). Phoenix, AZ: American Council on Education and Oryx Press.

Mestenhauser, J. A., & Ellingboe, B. S. (Eds.). (1998). *Reforming the higher education curriculum: Internationalizing the campus.* Phoenix, AZ: American Council on Education and Oryx Press.

Mezirow, J. (1997). Transformative learning: Theory to practice. *New Directions for Adult and Continuing Education, 74,* 5–12.

Mohammed, R. (2001). "Insiders" and/or "outsiders": Positionality theory and praxis. In M. Limb & C. Dwyer (Eds.), *Qualitative methodologies for geographers* (pp. 101–117). London: Arnold.

Montrose, L. (2002, Winter). International study and experiential learning: The academic context. *Frontiers: The Interdisciplinary Journal of Study Abroad, 8,* 1–15.

NAFSA: Association of International Educators. (n.d.). Home page. Retrieved May 5, 2009, from http://www.nafsa.org.

NAFSA: Association of International Educators. (2003). *Securing America's future: Global education for a global age: Report of the strategic task force on education abroad.* Washington, DC: Author.

NAFSA: Association of International Educators. (2008). Internationalization at home. Retrieved July 21, 2008, from http://www.nafsa.org/knowledge_com munity_network.sec/teaching_learning_and/internationalizing_the_3/practice_resources_24/iahinternationalization/iah_overview_and_background.

Narayan, K. (1993). How native is a "native" anthropologist? *American Anthropologist, 95*(3), 671–686.

Nilsson, B., & Otten, M. (Eds.) (2003). Special issue: Internationalisation at home. *Journal of Studies in International Education, 7*(1).

Ogden, A. (2006). Ethnographic inquiry: Reframing the learning core of education abroad. *Frontiers: The Interdisciplinary Journal of Study Abroad, 8,* 87–112.

Ogden, A. (2007–2008, Winter). The view from the veranda: Understanding today's colonial student. *Frontiers: The Interdisciplinary Journal of Study Abroad, 15,* 35–55.

Olson, C. L., Evans, R., & Shoenberg, R. F. (2007). *At home in the world: Bridging the gap between internationalization and multicultural education. Global learning for all.* Working Papers on Internationalizing Higher Education, 4. Washington, DC: ACE.

Paige, R. M. (1993). On the nature of intercultural experiences and intercultural education. In M. E. Paige (Ed.), *Education for the intercultural experience* (pp. 1–20). Yarmouth, ME: Intercultural Press.

Paige, R. M., Cohen, A. D., Kappler, B., Chi, J. C., & Lassegard, J. P. (2002). *Maximizing study abroad: A student's guide to strategies for language and culture learning and use.* Minneapolis, MN: CARLA.

Perry, W. P. (1968). *Forms of intellectual and ethical development in the college years: A scheme.* Austin, TX: Holt.

Pizzolato, J. E. (2007). Assessing self-authorship. *New Directions for Teaching and Learning, 109,* 31–42.

Pusch, M. D., & Merrill, M. (2008). Reflection, reciprocity, responsibility, and committed relativism: Intercultural development through international service-learning. In V. Savicki (Ed.), *Developing intercultural competence and transformation: Theory, research, and application in international education* (pp. 297–321). Sterling, VA: Stylus.

Savicki, V. (Ed.). (2008a). *Developing intercultural competence and transformation: Theory, research, and application in international education.* Sterling, VA: Stylus.

Savicki, V. (2008b). Experiential and affective education for international educators. In V. Savicki (Ed.), *Developing intercultural competence and transformation: Theory, research, and application in international education* (pp. 74–91). Sterling, VA: Stylus.

Selby, R. (2008). Designing transformation in international education. In V. Savicki (Ed.), *Developing intercultural competence and transformation: Theory, research, and application in international education* (pp. 1–10). Sterling, VA: Stylus.

Stohl, M. (2007). We have met the enemy and he is us: The role of faculty in the internationalization of higher education in the coming decade. *Journal of Studies in International Education, 11*(3/4), 359–372.

Taylor, E. W. (1994). Intercultural competency: A transformative learning process. *Adult Education Quarterly, 44,* 154–174.

Vande Berg, M. (2007). Intervening in the learning of U.S. students abroad. *Journal of Studies in International Education, 11*(3/4), 392–399.

2

LESSONS FROM GEOGRAPHY

Mental Maps and Spatial Narratives

Darren Kelly

I n my experience working with American students in Dublin, Ireland, and visiting study abroad programs across Europe, Africa, Asia, and South America, I have found that self-created and self-maintained physical and cultural comfort zones by study abroad students are, to varying degrees, a norm. These zones, which could also be labeled "life worlds" or "nested environments," may include the international housing on campus as well as a limited number of places, such as coffee shops, located close to the campus.

This behavior can be seen in the United States as well. Students at many colleges and universities talk about their campus "bubbles," and international students often are said to close spatial and cultural ranks. Although this exclusionary behavior can be comforting for students remaining on their home campuses as well as students studying abroad, if not modified over time, the behavior takes away from students' engagement with their host sites. In turn, the lack of engagement can stunt the potential that study abroad offers in terms of academic growth, language acquisition, the development of critical thinking skills, personal maturation, and intercultural learning.

Although some students break through their comfort zones to explore by themselves, the argument made here is that, to a large degree, a student's engagement with the host environment produces more robust results if it is facilitated by curricula and an experiential pedagogy that enable students to break free from their safety zones to self-consciously enter and engage with their host environments. Ideally, such curricula should begin before students depart and continue during and after the study abroad experience.

This chapter explores how lessons from geography and related fields of knowledge such as philosophy, sociology, and literary and cultural studies can be brought to bear on study abroad. These disciplines are particularly appropriate as their methodologies can encourage students' awareness of their conscious and unconscious sense of place and space, their cultural norms, spatial narratives, and stereotypes. Further, when used to critique and better understand new environments, their forms of analysis can be linked to the development of study abroad students' sociological and geographical imaginations. This chapter therefore draws on these fields to suggest strategies, activities, and tools to engage students with off-campus learning at home and abroad.

Many study abroad programs are located in cities. City living offers different realities for students more accustomed to living on bordered college campuses or who have rural or suburban backgrounds. Such students in particular profit from an introduction to urban theory, an awareness of the dynamics of living in cities, and instruction in tools with which to physically and culturally navigate cities. The physical, socioeconomic, and cultural transition of countries is, arguably, most prominent in cities. Students may lament transitions that have made their study abroad cities less "authentic" than anticipated. However, if they are able to unpack these transitions, they will better understand the past, present, and future of their study abroad sites and the plural causes and effects of transitions at home and abroad. This chapter therefore often takes the city as the sphere in which study abroad takes place, although the lessons from the chapter can be applied to non-urban sites as well.

The Creation of Comfort Zones

Two variables can be said to contribute to the creation of physical and cultural comfort (safety) zones by students studying abroad. The first variable is linked with the maintenance of cultural norms. The second is linked with students' fears of getting lost and, by association, a possible fear of urban space and city dwellers.

Student comfort zones are established and governed by the cultural norms of home. These norms, or rituals and codes of behavior, can range from food, dress, music, political correctness, and language to etiquette around discussions and dating. Students' perceived need for the upkeep of their culture can be based on a fear of the host culture or a fear of losing their own culture or sense of self. The latter may be tied up with their new-found and possibly uncomfortable status of being a minority in their host site. By socializing with similar people in dedicated, culture-specific spaces, students can screen out their new host environment. This behavior is exacerbated by the proliferation of establishments catering to expatriates, including study abroad students, about which Engle and Engle (2002), among others, have written. Further, global high speed Internet access is a factor in the cocooning of study abroad students. For example, Skype allows students to call other Skype users free of charge and call home and cell phones at reduced rates. Some study abroad students spend a considerable amount of time calling family, partners, and friends, and surfing the Internet. The result can be the creation of a kind of ambilocation, whereby students coterminously inhabit two psychosocial realms, reducing their engagement with and understanding of their host society and culture.

On the other hand, engaging in the host culture and language can be exhausting. Tönnies (1887/1957) and Wirth (1938/1996) argue that people (in our case, students) living in cities need to defend themselves against and retreat from the constant bombardment of a city's stimuli such as human and automobile congestion, the explosion of colors and smells, and the cacophony of loud noises. Additionally, navigating cities, particularly for students who rarely walk at home, can be physically and emotionally tiring, contributing to a need to retreat to comfortable surroundings to relax. More positively then, comfort zones can give students space to recharge their batteries. Furthermore, spending time with fellow study abroad and international students discussing their day and particular events can lead to self-reflection and critical analysis of experiences with host communities.

The fear of being lost can be linked with students' perceptions and fears of new environments, particularly urban spaces. Cities can intimidate students and exacerbate their fears of getting lost. To allay this fear, students may "keep to the well-beaten path," thus restricting the places and spaces they inhabit. Lynch's research of the spatial practices of inhabitants of three American cities found that once people traveled unknown routes they became disoriented:

The sense of anxiety and even terror that accompanies [being disoriented] reveals to us how closely [the need to know where we are] is linked to our sense of balance and well-being. The word "lost" in our language means much more than simple geographical uncertainty; it carries overtones of utter disaster. (1960, p. 4)

Being lost in a foreign country can be even more terrifying, similar to the discussion of high-intensity dissonance in chapter 1. However, the stresses associated with physical and emotional disorientation can be alleviated through practical and emotional means. Students who receive an introduction to the host city's geography and transport routes with group and individual practice can build up their confidence to go out and explore the city. The "emotional means" of alleviating stress is related to perception. "Lost" connotes a sense of permanence, thus leading to panic. However, students might avoid this panic if they can understand "lost" as representing a challenge (to find their way), and an opportunity (to explore). Having the communication skills and confidence to approach their hosts will help them find their way, and confidence and curiosity may lead them to places formerly hidden to them and frequented by locals rather than tourists.

Sibley's *Geographies of Exclusion* (1995) contains an effective and student-accessible discussion of this phenomenon. One of Sibley's central arguments is that residential and social exclusion can be manifested by moral panics or fear of different subgroups, based on, for example, age, race, and social class. It follows that students may fear unknown places because they are inhabited by people different from themselves. Raban, referring to London, writes, "One man's village is another man's ghetto" (1974, p. 219). Smith (1996) argues that American culture has traditionally been anti-urban, with cities and their inhabitants maligned in journalism and popular media, which often use the terms *city* and *urban* as pejoratives. On the other hand, gentrification has given rise to radical physical and cultural juxtapositions in urban space. When students understand the processes that lead to urban renewal and gentrification, cities' rapid physical expansion, and the causes and effects of rapid rural migration to the city, they gain a well-grounded interdisciplinary understanding of the complexity of the cities and nations in which they are studying. Such studies are fertile ground for research projects anchored in students' major fields of study. Such projects can provide an important academic link back to students' home institutions, as discussed by Pablo

Toral in chapter 11. The project's value lies in fieldwork that requires interaction with local environments and people and takes into consideration the local, national, and international context of their research, in turn testing and adding to their disciplinary learning.

Deconstructing Maps and Challenging Stereotypes: From the Global to the Local

Having students compare the Mercator and Peters maps and other projections is a good place to start a conversation about the messages and power inequalities that maps convey. Furthermore, this exercise can make students self-conscious about their unconscious acceptance of the distorted shape of the world common in the maps they use, and encourage them to discuss the effects of geographic and sociocultural misrepresentation. Such exercises can be extended to include an analysis of the images that travel guides and other literature use to represent countries, as discussed in chapter 6.

The Mercator map is one of the most popular or recognizable world maps for American students; it hangs on the walls of many high schools. Although it was created by the Flemish cartographer Gerardus Mercator in 1569 for nautical purposes, the shape and size of the continents is often commonly accepted as representative of what the world looks like. However, although the continents' and countries' shapes on the map are relatively accurate, their relative area sizes are not. Greenland and Africa are shown to be almost equal in size; in reality, Africa is more than ten times the size of Greenland. Thus the Mercator map can be categorized as being Eurocentric, symbolizing a world order with an attendant unequal balance of power. The Peters map, created by Arno Peters in 1974, illustrates for students that how we view the world can be illustrative of our position in it. Because the shape of the continents in the Peters map is drastically different from the Mercator, it was heralded by many people and social justice organizations as righting the Mercator's Western-dominated perception of the world.

Students can be asked to draw maps, before looking at standard ones, to elicit their perceptions of the world around them. A student planning to study abroad in an Asian country may render the country smaller or larger in comparison to the United States depending on the student's unconscious prejudices and ignorance of the two countries. Harmon, in *You Are Here: Personal Geographies and Other Maps of the Imagination* (2004), illustrates the research completed by artist Kim Dingle in 1990 in which American high school students were asked to draw the outline of the United States. The resulting drawings illustrated vast differences in the students' perceptions of the country in terms of size and shape. For example, in some maps the southern states were largely missing, whereas others lacked northeastern states. Harmon's book is replete with wonderful examples of different thematic maps, including mental maps. For further information on mental maps, see *Mental Maps* (Gould, 2002). Websites dedicated to mental mapping include http://geography.about.com/cs/culturalgeography/a/mentalmaps.htm and http://www.mentalmaps.info.

Reducing the scale of analysis of space to that of the local can challenge students' assumptions about where they live. Students can be asked to make sketches or maps of where they live and to include in them places and spaces they consider to be important to their lives and those they most often frequent. The next step is to ask them to analyze these personal or mental maps in terms of what they contain and what they do not. Very often, the maps resemble Steinberg's well-known *New Yorker* cover, "View of the World From 9th Avenue," in which the streets between 9th Avenue and the Hudson River are well-populated and lined with buildings and cars, but the rest of the United States and the world are reduced to a few lines and words.

I gave this mental mapping exercise to approximately 35 students at different class levels enrolled in three courses (theater, writing, and study abroad preparation) at Beloit College, Wisconsin, in 2007. Most of the students did not include Beloit's downtown in their maps, although it is roughly a five-minute walk from the college campus. The exercise illustrated in graphic form the existence of geographies of inclusion and exclusion known locally as the "Beloit bubble." Students tend not to frequent the downtown because relatively few of its businesses cater to students and most of their needs are met on campus. Further, the grocery store they most frequently use is located several blocks away from the central downtown area, and they can walk to the bookstore they use without passing other shops. The college itself contributes to this by providing transportation to strip malls to do errands.

To help the students learn to negotiate and investigate the city, I therefore set a number of assignments that encouraged them to venture away from the college. These exercises included writing travelogues based on their walks in the city, conducting interviews with locals, visiting the city archives, and creating thematic-based photo essays. These latter took as their subject matter Beloit's natural environment, architecture, history, religion, recreation, murals, and race and ethnicity. As a result, Beloit and its residents became more complex and meaningful to the students, several of whom subsequently elected to carry out independent projects in the following semester that further engaged them with the city.

The Image of the City

My use of mental maps with students in Beloit and Dublin, Ireland, has been heavily influenced by Kevin Lynch's seminal research, which culminated in the publication of *The Image of the City* (1960). I have also used the concept of mental maps to introduce students to the concept of how space is "produced." This discourse is connected with the work of French philosophers Henri Lefebvre (1939/1996, 1970/2003, 1974/1991) and Michel Foucault (1986, 1991), the so-called spatial turn in New (postmodern) Geography, and the work of geographers such as David Harvey (1973, 1990) and Edward Soja (1989, 1996). In the following pages Lynch's work is outlined, followed by a discussion of how his work has been adopted for study abroad through the use and analysis of student mental maps.

Although relatively small in scale, Lynch's research became highly influential in a range of areas, particularly urban planning. His work furthered the concept of the legibility and symbolic nature of urban space and the value of perception within qualitative research. Over a five-year period, Lynch studied how people locate themselves in contemporary cities and the factors that dictate their spatial (and social) activities. Lynch concluded that historically, regardless of geography, people have adapted themselves to and mastered their environments. "Structuring and identifying the environment is a vital ability among all mobile animals" (Lynch, 1960, p. 3).

Lynch's research focused on Boston, Jersey City, and Los Angeles, with a team of researchers surveying people's different uses of city space, such as the routes used to travel to work and the reasons for "choosing" these routes. To aid this process, people were asked to sketch—that is, create mental maps—of their journeys through the cities. These were then used to create a composite image of the cities.

Lynch concluded that there are five at times interconnected elements that contribute to a city's legibility: the *landmark; paths* or common routes that people use to travel, for example, a highway into the city; *districts* or spatial areas recognizable by location and image (Greenwich Village is an example); *nodes* or central points through which large groups of individuals traverse, such as a main transport station; and finally, *edges,* that is, natural or artificial borders that encourage people to travel along a certain route over another, for example, a river or tall buildings lining a street. In Lynch's study, some respondents intentionally did not travel the most direct routes to work so they could pass green spaces and waterfronts. In this case, the physical landscape positively affected their emotional well-being. On the other hand, one reason respondents did not travel through certain areas was the difficulty of negotiating the confusing layout of the streets; there did not seem to be obvious pathways with which to travel from point A to B.

Students who study Lynch's work can begin to critique a city's urban plan and its inhabitants' daily activities. They can do this by studying a map of the city to find its main transport arteries and nodes, overlaying census data onto a map, and interviewing people about their routes and uses of space in the city. In the past I have had a team of American study abroad students interview inner-city residents in Dublin, Ireland, about their daily routes and activities. The students, as part of the project, mounted a large-scale map of the city on a hard board and used pins and thread to illustrate the routes taken by the residents.

Using Lynch's Research to Critique the Spatial Narratives of Study Abroad Students: Two Examples

The ability of the built environment to influence the spatial behavior of study abroad students was made clear to me on a 2008 visit to Beloit College students studying at the Universidad San Francisco de Quito in Ecuador. I and other faculty members strolled around the vicinity of the university to acquaint ourselves with the students' new environment. A large paved road borders the university with cafes and fast-food restaurants that cater to the students and the international community connected to a larger process of gentrification in the area called Cumbaya. At one stage we wandered away from the campus along narrow streets to find Cumbaya's original plaza and the beginning of a bicycle path that follows an abandoned railway line that was close by. I asked the students if they went to the plaza or used the bicycle path, but none of the students were aware of them.

The following map (Figure 2.1) is of Cumbaya. The main roads that surround the university have been highlighted. The bike path is indicated by a circle close to the southeast corner of the highlighted roadway and the plaza is located to the bottom right of the map. The dotted square partially inside this rectangle on the left is the university, and to the right are gentrified gated communities. The shops and services in front of the university act as a centrifugal force, magnetizing students to the immediate area. Based on Lynch's work, one could label the outlined area, the university *district*. The road is a *pathway* that also acts as an *edge* or border, which seemed to have shepherded the students away from the smaller, and possibly for them visually intimidating, winding streets that lead to the plaza. The roundabout at the southwest of the highlighted road is next to the entrance of the university and serves as a transport *node* for many of Cumbaya's workers and students traveling to and from other parts of Quito.

FIGURE 2.1
Path, edge, and border around Universidad San Francisco de Quito. Map produced by author with the use of Google Earth.

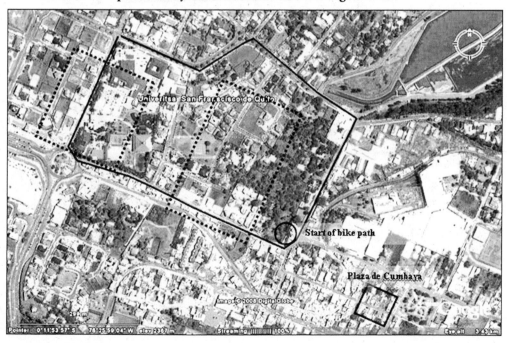

Based on the changing nature of services and functions of the plaza, such as a newly opened expensive salon and jewelry store, it was apparent that the plaza was in the process of being gentrified.

In Quito, some private as well as semipublic places, such as shopping malls, are guarded by security personnel. This is true at the Universidad San Francisco as well, which can only be entered by a main gate patrolled by armed guards. The existence of guards and gates can be used to help students become aware of the functioning duality of invisible–visible borders in cities. Such borders are visible to the marginalized in society, such as the homeless and immigrants, because, depending on the city, they may be ejected or moved away by security personnel. In contrast, the borders are invisible to the privileged in society, including tourists and study abroad students, because they often are free to frequent these guarded spaces, whose beautification and relative safety are, in the mode of Lynch, a forceful attraction.

Another example of students not traveling off the beaten track occurred when I visited Beloit students studying in the city of Jinan, in China's Shandong province in 2007. Beloit College professor Daniel Youd (see chapter 8) had not initially alerted his students to the picturesque beauty of the river that runs through the city, which is famous for its thermal springs, because he wished to know if the students would find the river by themselves. The answer was no, and the river's location may have contributed to this. Although it cuts through the heart of the city, it is both half an hour's walk from the campus where the students live and is accessed by descending some 20 feet via unobtrusive steps. Again, in line with Lynch's work, although the students had walked above the river along a main thoroughfare, the thoroughfare had acted as a path and an edge. For the insiders who know about the river, however, it is not only a place of beauty and rest from the busy streets above, but a social space for the local people of Jinan and, therefore, an ideal place for the students to observe and engage local people in a comfortable atmosphere. The students now receive an assignment requiring them to visit the river and its springs and record their observations.

To help study abroad students move beyond restrictive edges to understand their study abroad sites, over a six-year period I have asked the study abroad students enrolled in a class I teach in Ireland for the study abroad provider IES Abroad to create mental maps of Dublin. The following section of this chapter discusses the creation of those maps as well as follow-up field research assignments used to encourage the students to engage more comprehensively and critically with the city of Dublin.

Mental Maps and Field Research With Students in Dublin, Ireland: A Case Study

Mental maps are usually hand-drawn sketches or maps that illustrate an individual's familiarity with a place, as well as that person's uses and perceptions of space. In *Soft City*, Jonathon Raban articulates this relationship to great effect when he writes, "the sum of one man's route through the city is as unique as a fingerprint or a spur" (1974, p. 94). It might be argued therefore that "where you are" is, or at least contributes to, "who you are." Mental maps could be considered "spatial narratives" because they tell the first-person narratives of the maps' protagonists. James Joyce's *Ulysses* (1922/1986) tells the story, or spatial narrative, of Leopold Bloom's route across Dublin on June 16, 1904. Likewise, for students studying abroad, the routes that they habitually take become a spatial narrative or story of their study abroad experience.

During the second week of class the American students in Dublin are asked to draw a mental map of the city. Many students are hesitant to draw a map, so they have to be reassured that this exercise is not about re-creating an accurate street map to scale, but rather getting down on paper a record of the general spaces and routes they take each day and specifically, the places that they have begun to frequent, such as the local convenience store where they get their coffee and bread roll each morning on the way to class. I reassure the students that this is not a test and that they don't have to share their maps with the group, but rather that they should see the exercise as fun and do it as quickly as possible without fear.

As outlined in the introduction to this chapter, it might be assumed that young, confident students, many of whom are proud of their individuality, would branch out and explore their new surroundings and thus have different mind maps. However, based on the students' maps in my course, this is by and large not the case, despite their speaking the same language as the local population. The maps are quite restricted in scale and mostly are identical in depicting the routes traveled and places visited. Further, without exception, the student maps center on the beautiful St. Stephen's Green and the exclusive shopping zone around Grafton Street, both of which are located on Dublin's fashionable south side. The River Liffey runs through the center of Dublin City, separating it into a north and south side. Most of the maps include neither the north side of the city nor the river, and when they do, the map is placed at the edge of their life-worlds as a border, as illustrated in the student map in Figure 2.2. Figure 2.3 shows the location of the places identified on the student map on a Google map of Dublin. The Google map makes clear that the student created a comfort zone, marked by a dotted line, in the southeast of the city.

Mental maps can be likened to global positioning system (GPS) screens, whereby anything peripheral to the streets traveled, such as the plaza in Cumbaya and river in Jinan, are literally "off the map." In essence, they are invisible blank spaces, as can be seen in the student's map (see Figure 2.2). The difference between a mental map and a GPS map is that the former lacks exact distances and some street names, and a mental map does not necessarily

FIGURE 2.2.
Student mental map of Dublin after 2 weeks.

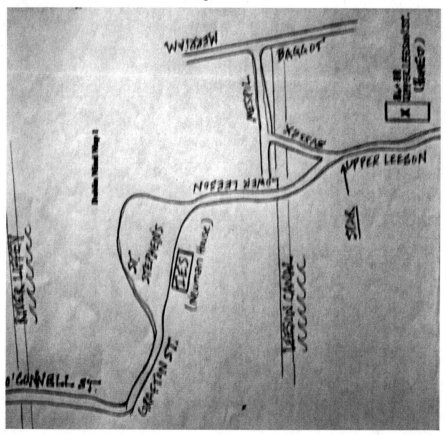

FIGURE 2.3.
Dublin's city center with student map locators.

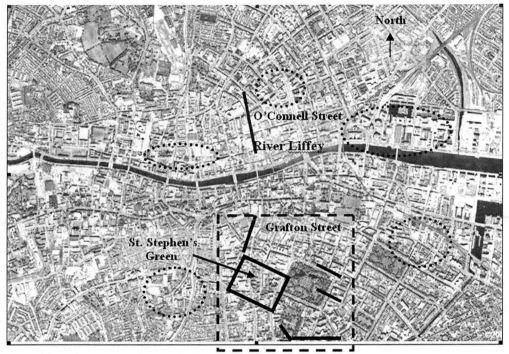

The heavy blackened lines are the places indicated on the student's mental map and the large square indicates the student's comfort zone. The dotted shapes indicate spaces where students took class walking tours and conducted research projects.

show the shortest or most logical route between destinations. The mental map can be compared with a cubist collage in which many of the images are spatially cut and pasted to create a nonscaled picture or image. Notice, for example, the size of St. Stephen's Green in the student's perception of Dublin (see Figure 2.2) as compared with its actual size in the city map (see Figure 2.3), and how the Green's size and location are reduced in students' later mental maps (see Figure 2.3, and Figure 2.4 on page 37).

Free mapping software such as Google Maps now makes it possible for students to transfer items from their mental maps to a map created using satellite imagery. In a next step, the students can photograph and video the items and upload the images onto the map to create a "mashup." Over time students can further develop their maps to create a visual diary of the spaces and places they have inhabited during their study abroad experience. It is of critical importance, however, that students begin with a mental map, because it explicates the students' perceptions of city space. Transferring the mental data onto the computerized map illustrates to the students how geographically and culturally skewed their engagement with the study abroad site has been to date. Lynch's work, in turn, can help the students analyze the ways in which they have traversed the city by locating the spatial funnels through which they have been consciously and subconsciously shepherded.

A further aim of the course in Dublin is to realign the students' cosseted engagement with the city by having them explore different neighborhoods each week via walking tours and individual and group research; the students then shade these districts and attach images of places in them on their personal Google maps of Dublin. When it is not feasible to use Google maps, students can work with paper. Another aim is to make the students aware of the different subgroups inhabiting certain maligned spaces in Dublin.

Unlike a city such as Los Angeles where rich and poor places are geographically separated, in Dublin such subcultural populations are literally juxtaposed. For example, a few minutes' walk from Grafton Street, which is on every student's mental map, are small communities characterized by extraordinarily high unemployment and high instances of HIV and drug-related deaths. The first walking tour that I do with the students goes to one such neighborhood; usually the students are amazed by the proximity of the different social groupings that reside there, which includes an immigrant subgroup.

This walking tour introduces the students to issues around gentrification, what I term *ethnification*, and the possible displacement of Dublin's indigenous inner-city residents. It also introduces students to a discussion of Irish identity politics and the meteoric rise in the Irish economy, a phenomenon called the "Celtic Tiger." Students consider how this phenomenon directly relates to gentrification and immigration as well as to the physical and sociocultural morphology of Dublin's inner-city spaces. As part of these tours, students meet local residents and community leaders to discuss the effects of rapid transition on the local population. Despite their negative stereotypes, Dublin's disadvantaged communities have been in fact very closely knit and matriarchal. The interviews help the students come to appreciate the residents' strong sense of place and community. Depending on the semester and circumstances, students may spend a morning in Dublin's Mountjoy Prison meeting prisoners involved in a drama project; or they may visit a halting site, home to some of Ireland's indigenous traveling community. One class walking tour visits the city's docklands and the Irish Financial Services Center (IFSC), which has radically altered the physical and sociocultural makeup of the docklands area. Discussions of political economy and the relationship between the Celtic Tiger and investment in Irish companies on the part of American companies raise the issue of globalization, and teach the students to think globally as they investigate the local.

The work of Michel Foucault (1986) informs the students' discussions. Foucault labels spaces in transition *heterotopias,* "capable of juxtaposing in a single real place several spaces, several sites that are in themselves incompatible" (p. 25). Foucault's discourse is balanced by a discussion of Allport's (1954/1958) contact hypothesis thesis, which claims that the stigmas or attitudes individuals or groups have of each other will be changed through contact. Based on this discourse students discuss terms such as the *melting pot* and what it means to them in relation to American society.

During the middle of the course students are sent to research other invisible communities in Dublin. I identify the neighborhoods, give them some academic sources, and act as a gatekeeper to these spaces by providing them with contacts in various organizations who can aid their research. The main aim for the students is to identify the subcultural populations in each location and to examine the factors, some of them global, that gave rise to the rapid transformation of the area, as well as particular issues that have arisen because of this transformation. The research must include statistics, photographs, and interviews. The students prepare a presentation for the final week of class. For this, they often use PowerPoint presentations and, at times, recorded interviews.

Spatial Narratives: Making the Unconscious Conscious Before the Conscious Becomes Unconscious

When faced with their overlapping, coterminus uses of space, as illustrated by their first mental maps, the students in Dublin are surprised and, in some cases, quite defensive because they do not wish to be perceived as being predictable and unadventurous. Most of the students are surprised at how unconscious they are when they travel. In the students' defense, their spatial narratives are influenced by their study abroad program's safety briefings. Also, patrons of bars and restaurants sometimes warn the students to avoid the city's north side, and guidebooks steer other students away from the north to the more touristy sections of the city. However, once the course has raised their consciousness about their uses of space, they make more active and conscious choices about their activities and behavior.

To facilitate the students' understanding of their unconscious use of space, they are given a blank sheet of paper and asked to design, in 30 seconds or less, a high school classroom using *x*'s for the seats. They are also told to include the teacher's desk. The overwhelming majority of student maps locate a small teacher's desk at the top of the classroom and place uniform lines of *x*'s across and down the classroom. The students are then asked to repeat the exercise, but to design the boardroom of a high-powered business. In this case, most of the students place a very large oval shaped table in the center of the room and place the *x*'s around the table. In essence, they have created "maps" of these two locations, with the rooms as the "spaces" and the chairs as the "places," as well as spatial expressions of two different cultures, one educational and the other business. As with their initial mental maps of Dublin, the exercise reveals a uniformity in the students' conceptions of two different places, and helps them better understand how internalized spatial behavior is.

Exploring the City: Mental Maps 2 and 3 and Self-Reflection

During the middle and final week of the students' course in Dublin, the students repeat the mental mapping exercise to include the places and spaces they now most frequent. As seen in Figures 2.4 and 2.5, produced by the same student who drew the map in Figure 2.2, the territory depicted grows dramatically, thus representing the student's exploration of and engagement with the city. In their course evaluations most of the students claim they would not have explored Dublin to such an extent if they had not taken the class. In fact, according to the students, program students who do not take the class do not go far beyond their original comfort zones.

Perhaps surprisingly, some of the students' third and final mind maps, although identifying more *spaces* in the city, do not include as many *places* compared with their second mental map. Hertmans suggests an answer: "As

FIGURE 2.4.
Second student mental map.

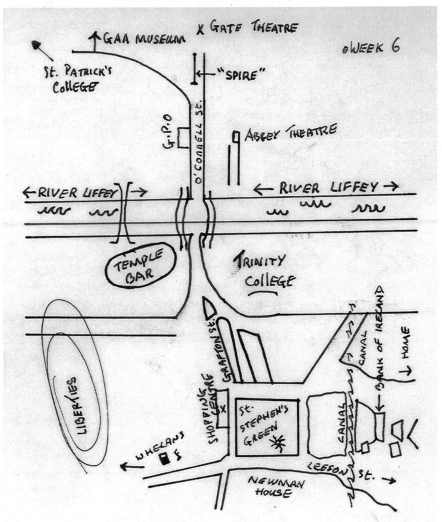

soon as we start to feel at home in a foreign city, that city also starts working on its disappearance" (2001, p. 206). In the case of the Dublin students, in the middle of their stay they explored extensively, whereas in the last period of their stay, they began to reduce their activities to a certain number of places and spaces.

FIGURE 2.5.
Third student mental map.

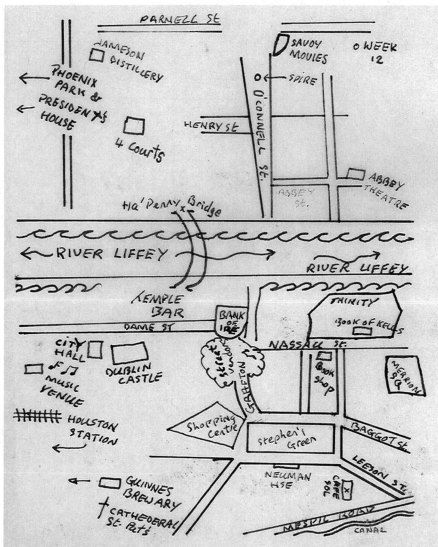

Students' Final Reflections on Mental Maps

Before the term ends the students write a short critique of their three mental maps as these reflect their engagement and understanding of Dublin. This task facilitates a measure of self-reflection and critical analysis, analogous to being both the mouse walking through a wooden maze and the observing scientist. The students support their critique with quotes from class readings, thus balancing the subjective with objective and interdisciplinary analysis. To prepare the students for reentry as well as help them make the connection to their hometowns and college campuses, they are asked to include these in their discussion of Dublin, and anticipate how their special narratives of the places they left may now change when they return to them.

Conclusion

The establishment and maintenance of student comfort zones seems to be the rule rather than the exception in many study abroad sites. Their creation is partially related to cultural and physical factors. The latter is related to students' fears of being lost and of engaging with new spaces, particularly in cities, which can be based on stereotypes about urban spaces and their inhabitants. To counteract this unwillingness to explore, students need to be encouraged to go out into the city through an interdisciplinary and experiential curriculum. The work of Kevin Lynch (1960), particularly in its relationship with the concept of mental mapping, can serve as a means for understanding and critiquing student spatial behavior. The creation of mental maps can help students reflect on their engagement, or lack thereof, with the study abroad site or city. Walking tours in areas that have remained unknown or forbidden, as well as individual and group field research, can show students the multifaceted nature of the production of space and its interconnectedness with the global economy. Furthermore, having students critique their spatial narratives and the modus operandi of urban space encourages them to reflect on the places and spaces where they have lived in the United States. Such exercises and assignments also encourage students to look at their study abroad experiences through different academic lenses.

References

Allport, G. (1958). *The nature of prejudice.* Garden City, NY: Doubleday. (Original work published 1954.)

Engle, J., & Engle, L. (2002). Neither international nor educative: Study abroad in the time of globalization. In W. Grünzweig & N. Rinehart (Eds.), *Rockin' in Red Square: Critical approaches to international education in the age of cyberculture* (pp. 25–39). Münster, Germany: Lit Verlag.

Foucault, M. (1986). Of other spaces (J. Miskowiec, Trans.). *Diacritics, 16,* 22–27.

Foucault, M. (1991). *Discipline and punish: The birth of the prison* (A. Sheridan, Trans.). London: Penguin Books.

Gould, P. (2002). *Mental maps.* London: Routledge.

Harmon, K. (2004). *You are here: Personal geographies and other maps of the imagination.* New York: Princeton Architectural Press.

Harvey, D. (1973). *Social justice and the city.* London: Edward Arnold.

Harvey, D. (1990). *The condition of postmodernity.* Oxford: Blackwell.

Hertmans, S. (2001). *Intercities.* London: Reaktion.

Joyce, J. (1986). *Ulysses.* New York: Vintage. (Original work published 1922.)

Lefebvre, H. (1991). *The production of space* (D. Nicholson-Smith, Trans.). Oxford: Blackwell. (Original work published 1974.)

Lefebvre, H. (1996). *Writings on cities* (E. Kofman & E. Lebas, Trans. and Eds.). London: Blackwell. (Original work published 1939.)

Lefebvre, H. (2003). *The urban revolution.* (R. Bononno, Trans.). Minneapolis: University of Minnesota Press. (Original work published 1970.)

Lynch, K. (1960). *The image of the city.* Cambridge: Massachusetts Institute of Technology.

Raban, J. (1974). *Soft city.* London: Hamilton.

Sibley, D. (1995). *Geographies of exclusion.* London: Routledge.

Smith, N. (1996). *The new urban frontier: Gentrification and the revanchist city.* New York: Routledge.

Soja, E. W. (1989). *Postmodern geographies: The reassertion of space in critical social theory.* London: Verso.

Soja, E. W. (1996). *Thirdspace: Journeys to Los Angeles and other real and imagined places.* Oxford: Blackwell.

Tönnies, F. (1957). *Gemeinschaft und Gesellschaft* [Community and Society]. (C. P. Loomis, Trans.). Lansing: Michigan State University Press. (Original work published 1887.)

Wirth, L. (1996). Urbanism as a way of life. In R. T. LeGates & F. Stout (Eds.). *The city reader* (pp. 97–104). London: Routledge. (Original work published 1938.)

3

PREPARATORY COURSES FOR STUDENTS GOING TO DIVERGENT SITES

Two Examples

Elizabeth Brewer and Jan Solberg

"Let him go. He's bound to get something out of it," was once a common reaction to applicants displaying neither academic preparation for a study abroad program nor understanding of what it means to live abroad. However, doubts about the wisdom of sending unprepared students abroad were voiced as early as 1980 (Burn), when U.S. study abroad enrollments were beginning to rise. The doubts have only increased (Hunter, 2008; Savicki & Selby, 2008). Indeed, many argue that not only is preparation necessary, but that guidance and intervention must occur during the study abroad if students are to truly learn (Savicki, 2008; Vande Berg, 2007).

The Case for Preparation

For study abroad to work, it can be argued that students need to have and be able to integrate three kinds of learning: content (Kulacki, 2000; Pusch & Merrill, 2008), intercultural (Deardorff, 2008; Vande Berg, 2007), and experiential (Bennett, 2008; Pusch & Merrill, 2008; Selby, 2008). Foreign language study, which is traditionally emphasized as well (Burn, 1980; Gore, 2005), remains but is not as central as it once was (Hoffa, 2002), whereas the role of affective learning has gained support (Bennett, 2008; Chambers & Chambers, 2008; Savicki, 2008). The traditional preparation for study abroad has consisted of taking one or more courses related to the study abroad country or program focus and a language class as needed, along with an orientation organized by a study abroad advisor that focuses on logistics, safety and security, and cultural adjustment.

As pointed out in chapter 1, however, these separate approaches to preparation have left too many students arriving on site unprepared for what faces them and returning to campus no wiser than before they left. As a result, a variety of both credit-bearing and noncredit orientation courses, taught both on campus and virtually, have been introduced. Virtually all include an emphasis on cross-cultural or intercultural concepts. Examples include a cross-cultural training course developed by Bruce LaBrack (n.d.) more than 20 years ago, which in turn helped lead to Loyola Marymount University's online courses (Center for Global Education, 2008). The University of Minnesota's Center for Advanced Research on Language Acquisition publishes student and faculty guides to advance language and cultural learning in study abroad (Cohen et al., 2003; Paige, Cohen, Kappler, Chi, & Lassegard, 2002); elsewhere consortial initiatives have encouraged the development of predeparture courses (Global Partners Project, 2005). A measure of the importance of the courses, both government (Fund for the Improvement of Postsecondary Education [FIPSE]) and foundation (Mellon) funding have supported their development.

The Origins of Preparatory Courses at Beloit College and Kalamazoo College

In 2002, Beloit College began to shift from a focus on study abroad and international student enrollments to campus internationalization. A liberal arts college, Beloit's international engagement began shortly after its founding in 1846 and solidified when formal study abroad programming began after 1960. Only with internationalization, however, did the college adopt an international education mission statement and learning goals for study abroad. The goals ask students to gain new perspectives on their fields of study, develop intercultural competencies and communication skills, learn others' perspectives, reflect on their assumptions and values, and learn about and from the study abroad site.

At this point, in campus discussions and conferences the college also asked itself the degree to which study abroad was adding value to its educational program. At the time, approximately 40% of Beloit students spent one or two semesters abroad; by 2008 the percentage was closer to 50. Other 2002 factors hold today. About two-thirds of Beloit's students study abroad as exchange or direct-enrollment students, with the other third enrolled in programs offered by study abroad providers. Although some exchange programs enroll as many as ten students, the majority of students are the only Beloiters at their sites, and Beloit operates a faculty-led semester program only every second year. Together these factors mean that the normal experience of a Beloit study abroad student is truly to be away from campus.

In the spring 2003 semester, an ad hoc group of faculty members and the director of international education convened over several weeks to discuss the creation of a study abroad preparation class. Study abroad applications and interviews suggested there were gaps in students' preparation for study abroad. As well, returned study abroad students, as evidenced by their study abroad evaluations and performance in classes, had not learned as much as anticipated. The faculty group's consensus was that at present, the preparation students were receiving in the curriculum and orientation programs was not sufficient for all students to succeed in study abroad. Some would need further intervention. They therefore decided to establish a two-semester hour, elective study abroad preparation course meeting once weekly over the semester, to be taught from year to year by different members of the group as their teaching schedules permitted.

Most intercultural specialists agree that intercultural competency involves "the ability to communicate effectively and appropriately in intercultural situations based on one's intercultural knowledge, skills and attitudes," with a close second definition involving "the ability to shift one's frame of reference appropriately, the ability to achieve one's goals to some degree, and the ability to behave appropriately and effectively in intercultural situations" (Deardorff, 2008, p. 23). Consistent with the first definition, the Beloit course, Developing Intercultural Competencies, employed comparisons between the United States and the students' anticipated study abroad sites to help the students understand abstract and concrete differences between these; develop the ability to recognize, analyze, and understand multiple perspectives; and negotiate different modes of communication. Reflection helped the students understand their own assumptions and values.

Because the course was taught over several semesters, consistent with Dear-dorff's second definition, modifications were introduced to help students gain skills needed to learn experientially and perform tasks in another cultural context (Lambert, 1994). The course also was modified to allow for more explicit connections to students' other studies, so as to help them mature in those areas as well.

Coincidentally, in 2002 a similar initiative was undertaken at Kalamazoo College, a small liberal arts institution founded in 1833. Kalamazoo has long prided itself on being forward-thinking, and over the past 50 years, approximately 85% of all its students have studied abroad. However, although a 2002 *U.S. News & World Report* article had ranked "K" College and its Center for International Programs first in the nation in the percentage of its students studying abroad, Kalamazoo faculty and administrators were concerned that study abroad was often bracketed off from students' other academic and life experiences. Students needed theoretical frameworks to help structure the experience, opportunities for significant reflection on the experience, and venues in which to share that experience upon their return. To address these needs, Kalamazoo College launched a new initiative, *Reclaiming International Studies: Helping the Campus Benefit From International Programs,* which was supported by the Andrew W. Mellon Foundation and the McGregor Fund. Citing many of the same goals as Beloit, the initiative included the development of a program to help study abroad students better prepare for, participate in, and reflect upon their experience. This program was christened the Kalamazoo Project for Intercultural Communication, generally referred to by its acronym, KPIC.

Most Kalamazoo students study abroad through programs administered by the college. A central feature of these programs is the Integrative Cultural Research Project (ICRP). In consultation with the resident directors of their programs, ICRP students select an activity (a service or volunteer project, a cultural internship, the collecting of life histories, etc.) requiring them to work with local people on local projects of local importance using the local language and employing local means and methods in a locally acceptable manner. Through a structured process of observation, interaction, research, and reflection, students ideally learn to perform tasks in another cultural context, and experience profound changes in cultural perspective. KPIC was thus born partially of a desire to strengthen the ICRP, but as it evolved, the ICRP came to be only one of several foci of study. Because it was not practical for a study abroad administrator to assume responsibility for the direction of this project, and no Kalamazoo College faculty member was a specialist in intercultural communication, a foreign language teacher with a strong interest in this area was selected to design and run the KPIC program in consultation with the college's Center for International Programs. In addition to her own independently selected readings on intercultural theory and training, as preparation the faculty member attended a summer seminar on teaching intercultural communication, taught by Stella Ting-Toomey and Leeva Chung at the Summer Institute for Intercultural Communication (SIIC).

Starting Points for the Courses

One starting assumption for both preparation courses is that their participants will be heterogeneous in background, interests, and destinations, and are unlikely to be supervised while abroad by a faculty member from one of the colleges. A second is that the course should help the students acquire habits (inquiry, observation, reflection), skills (observation, documentation, analysis, communication), and knowledge (factual and conceptual) to prepare them to learn while abroad. Savicki and Selby (2008) point out that much of the learning in study abroad is unplanned and serendipitous. The larger aim of the course, then, can be said to help students learn to get lost intelligently, so that they can manage and perhaps enjoy the experience of being an outsider in unknown places, learn from this experience, and reflect on it to grow personally, emotionally, and intellectually. Solnit writes about the value of getting lost as lying in the discovery it brings, but only if you know how to get lost: "[When] you get lost, the world has become larger than your knowledge of it" (2005, p. 22). This involves a loss of control, but if one is prepared, one can navigate that loss of control to learn and grow. This is a point repeatedly stressed by Darren Kelly in chapters 2 and 6 of this book, drawing on lessons from geography, among others.

Beloit College Course Structure and Assignments

Based on the starting points for the Beloit course outlined previously, students have weekly assignments involving reading, research, and writing, punctuated by assignments that involve gathering and recording information obtained in interactions with environments off campus. At the end of the course, they create a photo essay to synthesize and present what they have learned about their study abroad country.

In the first class period, we generate definitions of culture and establish baselines of the students' knowledge by drawing maps or visual representations of the countries to which they are going. Some of the students' maps contain outlines of the countries' borders, major rivers, and cities, whereas others contain images of people and things they associate with the country. Some are densely filled with information; others lack detail. Looking at the maps together permits the students to see how each thinks about the countries. A follow-up writing assignment asks them to think about what the map tells them about their knowledge of the country, what the other students' maps told them, and what they would like to explore over the course of the semester. As one student wrote, "The mapping exercise allowed me to compile my knowledge, thoughts, and fears about the Galapagos, so I could see what I already know, and what I should research more thoroughly. Most of the information on my map related to biology, my major, but I realize the islands have a sizable human population as well, and I will need to focus my research on that."

Writing assignments are organized into two kinds, both involving research. The first is "news" reporting, that is, a short essay on a topic the students have investigated that week. They can report on contemporary news, historical events, or cultural events; the choice is the student's. However, over the course of the semester they must use at least five different sources for the news they report, and must connect several of the news reports to their major studies. One paragraph reports on the news as objectively as possible, with a second devoted to a discussion and analysis of the news, including a reflection on the possible implications for their study abroad. The minimum requirement is two well-written paragraphs; however, the students frequently write more and often use multiple sources as well. A roundtable at the start of each class allows the students to report on their findings; this allows the students to find out about each other's countries and triggers ideas for their research for the next week as well as ideas for sources to use. The assignment quickly allows students to discover things they had not known about their study abroad countries and to reexamine what they think they know. "The traditional British Sunday culture is apparently stronger than I thought it was," wrote one student. "Perhaps British traditions, such as gardening and the Sunday roast, occupy the symbolic cultural role that church occupies in the U.S." This assignment also encourages habits that are useful while they are abroad: "My [host] family is always talking about current issues, and to be able to participate I check the world news every time I'm online. The class taught me to."

The second kind of writing is one- to two-page essays in response to the readings, research undertaken related to the course reading, and experiential learning assignments. So that students can better understand who they are and how they came to be that way, many of the readings assigned come from U.S. sources, both contemporary and older ones; for international students enrolling in the course, this provides windows into the United States, and points of comparison with both their own country and the third country that they now are studying. Part of the idea is to help the students realize that what they know as "normal" was not always so.

For example, when the course looks at concepts of cleanliness and tidiness, the common text is Suellen Hoy's *Chasing Dirt: The American Pursuit of Cleanliness* (1995), which chronicles the relationship of the United States to cleanliness from the early 19th century, when Americans were rather comfortable with dirt, into the modern period, by which time standards for both personal and public cleanliness had advanced. In the course we read excerpts from the book on the work of the Sanitary Commission in the Union North during the U.S. Civil War, and how the commission's work teaching soldiers and their officers basic sanitation concepts (constructing and using latrines) and habits of personal hygiene (daily washing of face, hands, and feet) not only limited death from disease and kept soldiers out of field hospitals, but also spread these concepts and habits to the farms and other homes to which they returned at war's end. We also read an excerpt from the book on how the lessons from the Sanitary Commission were subsequently adapted by civic leaders to mobilize efforts and institute measures to increase the health and cleanliness of U.S. cities. These readings help the students understand that what constitutes "clean" in the United States has changed over time, and that just as they were taught as children to wash themselves and keep themselves neat, a young nation was taught to do so as well. The texts then serve as a springboard for the students to conduct their own research into cleanliness as it is understood and practiced in their study abroad countries. The students have considerable latitude as to what they choose to investigate for this assignment; one semester a student looked at bathing in Japan, and another followed an environmental campaign in Australia. This enabled the first student to see how ideas about togetherness, nature, resources, time, and relaxation are embedded in Japanese approaches to bathing, and the second student began to see how environmental realities would shape her day-to-day activities in Australia. The Australia campaign also made her wonder how its lessons might be applied in the United States.

If some assignments allow students to explore concrete and abstract differences between their home and study abroad countries, others allow students to test experiential learning methods. Following an in-class exercise intended to sharpen students' observation skills, the students walk along a specific route in Beloit to observe and record as much as they can. The students can go singly or in pairs and choose when to take the walk. The route deliberately takes them to streets they probably have traveled before, as well as to streets they probably have not. Along the way, they are asked to look for clues to Beloit's past, present, and future, and to record information about infrastructure and natural, human, and animal worlds. Although most elect to take a camera along as well as a notebook, the occasional student instead relies on notes and sketches. Presentations in class the following week show them that they each see and notice differently, and that a city they hitherto may have largely ignored also offers its share of discoveries: "This walk gave me a new sense of the town. . . . I was able to see neighborhoods where I would never go otherwise." They also learn the degree to which they are comfortable taking photos and notes and what it feels like to enter a new neighborhood. In short, they evaluate themselves as observers.

The students then read texts in which others have documented their experiences and observations (see Appendix A in this chapter for examples of texts), after which they first document their fall or spring break using three or more techniques, and then write an essay on what they documented, the techniques they used and their effectiveness, and the implications for their study abroad.

Theories related to living in another culture and cultural adjustment are introduced at several points during the semester. Classroom exercises simulate the experience of cultural dissonance, as does the assignment described by Nancy Krusko in chapter 9 in which students spend an hour in an unfamiliar setting as participant observers. Narrative also helps the student see how theory applies to experience. For example, near the end of the course, the students read Jane Smiley's short story, "Long Distance" (1987), to see how Adler's (1981) theory of reentry adjustment can be used as a tool for analysis; they are then asked to think about their own experiences of adjustment (for example, to college in a distant state) and readjustment (to home after being away at college). An essay on a Peace Corps volunteer's experiences in Mauritania prompts the students to think about their own positionality (Dahlgren, 2005), and an essay in *Distant Mirrors* (DeVita & Armstrong, 2002) helps them think about cultural differences and adjustment, how they might be viewed as Americans while abroad, and their own biases and assumptions.

Finally, as referenced earlier in this chapter, the concluding assignment for the class involves a photo essay about the students' study abroad countries, which the students present in the final class session. This assignment allows the student to see how much they have learned since the start of the class, order it, and share it with others, and serves as practice for similar work when they are abroad and return home.

Kalamazoo College Course Structure and Assignments

KPIC was designed as a three-part course with students receiving credit after completing all three segments. Part II takes place abroad and is facilitated by the study abroad program. The discussion here, therefore, focuses on parts I and III. Part I consists of a short course in intercultural communication and training in how to become competent participant observers in another culture. The main components of the intercultural piece are (as summarized by Lustig & Koester, 2005) definitions of culture, Hall's notion of high- and low-context cultures, Kluckhohn and Strodtbeck's value orientations, Hofstede's cultural patterns, verbal and nonverbal codes, cultural aspects of rhetoric (what is a culture's preferred mode of organization for an oral or written "document," such as a student paper or presentation, and what constitutes "evidence" across cultures), "rules" for conversation, and the notions of "face" and "saving face." Students also read Craig Storti's *The Art of Crossing Cultures* (2001).

To learn how to observe another culture and to analyze "cultural incidents," the course's point of departure is Raymonde Carroll's *Cultural Misunderstandings* (1988), which discusses the need and procedures for cultural analysis, and then provides excellent models in essays on such subjects as "Home," "Parents and Children," "Friendship," "The Couple," and so on. Heeding Carroll's admonition to validate any interpretations of a culture by finding other evidence that supports the initial interpretation, the KPIC instructor and students modified the common mnemonic for cultural analysis, DIE (describe–interpret–evaluate), by adding "V" for "validate," thus yielding the acronym "DIVE" referred to in chapter 1.

Each week students write short papers, many of which are accounts of observation assignments they are given. One such assignment might be to visit a large American supermarket, noting what its layout and merchandise suggest about American individualism (e.g., chunky spaghetti sauce, sauce with meat, without meat, with garlic, without garlic, with extra garlic), attitudes toward time (e.g., microwaveable precooked pancakes, scrambled eggs, mashed potatoes; hours when the store is open), and cleanliness (What foods can one actually touch? Why might one find anti-bacterial wipes at the entrance to the market? etc.). Opportunities for observation are also offered through the media of fiction, nonfiction, and film. In fact, one of the most powerful experiences of the KPIC course is the viewing of the award-winning documentary, *Daughter from Danang* (Franco & Dolgin, 2002), which chronicles the reuniting of an Amerasian child and her Vietnamese mother after 22 years of separation. This reunion is rife with cultural disasters, offering a dramatic example of the importance of intercultural communication, demonstrating to students how much they have learned in the course ("I saw everything we had talked about during this class in that film") and renewing their resolve to prepare as well as they can for their own upcoming intercultural encounters.

Part III of the KPIC course contains roughly equal amounts of continued reflection on the study abroad experience and of sharing that experience with others. During the spring quarter, students discuss their essays with the instructor and their classmates, continue the process of reading and reflection, and contemplate the difficulties inherent in talking about their experiences. To this end, they read texts by other culture-crossers, observing how good writers express the complex and shifting emotion and cognition that their journeys have produced. In the spring of 2008, for instance, they read *The Village of Waiting* (2001), George Packer's painful account of his Peace Corps stint in Togo; and *36 Views of Mt. Fuji* (2006), Cathy Davidson's skillful synthesis of her ongoing relationship with Japan. It is valuable for Kalamazoo students to read at least one account of a difficult or "unsuccessful" experience abroad (like Packer's); Kalamazoo College culture seems permeated with the assumption that all of its students have a "transforming experience," and many students feel guilty or inadequate if theirs was not.

Acknowledging this reality has made students more free to talk about all aspects of their study abroad; in recent years, the class has even served as a sounding board for a few non-KPIC students enrolling in the course who are seeking to put negative experiences in a larger context.

A second component of the course puts the KPIC students in contact with a wider audience. When they return, they complete a brief unit on public speaking and then present a poster session, the focus of which is the Integrative Cultural Research Project (ICRP) they conducted in their host country. These sessions are offered to members of the Kalamazoo College community (a) in the early spring, when the sophomores have confirmed their study abroad placement and are thinking about the ICRP; (b) later in the same spring, when those sophomores' parents are on campus for the Parents' Orientation program; and (c) the following fall, during Family Weekend, when many first-year students' parents are beginning to contemplate the study abroad component of their sons' and daughters' college careers. Although the student presentations use the ICRP as their point of departure, conversations range far and wide, stretching to such subjects as history, geography, politics, culture, safety, homestays, and the academic experience.

In addition, students present their experiences to audiences in a variety of venues beyond the campus, both in Kalamazoo and in their own hometowns. In addition to the general audiences in churches, elementary schools, middle schools, high schools, and retirement centers, the specialized nature of the ICRPs also attracts more specialized audiences, for example:

- A nature center (the rehabilitation of injured raptors in France)
- The Salvation Army or the Gospel Mission (work in homeless shelters and restaurants for the homeless)
- Free Burma Association and Amnesty International (projects serving refugees)
- Local environmental organizations (internships with the Green Party in Germany)
- Local or organic food organizations and various ethnic cultural organizations (projects involving cooking, growing, or selling local foods abroad)
- Education classes and organizations serving people with disabilities (services projects abroad with the blind, the deaf, the physically or developmentally disabled with similar organizations)

Such speaking engagements allow students to share their newly acquired knowledge with particularly interested parties. During the reentry period, students are often frustrated to realize that any anecdote taken out of context seems somehow to be a false representation of their experience; they do not know "where to start." When the conversation is rooted in the concrete details of a shared interest, though, it often flows effortlessly.

During KPIC's part III, as students revise older essays and write a new one on reentry, they all become aware of the ways in which they continue to reframe their experiences. They all express appreciation for the opportunity KPIC offers them to shape—and reshape—their experiences.

Lessons Learned

The assignments submitted in the Beloit class and subsequent self-reports indicate that students in the preparatory course do, indeed, learn quite a bit. One student wrote, "I was listening to an interview by someone who had just returned from London who said it was perfect, she wouldn't change a thing about it. It made me think of everything that isn't perfect about London: terrible traffic, rainy weather, cramped houses, etc., and then I realized, my view of London is more well-rounded!" As they "write home," Kalamazoo students also have routinely shown that they retain and apply concepts they have learned in the KPIC class. One group even coined the phrase "KPIC moment" to describe those flashes of insight that came to them as the "bizarre" became "normal" when viewed through the lens of intercultural analysis.

The logistics of the course are another matter, however. At both Beloit and Kalamazoo, because the course is worth fewer credits than most courses, most students are obliged to take it as an overload, which limits the pool of students who take it. At Kalamazoo, it was originally thought that the students in the course would take an underload during the quarter following their return from study abroad, because they had taken part I of the course as an overload. However, most do not. In Beloit's case, the course was to be paired with a course for returned study abroad students, making it possible for students to take an underload in one semester as well. In the Beloit case, students tend to take either the pre- or post-study abroad course, but not both. Furthermore, since the course's inception, Beloit has adopted a reduced teaching load, and many of the original faculty members involved in the project are unavailable to teach it. Instead, the director of international education teaches the course as her regular duties permit. Kalamazoo has been able to cover the KPIC course by hiring foreign language adjuncts to cover the instructor's regular teaching responsibilities, but if good adjunct instructors are not available to cover the courses, this practice can be detrimental. In addition, the Kalamazoo course's many extra administrative and teaching responsibilities (corresponding with students, maintaining a website, arranging and providing transportation to speaking engagements, etc.) have made it difficult for one person to handle.

More positively, however, faculty and curriculum development activities, including the collaboration of Beloit College and Kalamazoo College that led to this book, have allowed practices from the course to spill over into other courses taught on campus. For example, some Beloit faculty now are more intentional in their teaching of the skills required of participant observers, as evidenced by Daniel Youd's course on Chinese cities and Nancy Krusko's Nicaragua course (see chapters 8 and 9, respectively). The chapters by Nancy Krusko (chapter 9), Marion Fass and Anne Fraser (chapter 10), and Pablo Toral (chapter 11) demonstrate how courses and advising can bring the emotional learning of study abroad into play, and all contributions by Beloit faculty in this volume offer examples of how to advance intercultural learning. More Beloit College first-year seminar instructors are now using explorations of the city to both introduce students to experiential learning techniques and help them think about their relationship to the city and its residents; both entry-level and advanced courses are now focusing more on intercultural learning. At Kalamazoo, the KPIC course was a natural complement to the work of its Internationalization Task Force, as were other courses, such as the religion course discussed by Carol Anderson and Kiran Cunningham (chapter 4) in this volume. Other Kalamazoo faculty members are using readings, techniques, and terminology that originated with KPIC. Kalamazoo College is now engaged in a process of curricular reform that will include the development of several sophomore seminars, many of them focused in some way on the intercultural experience. These will be taken as a part of the students' full course load, and may well come to take the place of KPIC.

Study abroad preparation courses can continue to play an important role in strengthening study abroad. However, one of their most important roles may be to help transform the larger curriculum, in the process rendering themselves obsolete.

References

Adler, N. (1981). Re-entry: Managing cross-cultural transitions. *Group and Organizational Studies, 6*(3), 341–356.

Bennett, J. M. (2008). On becoming a global soul: A path to engagement during study abroad. In V. Savicki (Ed.), *Developing intercultural competence and transformation: Theory, research, and application in international education* (pp. 13–31). Sterling, VA: Stylus.

Burn, B. B. (1980). *Expanding the international dimension of higher education.* San Francisco: Jossey-Bass.

Carroll, R. (1988). *Cultural misunderstandings: The French-American experience* (Carol Volk, Trans.). Chicago: University of Chicago.

Center for Global Education. (2008). Course information: Steps to become a global scholar. Retrieved July 24, 2008, from http://globalscholar.us/course_description.asp.

Chambers, A., & Chambers, K. (2008). Tuscan dreams: Study abroad student expectation and experience in Siena. In V. Savicki (Ed.), *Developing intercultural competence and transformation: Theory, research, and application in international education* (pp. 128–153). Sterling, VA: Stylus.

Cohen, A. D., Paige, R. M., Kappler, B., Demmessie, M., Weaver, S. J., & Chi, J. C., et al. (2003). *Maximizing study abroad: A language instructor's guide to strategies for language and culture learning and use.* Minneapolis, MN: Center for Advanced Research on Language Acquisition.

Dahlgren, K. E. (2005, Fall/Winter). Waiting for rain in Mauritania. *Beloit College Magazine,* 24–27.

Davidson, C. (2006). *36 Views of Mt. Fuji: On finding myself in Japan.* Durham, NC: Duke University.

Deardorff, D. K. (2008). Intercultural competence: A definition, model, and implications for education abroad. In V. Savicki (Ed.), *Developing intercultural competence and transformation: Theory, research, and application in international education* (pp. 32–52). Sterling, VA: Stylus.

DeVita, P. R., & Armstrong, J. D. (Eds.). (2002). *Distant mirrors: America as foreign culture* (3rd ed.). Belmont, CA: Wadsworth.

Franco, V., & Dolgin, G. (Directors). (2002). *Daughter from Danang* [Motion picture]. (Available from Balcony Releasing in association with Cowboy Pictures, 103 Hardy Pond Road, Waltham, MA 02451, or from the Public Broadcasting Service at http://www.shoppbs.org)

Global Partners Project. (2005). Symposia on pre-departure and reorientation programs. Retrieved July 24, 2008, from http://www.global-partners.org/best prac/reorientation.html.

Gore, J. E. (2005). *Dominant beliefs and alternative voices: Discourse, belief, and gender in American study abroad.* New York: Routledge.

Hoffa, W. W. (2002). Learning about the future world: International education and the demise of the nation state. In W. Grünzweig & N. Rinehart (Eds.), *Rockin' in Red Square: Critical approaches to international education in the age of cyberculture* (pp. 57–72). Münster: Lit-Verlag.

Hoy, S. M. (1995). *Chasing dirt: The American pursuit of cleanliness.* New York: Oxford University.

Hunter, A. (2008). Transformative learning in international education. In V. Savicki (Ed.), *Developing intercultural competence and transformation: Theory, research, and application in international education* (pp. 92–107). Sterling, VA: Stylus.

Kulacki, G. (2000, Winter). Area studies and study abroad: The Chinese experience. *Frontiers: The Interdisciplinary Journal of Study Abroad, 15,* 23–46.

LaBrack, B. (n.d.). Orientation courses. Retrieved July 26, 2008, from http://www.globaled.us/safeti/orientation.html.

Lambert, R. D. (1994). Parsing the concept of global competence. In R. D. Lambert (Ed.), *Educational exchange and global competence* (pp. 11–24). New York: Council on International Educational Exchange.

Lustig, M., & Koester, J. (2005). *Intercultural competence: Interpersonal communication across cultures* (5th ed.). Columbus, OH: Allyn & Bacon.

Packer, G. (2001). *The village of waiting.* New York: Farrar, Straus and Giroux.

Paige, R. M., Cohen, A. D., Kappler, B., Chi, J. C., & Lassegard, J. P. (2002). *Maximizing study abroad: A student's guide to strategies for language and culture learning and use.* Minneapolis, MN: Center for Advanced Research on Language Acquisition.

Pusch M. D., & Merrill, M. (2008). Reflection, reciprocity, responsibility, and committed relativism: Intercultural development through international service-learning. In V. Savicki (Ed.), *Developing intercultural competence and transformation: Theory, research, and application in international education* (pp. 297–321). Sterling, VA: Stylus.

Savicki, V. (2008). Experiential and affective education for international educators. In V. Savicki (Ed.), *Developing intercultural competence and transformation: Theory, research, and application in international education* (pp. 74–91). Sterling, VA: Stylus.

Savicki, V., & Selby, R. (2008). Synthesis and conclusions. In V. Savicki (Ed.), *Developing intercultural competence and transformation: Theory, research, and application in international education* (pp. 342–352). Sterling, VA: Stylus.

Selby, R. (2008). Designing transformation in international education. In V. Savicki (Ed.), *Developing intercultural competence and transformation: Theory, research, and application in international education* (pp. 1–10). Sterling, VA: Stylus.

Solnit, R. (2005). *A field guide to getting lost.* New York: Viking.

Smiley, J. (1987). Long distance. In *The age of grief: A novella and stories* (pp. 71–92). New York: Knopf.

Storti, C. (2001). *The art of crossing cultures* (2nd ed.). London: Nicholas Brealey.

Vande Berg, M. (2007). Intervening in the learning of U.S. students abroad. *Journal of Studies in International Education, 11*(3/4), 392–399.

Appendix A: Examples of In-Class Activities and Course Assignments, Developing Intercultural Competencies

What Does My Mental Map Tell Me?

Activity (first class period)

Draw a visual representation (mental map) of your host country, incorporating as much detail as you can. Share your map with others in the class.

Short Essay

Reflection on the mapping exercise. What did my map teach me? What do I know? What do I need/want to learn? What did I learn from others' maps?

Purpose

Establishes baseline of knowledge; encourages dialogue among the students and learning from each other, and raises questions for the students about what more they need to learn.

What Do We Mean By Home?

Reading

Rybczynski, W. (1987). *Home: A short history of an idea* (chapter 2 and pp. 61–62). New York: Penguin Books.

Short Essay

Chapter 2 discusses the absence of the notion of "home" in medieval Europe, and pages 61 and 62 note the embrace of the concept by the Dutch in the 16th century. Referring to the concrete and abstract notions of dwellings and home in the text, do research on where people live in your study abroad country and how they conceive of home. To prompt your research, you can use the research questions we generated in class. Write an essay on this, making reference to the excerpt from *Home*. Make sure to cite your sources. *Note:* You do not need to produce an essay of the depth and detail equivalent to the chapter in *Home*. You do want to begin to develop an imagination for the houses and homes you will become a part of when you study abroad.

Purpose

Establishes baseline of knowledge; encourages dialogue among the students and learning from each other, and raises questions for the students about what more they need to learn.

City Exploration

Field Research

You can do this by yourself or with one or two other students from the class. If possible, take a camera with you. Your job is to be the explorer, observing as much as you can and recording it. Using the map distributed in class, walk the route taking in as much as you can. (You may explore beyond the route, but you must use the route as the basis for this assignment.) Use a notebook to jot down your observations. Use a camera to take photos of things that seem significant to you, that tell a story, and that raise questions for you.

Here are some questions you might want to consider. You might also consider additional questions of your own.

What is here now? What might have been here in the past? What might be here in the future?

Infrastructure: What buildings do you see? What are they made of? What is their condition? What are the buildings used for? How might they have been used in the past? How do people get around? Are there roads? sidewalks? paths? public transportation? private transportation?

Natural world: How present or absent is the natural world along the route? What of the natural world is visible? What of the natural world is heard? smelled? felt?

Human world: Who occupies the spaces along the route? How do they occupy them? Are they residents? building owners? renters? Do they live here? do business here? How old are they?

Animal world: Are there any animals along the route that are indigenous to the area? Are there animals (pets or other) that have been introduced to the area?

Class Presentation

If you used a camera to document your experiences, select up to ten photos to bring to class to present your "essay" on what you observed. You can do this with the others on your team. If you do not use a camera, write in your notebook a description of 10 things you might have photographed.

Presentation

What story do the photos tell? (If you do not have photos, describe ten things you found significant.) Why did you select them? Did you learn anything new about Beloit by doing this? Did this exercise raise questions for you about what you saw or about Beloit? If you did this exercise again, how might you do it differently? What did you learn about being an explorer? What lessons do you draw from this exercise for your study abroad experience?

Short Essay

Write an essay responding to the questions for the presentation. You may want to illustrate it with your photos or with drawings or descriptions of the ten things you selected for the presentation.

Purpose

Teaches students some techniques for experiential learning (observation, documentation, reflection), helps them anticipate their role as outsiders and observers in another country, encourages critical thinking, and allows them to practice presentation skills.

Documentation

Readings

Agee, J., & Evans, W. (2000). *Let us now praise famous men* (pp. 170–176, photos of bedstead and front of house with two seated adult women and six children gathered on the porch). New York: Houghton Mifflin. (Original work published 1941.)

Ambrose, S. (1996). *Undaunted courage* (chapter 28). New York: Simon and Schuster.

Bennett, S. (n.d.) Unpublished e-mail journal.

DeVoto, B. (Ed.). (1997). *The journals of Lewis and Clark* (pp. 154–159, 324–325, 327). New York: Houghton Mifflin. (Original work published 1953.)

Page, L. G., & Wiggington, E. (1984). *The Foxfire book of Appalachian cookery* (pp. 44–48). New York: Dutton.

Theroux, P. (2003). *Dark star safari* (Chapter 11). New York: Penguin.

Short Essay

Reviewing the different ways in which experiences and environments were recorded in the readings, apply these to your experiences during the semester break. Use three or more techniques to record your activities, observations, interactions with others, and the environments in which you spend fall break. Write an essay summarizing the techniques you used and why, and discuss the implications for your study abroad.

Purpose

Teaches students some techniques for experiential learning (observation, documentation, reflection), helps them anticipate their role as outsiders and observers in another country, encourages critical thinking, and allows them to practice presentation skills.

Appendix B: Student Writing, Kalamazoo College

In this essay, "Mai Khao Jai Kreng Jai!" written during his junior year in Thailand, Kalamazoo College graduate Matthew Pieknik describes the bewilderment of an American student trying to navigate a high-context Asian culture.

Almost everything I had learned about Thai culture before coming here suggested that American and Thai cultures were about as opposite as possible. If Americans seem time-obsessed, then Thais seem never to have grasped the concept in the first place. American culture is characterized as very individualistic, whereas Thai culture is characterized as very collectivistic. Given these and other seemingly polar opposites, I expected a challenging degree of cultural misunderstanding.

Therefore, after spending a couple weeks with my homestay family, on campus, or on rarer occasions, around the city, I was surprised at how easily I'd seemed to slide right into Thai culture with apparently only the most minor of cultural faux pas. The first time I walked into my family's house I forgot to take off my shoes, but that was a one-time affair. . . . Overall, I was secretly thrilled with myself for being such a prepared, observant, and respectful visitor. I'd never expected that my powers of intercultural understanding included the ability to perceive the potentiality of a cultural misunderstanding in any situation and avoid it as skillfully as any superhero sidesteps a trap set by his archenemy. So what if I didn't know the language? I apparently had an understanding that transcended language.

Foolishly convinced of my sensitivity and consequent invincibility, it wasn't until I began to interact with more Thai people and try to befriend them that I realized there was something larger and subtler at work than I had previously conceived: *kreng jai.*

Americans are said to highly value honesty; but, as is true in other Asian countries, Thais value social harmony over honesty and respect the concept of "saving face," wherein honesty is often more of a possibility than a prerequisite in interaction with other people. In Thai the concept is defined as *kreng jai,* which might be roughly translated as "strict heart" or "careful heart." It refers to rules of behavior that all Thais practice and deeply respect. To practice it is to be constantly aware of how what you say or how you act will be interpreted by other people, and of how important it is to avoid straining the social harmony that makes communication and interaction in Thai culture as respectful, friendly, generous, and free-and-easy as it is.

In my time here I have probably committed many more cultural faux pas than I am conscious of, and though I expected people to inform me if I did something wrong, correcting the *mai kreng jai* (*un-kreng jai*) behavior of a visitor to this culture would be extremely *mai kreng jai* in itself. Except for a few things my American program director has pointed out to me, and the shoe incident my first night in Thailand, I have never been corrected for anything, which explains my false sense of security.

Aside from making it more difficult to be aware of my own cultural faux pas, *kreng jai* has also made it difficult for me to build friendships, that is, to gauge honesty and authentic behavior. Granted, there is the language barrier. When I have been in the company of someone I'm trying to become friends with, even basic conversation is difficult. I find myself desperately searching for anything to say just to keep a conversation flowing, but the Thai on the other end seldom initiates conversation unprompted. When I am initiating all the dialogue, I feel like I am imposing, forcing that person to talk to me.

And there's an important distinction between knowing no Thai and knowing only "some." It doesn't really help too much to know only "some" Thai. I can start a simple conversation about sports or food or school, but after the initial question I have no idea what's being said. So then I try in English and the Thai person doesn't understand. This explains partially, I think, why a lot of the Thais I know don't initiate conversation—they know just as little English as I do Thai, and are probably just as intimidated to try and use it as I am.

Kreng jai just adds to my relationship-building difficulties. There's always hesitation to say or do anything that might go against the other party's wishes, opinions, or feelings. At home 99% of the people I encounter every day speak my native language. In addition, I am so in tune to the ways in which other people act and present themselves that most of the time it isn't difficult to discern who genuinely enjoys your company and who's only "faking it." So far I can find no indication of that here. Take, for instance, my host-brother, Ahn, from the family I stayed with last week in Mae Tha; I don't know if Ahn genuinely enjoys my company or if he thinks I'm an annoying, inquisitive person and he's just wary of crossing me and saying, "No, I don't want to hang out with you" because that would be entirely too confrontational and *mai kreng jai.* When I found out that he goes to school just down the street from my university's campus and that he likes to eat dinner at the student market where my host parents work, and that we both liked a particular dance club here in Chiang Mai, that gave us a variety of ways to meet up and do things. Hoping to make my first real Thai friend, I made plans to go to the market the other night for dinner. However, another aspect of *kreng jai* is that half the time when you make plans with another Thai person, they're not necessarily real plans, but are actually agreed to out of a sense of social harmony, because to agree to them is *kreng jai.*

For example, if I were to say, "Hey Ahn, we should meet for dinner Tuesday night!" he might know very well that he cannot make it, but will answer yes, just as a way of indicating how much he would *like* to go with me if only he could. And then I might show up on Tuesday, but never find him there, because I only asked once, and he wanted me to know that he *wanted* to go, but I only asked once and didn't realize what was happening. Therefore, to make this plan with Ahn really materialize, I have to push the issue and say, "OK, do you really want to go? When are we going to go?" and reconfirm the details several times, all of which seems very rude to me.

And after all of this Ahn might say yes even if he doesn't want to go, even if he doesn't care for my company, because I should have realized that if he was offhanded about it, he didn't want to go. To be unaware of these subtleties leads to *mai kreng jai* behavior, and for him to decline after all my efforts would be *mai kreng jai* as well.

Not to mention the fact that when we finally sat down to dinner, I felt terribly inadequate anyway because all of a sudden I was sitting with someone I didn't really know, but wanted to, and wanted to talk to, but couldn't, and didn't even know if he really wanted to be there anyway, or if I just forced him to show up.

And thus, the biggest difficulty I have felt here emerges. I remember how excited I was about the book we read in class that illustrated the different models of American and French friendships [Raymonde Carroll's *Cultural Misunderstandings*]. I need the version of that book that will explain how *kreng jai* works in Thai relationships. I just don't know the in's and out's of how to be a Thai friend, the subtleties of interacting in this culture (my superhero powers are officially useless!), and no one seems to be willing to be honest, because it might cross me. That would be *mai kreng jai*.

4

CULTURE, RELIGION, AND NATIONALITY

Developing Ethnographic Skills and Reflective
Practices Connected to Study Abroad

Carol S. Anderson and Kiran Cunningham

As institutions prepare to send even more students abroad, it is imperative that as much attention be paid to preparing them to learn from their study abroad experience as is paid to crafting the experience itself. Students must be ready to learn and be equipped with an intercultural toolkit composed of essential knowledge, attitudes, and skills that they can draw upon as they enter into and live within a culture different from their own (see chapter 1 in this volume). They need not only knowledge of the place to which they are going, but also the conceptual and theoretical knowledge that will help them make sense of what they encounter there. They need attitudes that will allow them to suspend judgment, deal with ambiguity, and gain confidence. In addition to critical language skills, they need the ethnographic skills associated with active listening, close observation, description, and interpretation (Jurasek, Lamson, & O'Maley, 1996; Ogden, 2006). Without these fundamentals, students lack the foundation needed to productively and meaningfully engage with the people and institutions with whom they will be living and interacting, and therefore it is less likely they will achieve the kinds of transformative learning toward which most study abroad is aimed.

The course discussed in this chapter was originally designed to provide students about to study abroad with this critical intercultural toolkit and help returning juniors process the toolkit they developed while abroad as well as understand its relevance in the United States. (As seen in the discussion section at the end of this chapter, in the future it will enroll only sophomores.) Through a triple focus on theoretical/conceptual understanding, fieldwork, and self-understanding, and the connections and disjunctions that occur at the intersections of these foci, students develop crucial elements of the knowledge, attitudes, and skills components of the kit. After discussing the framework and structure of the course itself, we examine a sample of student work to determine the degree to which the course design engages students in the process of transformative learning.

Course Goals for "Culture, Religion, and Nationality"

The theoretical framework for the course is the intersection of culture, religion, and nationality. We use a variety of authors, leading toward postcolonial analyses toward the end of the course. We start by reading all of Thomas Tweed's *Our Lady of the Exile: Diasporic Religion at a Cuban Catholic Shrine in Miami* (1997). We then turn to Clifford Geertz's classic article, "Religion as a Cultural System" (1973), excerpts from Benedict Anderson's "Imagined Communities" (2001), and Arjun Appadurai's "Disjuncture and Difference in the Global Cultural Economy" (2002). Toward the end of the term, we have students read Talal Asad's 1983 article on Geertz and then a chapter out of Tweed's *Crossing and Dwelling: A Theory of Religion* (2006) as a way of returning to our initial conversations about definitions of religion. The course is designed with a tripartite structure: Students learn from the course readings and in-class discussions, conduct fieldwork, and connect these with their study abroad experiences, either in retrospect (for juniors) or in anticipation (for sophomores). We address the course goals and each of these components in turn, ending this section with a short discussion of how we seek to tie the components together at the end of the term.

The course goals begin with asking sophomores to anticipate their time abroad, and juniors to reflect on their time away. The second goal explicitly asks students to connect the global with the local by drawing on the emerging literature of culture, religion, nationality, and transnationalism to explore the diversity of the Kalamazoo area through fieldwork projects with local religious congregations. Our goals for theoretical learning include understanding the fundamental questions emerging in the fields of postcolonial studies in religion, nationality, and transnationalism. The final course goals are for synthetic learning: Outside the classroom, students learn how to conduct both ethnographic research and research in the history of religions, and will leave the course with an understanding of the ways that the dynamic processes of religion, culture, nationalism, and transnationalism play out in the dynamics of local faith communities and Kalamazoo.

As a means of helping students develop an intercultural toolkit linked to study abroad, and as an end in and of itself, we introduce the diversity of southwest Michigan to our students, and engage them in discussions about diversity and intercultural understanding abroad and at home. Although the bulk of our students are white and middle-class, increasing numbers are first-, second-, or third-generation students of color who share comparable class backgrounds with our Anglo students. This demographic means that we have a relatively wide array of experiences from which to draw during in-class discussions.

The course itself begins with a discussion of culture. What is it? How does it function in students' lives? In-class discussions and lectures introduce this concept, although we also examine each author's definition of culture as we work our way through the readings. Establishing the relationship between culture—we all have one—and intercultural understanding is the first task for the term. The interrogation of the dynamic of culture and the deliberate focus on intercultural understanding is our way of starting the conversation with students about their own positionality and dismantling student expectations that "sameness" is at home and "difference" is abroad. To design the course, we drew upon our own experiences with non-Anglo communities in Kalamazoo and the surrounding areas. Because Anderson is a historian of religions and Cunningham an applied anthropologist, it seemed natural to turn toward recently formed, largely immigrant faith communities as field sites for students to encounter diversity outside the classroom. This has worked well for us in the years that we have taught the course, although we have wrestled with the role of "immigrant" in our choice of faith communities in the past year or so.

It is a challenge for students who do not consider themselves to be religious to attend services in faith communities on a regular basis. There are a different set of challenges for students of committed faiths. This issue, however, is a reality for any class in a department of religion or religious studies, and thus we also introduce the students to the academic study of religion, and teach them that there is a way to set their own skepticism or faith commitments aside to examine the nature of religious commitment, practice, and faith. In this course, combining the academic study of religion with intercultural understanding provides students with a rare opportunity to have conversations with people about the various roles of the faith community in their lives—as a social network, as a source of faith and belief, as an identity, and as simply a relatively mundane habit. However, from the first week the class readings point students toward different definitions of religion and we use the question "What is religion?" as one of the themes throughout the quarter.

Importantly, we do *not* attempt to introduce each of the religions that students experience. To be candid, we tried that the first year; it was tedious and impossible given the complexity of, for example, the Sikh tradition. We explicitly tell students that they are not to seek to understand what they see in terms of faith tenets and doctrines, nor should they research the basic doctrines. Instead, out of a firm commitment to the writings of Pierre Bourdieu, we focus students' attention on the practices in which they share and observe at their congregations. (See, for example, Bourdieu, 1984.) The goal is to gain skill in ethnographic participant observation, not to figure out whether the Hindus at the Hindu temple are "really Hindu." When students come back after a site visit and ask us about a particular practice or doctrine, we tell them to ask someone in the congregation. This approach, rooted in Catherine Bell's (1992) analysis of the dynamic of power that has traditionally structured studies of religious rituals, is a useful way to subvert the "academic authority" versus "naïve participant" issue before it ever really emerges.

Finally, the question of nationality provides the class with the framework to examine assumptions about what it means to be an American, an immigrant, and to live abroad. We blur the lines of nationality and transnationalism, and, more recently, postcolonial interrogations of nationality. Our pedagogical goal for this component is to deconstruct monolithic identities of "American." Juniors who have returned from six months abroad are eager to talk about how they were identified as American—this doesn't really vary whether they were in Lancaster, Chiang Mai, Quito, or Dakar. Almost every student has a story to tell about how he or she was identified as American—one student of South Asian descent was told she couldn't be American because she was Indian (she went to Australia). The anecdotes provide a backbone of discussion for the term and become testing grounds for the theories we read about nationalism and transnationalism. They also demonstrate for sophomores what they will experience as they travel. In the future, we will do more to help students identify the construction of their own national identities from the start of the term by writing their own family autobiographies in response to the question, "When did your family become American?"

As we detail in the following section, the final exam seeks to draw all three of the dimensions of this tripartite structure together. Using the class readings, we ask students to analyze their experiences at the faith communities they are studying as sites of convergence and disjuncture in which culture, religion, and nationality are rarely a seamless whole, as they often expect at the start of the term. In the classroom, though, the conversations toward the end of the term are often quite synthetic and energizing as students begin to make the connections among (a) cultural diversity in Kalamazoo; (b) religious congregations as sites of dynamic negotiations of self-identity, identities of "others," national identities, and community identities; and (c) more complicated understandings of nationalism, both American and non-American.

Key Components of the Course

Three kinds of work are turned in during the term: field notebooks, reading notes, and the final exam. We also have a "fun" midterm, designed as an informal check on their learning, in which the students use crayons to draw a picture on large sheets of paper of how culture, religion, and nationality (as defined by particular authors) converge and diverge at their field sites. All of the assignments are woven together with class discussions. The reading load for the class is deliberately lighter than for other classes at this level, in recognition that we are looking for quality of analysis and thinking and in recognition of the fact that the site visits take up a fair amount of time outside of class.

The students begin by learning to do fieldwork in one of five or six religious congregations. We have made arrangements with a Sikh Gurdwara, one of two Islamic centers in the area, a Hindu temple and cultural center, a Spanish-speaking Catholic congregation, a Korean Presbyterian church, and, in various years, a Chinese American church, a Vietnamese Buddhist center, a Greek Orthodox church, and a Conservative Jewish synagogue. In future, we may include a more traditional Christian congregation that is *not* an immigrant congregation. Other congregations to which we have sent students in the past are not predominantly immigrant congregations—like the Greek Orthodox church and the Conservative Jewish synagogue. The difficulty with including nonimmigrant congregations is they make it more difficult to identify the role that nationality and transnationalism play. At the same time, however, it is important to demonstrate to students that the dynamics of culture, religion, and nationality are not present only in immigrant faith communities. Whatever the final list of congregations, on the first day of class students sign up by preference, and then one of us arranges the groups (in class), ideally, by year—we like a mix of sophomores and juniors at each field site—and by number. (It doesn't work if there is only one small car and seven students who need to get out to the field site across town.) Enrollments usually run around 25, so we try to get four or five students in each group. The students will make a minimum of six visits over the course of the next ten weeks to their sites, and use field notebooks to document the visits.

Field notebooks have two parts, starting with the fieldnotes themselves. These are observations, which must be (a) purely descriptive, including no personal commentary or interpretation; (b) vivid and detailed; and (c) a minimum of four single-spaced pages for each visit of about 1 hour. One classic example we use to illustrate the need for complete and full detail is a description of a man as "tall, wearing a turban, glasses, and tennis shoes." Was there nothing in between the turban and tennis shoes except for the glasses? The purpose is to get students to see not only what is foreign or unexpected, but also that which is familiar or expected (e.g., everything between the turban and tennis shoes). This is a learned skill that almost always improves during the course of the term.

The second part of the field notebooks is personal reflections. In this part, students are graded on each of the following topics: (a) depth of reflections on the process; (b) depth of reflection on their cultural assumptions and/or how they think about religion, either personally or in general; (c) discussion of learning related to study abroad (in hindsight or in anticipation); (d) any insights emerging out of the readings, class discussions, and fieldwork; and (e) reflections on the learning outcomes for international/intercultural understanding mentioned in the following text. Although the expectations for the reflection section are explicit, the quality varies substantially. The depth of reflection on the process varies among the students, especially early in the term, as does the depth of their reflections on their own cultural assumptions and/or religion. Often both of these insights improve significantly toward the end of the term as students become more adept at reflective learning generally and as they become increasingly comfortable writing about religion and gain a deeper understanding of themselves as cultural beings. The discussion of connections to study abroad can be very good; however, many students simply neglect this question—and miss out on the points allotted for that question. The emerging insights and connections between readings and their field sites also can be quite good. However, as seen in the following text, the students also take notes on the class readings each week in a separate assignment, and the remarks about their field sites included in their reading notes often are more insightful than those in their field notebooks, indicating, we believe, that students think more fruitfully from the text to the field site, instead of the reverse. This observation confirms the challenge of real experiential learning: It is much easier to start with a concept and find a "real-life" example to illustrate it than it is to start with the messiness of "real life" and interpret or explain it using concepts or theory.

Finally, the reflections on intercultural learning outcomes (included at the end of this chapter in the appendix) refer to a list that Kalamazoo College faculty drew up several years ago as part of Kalamazoo's comprehensive internationalization process. We ask that students go through the list to identify those skills that they have acquired or with which they are currently wrestling at their field site. As with the reflections on connections to study abroad, if they write on this question, their findings are illuminating. Indeed, we have found that students use it not only to develop their intercultural skills and attitudes, but also as a resource to help them make their way through the frustrations they often experience.

Students are always surprised at the amount of time fieldnotes take. To indicate our empathy, we have used video footage of the two of us and another colleague debriefing a visit to a temple in Kolkata, India, to show the students that we know precisely how much time is involved in writing fieldnotes.

The second ongoing assignment, due each week, is reading notes. The instructions for these are (a) three to four quotes (per article or chapter) that encapsulate the main arguments of the article or chapters they have read for the week, (b) one paragraph of reflection on new learning and/or new questions that emerged out of the reading, and (c) one to two paragraphs that connect the readings to observations at their field site. This is where we ask students for their tentative interpretations and emerging insights about what is going on at their field sites, particularly in terms of the dynamics of culture, religion, and nationality. Although students perceive the first couple of weeks of reading notes as quite burdensome in terms of workload, they soon get into a pattern of recording some interesting and fascinating connections. As mentioned previously, their emerging insights are often better in the third part of the reading notes than in the "connections to readings and class discussions" section of the field notebooks. Because students are far more accustomed to thinking from books and texts than thinking about what they are actually doing off campus, we would like to find ways to foreground this awareness, and encourage students to think *with* the authors we are reading while they are doing their site visits. Becoming adept at this more challenging way of linking what they are reading with what they are experiencing on site is critical to learning how to learn experientially, both in the context of study abroad and more generally.

These assignments form the backbone of class discussions. Each Monday, we begin by asking questions about that past weekend's site visits. We do a lot of small-group exercises, and ask the students to post their reading notes to the course management software, Moodle, by midnight Sunday night so that we can read them before class Monday morning. This enables us to start with the students' own understandings of the material instead of our own. This is not to say that we never lecture or lead discussion; however, we begin with the students' work and then move to other points that students didn't grasp. Similarly, we talk extensively about how to do the field notebooks—although we could do more with this, as our following discussion of the findings indicates. We talk loosely about experiences that students have had and things that make us laugh or cringe in sympathy. On an average, about 70% of the class is discussion based, including small-group exercises. The remaining 30% is devoted to short lectures. One of the interesting dimensions of the class is that it is team-taught. Team-teaching is not common at Kalamazoo College, and students are often uncomfortable when the instructors disagree. We deliberately use this discomfort, telling students that there *is* no right answer for this kind of analysis and that they need to learn from our disagreements.

The final exam provides for synthesis in the course, and we spend about 2 weeks preparing students for it. The exam question is almost always a variation on this question:

> Your task in this final exam is to conduct an analysis of your field site as a place of convergences and disjunctures in the dynamics of culture, religion, and nationality. You should choose at least four of the seven authors we have read in class, compare the strengths and weaknesses of each, and relate them to each other. In other words, you need to ground your analysis in the readings we have done in this course, but not simply by applying one quote to one finding from your field site. You should set your authors in dialogue with each other to elucidate the dynamics you found at your field site.

Here, we ask students not only to convey a theoretical understanding of culture, religion, and nationality, but also to understand how these are grounded in a local dynamic, in settings that are sites of disjuncture as well as convergence. In the final, they need to demonstrate their understanding of these as they apply to their particular field sites and we encourage them to work with other people in their group to prepare for the final, although they write the final draft on their own.

The three fundamental components of student work in this course— field notebooks, reading notes, and the final exam—provide students with enough structure to weave together their own ethnographic observations at their religious congregations with the theoretical and conceptual frameworks that we discuss in class. The ability to make connections between students' own positionality, the local setting of Kalamazoo, Michigan, and their study abroad experiences is developed through learning how to observe ethnographically and then learning how to conceptualize and analyze their experiences. In the following section, we examine a sample of student work to explore the degree to which students make these kinds of connections.

Analysis

At the end of the spring 2007 term, we explained to our students that we were planning on doing some research on student intercultural learning, and that we would like to use their reading notes and field notebooks from the class as data for this project. Eleven students agreed to let us use their work, providing us with electronic copies of their reading notes, personal reflections, and fieldnotes. The first and last set of personal reflections from each of those 11 students constitute the primary data for this analysis.

We began by coding the students' final set of reflections using a continuum of transformative learning developed by Cunningham and Grossman (2008). This continuum integrates research on transformative learning (Kiely, 2005; Mezirow, 1997) and intellectual development (Baxter Magolda, 1992; Erickson, 2007; Featherston & Kelly, 2007; Kegan, 1994; Pizzolatto, 2007). (See chapter 1 in this volume for additional discussion of these two bodies of research and the intersections between them.) It contains six levels of development: gains in knowledge, changes in attitudes, understanding of different perspectives, development of a structural understanding, development of a self-understanding, and changes in frames of reference. Within each level are a variety of more specific indicators. For example, under "attitude change" are "overcoming fear," "gaining confidence," and "letting go of control"; under "changes in self-understanding" are indicators such as "critically reflecting on one's perspective" and "taking responsibility for one's perspective." The indicators were the codes used in the analysis.

Table 4.1 shows the results of this coding. Each row reflects an individual student and each tick mark represents an instance of one of the indicators evident in their reflections.

Three groups representing different levels of learning emerged from the coding process. Group 1's reflections exhibited the lowest levels of learning, with relatively little in terms of structural and self-understanding. It is not that no learning was exhibited; rather, the learning was less far along the transformative learning continuum. One student in group 1, for example, discussing significant changes in attitude that had occurred as a result of her work in the class, linked these with her study abroad experiences:

> I made a lot of progress over the past weeks at the Hindu temple. I have learned a lot about culture not only from this class but from the visits to the temple. Much of what I've learned can be applied to my life. Especially being open-minded and not being scared to take chances. I like to take chances and challenge myself, but I think I choose the challenges that I want to do. This class and study abroad really force you to step out of your box and bridge gaps in your understanding of the world and cultures.

TABLE 4.1
Transformational Learning Levels Evident in Last Set of Personal Reflections

Student	Knowledge Gain	Attitude Change	Perspective Change	Structural Understanding	Self-Understanding	Change in Frame of Reference
Group 1	I					
				I	III	
		IIIIII		II	I	
	I	I	I		I	
		I		III	II	
Group 2				IIIIIII	III	
	I		I	IIII	IIIIII	
	IIII		IIII	IIIIIII	IIIII	
				IIIIII	IIIII	I
Group 3	I	IIIIII		IIII	IIIIIIIIIIIII	I
				I	IIIIIIIIIII	II

As a result of the course, this student described a greater willingness to take intercultural risks and a greater openness to intercultural learning, both of which are foundational to gains in structural and self-understanding further along the continuum.

The reflections by students in group 2 contained much more focus than those in group 1 on changes in their structural understanding and changes in their understanding of themselves. Although there was mention of these kinds of understandings in most of the group 1 reflections, group 2 exhibited a more sustained unpacking of structures and self. For example, one student made sense of her experience at the Islamic center by connecting it to a structural understanding of roles. In this quote, she discusses and processes the frustration she felt interacting with the Sunday school principal:

> He did not maintain eye contact for more than a second or two, he verbally questioned our presence, he told us—not asked us—where we would go and what we should do. . . . I had a hard time keeping an open mind—I didn't like him until the end of our visit. . . . Upon further reflection I

realized that his concern for our presence and his treatment of us was probably nothing personal but more related to the different roles he was playing as a male, Muslim, principal. Role as principal—concerned for the goings on of his school, who is there, what they are doing, how they are effecting [sic]/interrupting the classes. Role as a representative of a Muslim religious community to three white, obviously not Muslim, college students—are they getting an accurate, helpful portrayal of the Islamic center, are they in the classroom in which they will be able to learn the most? Role as an adult Muslim male in relation to young women—proper interaction is formal, much eye contact is not appropriate, commanding tone/language. This interaction was packed with gender/power/authority/age/insider-outsider dynamics. It's easy to forget that and take other people's behavior personally in reference to my own social/cultural script.

When this student was able to place the interaction in a structural context, she was able to make sense of it and de-charge the interaction by taking it out of her own cultural script embedded with assumptions about sexism and male power.

Another student in this group demonstrated a self-understanding by examining his own assumptions about religion and how they might have affected what he saw at the temple:

As someone who no longer attends a church or temple, but considers [himself] very spiritual, I am craving a place with which I can share and reinforce my religious beliefs. . . . Therefore I sort of projected this seriousness about practicing religion onto all of the people at the temple. Like as if attending temple is inherently the most important thing in one's life. But observing and talking to kids my age, I found that many are just as disinterested as I was with my time spent at a Christian church. To some of them it is just something their parents make them do. I don't know about other religion majors, but I tend to think of spiritual ideas as these ultimately important things in life and any chance to have serious reinforcement of them is fascinating and something I place so much value on in the world. But like I said about culture earlier, it is something personal and there is no reason to expect that one's own thoughts about religion are the same for any other person; in fact, doing this has caused some major problems throughout history.

This kind of reflection on one's own assumptions is a good example of the way that ethnographic methods can help students bracket their own assumptions, making them more visible for analysis in and of themselves.

Finally, group 3 shows more reflection occurring at the farther ends of the continuum. Both students in this category focus on unpacking and making visible their own frames of reference and approach the kinds of changes in frame of reference characteristic of transformational learning. One student, who spent the first half of the term being very frustrated with her field site because she couldn't find any religiosity, describes the shift required to see things differently:

> I have to start thinking again about my cultural upbringing and the fact that I am a cultural being. Whenever I went to church as a kid, or even now, when I go when I am back home, I always feel so uptight and stuffy. Wear your nice pants and a clean shirt, no flip flops because they make too much noise when you are walking down the aisle, don't talk in church, don't leave the pew unless absolutely necessary, always take away a crying baby or anything else that may cause distraction. . . . I could go on. Everything was always so formal and I always just felt smothered by rules. I think that before I really thought about this, that is why I was so frustrated at the church. Things are just so much more informal when I am used to such structure at church.

To get through the dissonance she was encountering, the student needed to examine her own assumptions, both in terms of what they were and their source. Once able to see these and understand how they were interfering with her ability to really see what was going on with the congregation, a new understanding was possible.

We considered a variety of explanations for the differences between groups. First, we wondered if students were starting at different places along the transformative learning continuum. Were those in groups 2 and 3 farther along to begin with than those in group 1? Did they have different attitudes toward intercultural engagement generally or fieldwork more specifically? Did they have less developed skills related to reflection? An analysis of the 11 students' first set of reflections suggests that none of these is the case. Although there is variation among the reflections along these lines, this variation does not seem to fall into these same groupings. In fact, almost all of the students expressed enthusiasm for the opportunity for intercultural interaction.

Further thinking about these students and examination of their first sets of personal reflections, however, revealed two distinct differences. The first was quite a surprise. The eleven students included seven sophomores, all of whom were about to leave for study abroad or study away experiences, and four juniors, all of whom had just recently returned from six-month studies abroad. All four juniors were in group 1. Second, there seemed to be a difference in the degree to which students acknowledged the challenge associated with the dissonance they experienced in their first site visit. Students in groups 2 and 3 were more likely to discuss the discomfort they felt and the challenge they would face in productively engaging in the community they were to study.

Taking the second observation first, students in groups 2 and 3 tended to spend a good deal of their first set of personal reflections discussing the discomfort they felt in their first visit. More significantly, however, they discussed the connection between this discomfort and their own learning, seeing the discomfort as a challenge and an important part of their learning. One student, for example, highlighted the challenge of the language barrier, writing:

> Right from the start, I knew that our single [biggest] challenge is the language barrier and struggles to communicate and understand each other. However, this is not a negative challenge, it only adds to the situation. . . . As we all struggled to communicate and understand what [others were] saying, that light went off in my head, that light that said, "ding, this is what this course is all about."

Another student wrote about approaching the door of the mosque, peering in, deciding that she couldn't muster the courage to enter, and then leaving and walking around the block before trying again. She summed up the challenges she will face in doing this fieldwork by enumerating four points:

1. It is a good thing for me to take time familiarizing myself with the Islamic center as a place. Now that I know the lay of the land, I will be more comfortable returning to challenge my wariness of Islamic gender/power dynamics.

2. I didn't initially realize how uncomfortable I am with those dynamics. Now I do and I can be careful to minimize the amount they distort my observations and analysis.

3. This experience was informative for me in terms of understanding my own personality and realizing what limits I need to push past and which I need to respect.

4. This was/is a good opportunity for me to understand what my own style of ethnographic research is. I can safely eliminate a caution-to-the-wind, jump-right-in style. If I were to take such an approach, my research might be disturbed by an over abundance of anxiety on my part, which I can reduce if I proceed in a different manner.

As exemplified by these two quotes, students in these groups tended to expect to be challenged and uncomfortable, but they also clearly understood that this was important to their learning. In contrast, the students in group 1, particularly the juniors just returned from study abroad, did not expect ongoing dissonance; rather, they expected that, compared with their study abroad experience, the fieldwork for this class would be fairly easy. One, for example, wrote:

I also think that having immersed myself into another culture for 5 months will really help me to immerse myself into the church and befriending the people. I am comfortable with surrounding myself in a new culture, and I think I have grown to be sensitive when trying to understand and learn something that I am unfamiliar with. And I realize my confidence and my strength because of study abroad more and more just by reflecting on this now. Further, even though Spanish culture is probably drastically different than Mexican, I look forward to recognizing those differences and learning along the way. I realize that this will be a lot easier than living in Spain because, even though I will be surrounded by a different ethnicity, we are still all united under the United States flag. We all have common ideals and beliefs, even if we have a different skin color. Therefore, I believe that connecting to and becoming a part of this congregation, and dealing with the intercultural dynamics, will be a lot easier than my life in Spain.

Similarly, another wrote:

To reflect again on my study abroad interactions and what I saw today, I feel like I was better prepared to handle this situation than I would have been before study abroad. Because of my language barriers in China I spent about 75% of my study abroad experience making a fool of myself or looking like an idiot or even worse not being able to communicate with people. So now that I am back in the United States my level of caring if I come off to people as stupid or not has gone way, way down and after spending so much time not being able to communicate with people effectively or coming off as illiterate I no longer worry (or at least not as much) about talking to people I don't know because at least I know they will understand me. So in that sense it is much easier to deal with intercultural dynamics here in the United States.

As illustrated by these two quotes, the returned study abroad students did not expect to encounter the cultural and linguistic difficulties in the United States that created the intercultural stumbling blocks abroad. Going into the experience with this assumption, they were less prepared for the dissonance they did encounter and probably less willing to admit it was there. Without being willing to confront the dissonance, there is little chance of working one's way through it in a way that leads to transformations in learning.

Discussion

There are two sets of conclusions to be drawn from these findings: conclusions about the effectiveness and design of the course, and conclusions about how we can better facilitate the learning of our returning juniors. Groups 2 and 3 tell us most about the former; group 1 helps us think about the latter.

At a general level, the work of groups 2 and 3 indicates that the design of the course, with its focus on fieldwork, theory and concepts, and personal reflections, does indeed provide a structure for students to engage in intercultural learning in productive ways. Learning and using the ethnographic tools of close observation and active listening forced them to really see what was going on and understand the group they were studying on its own terms. Becoming skilled at writing purely descriptive field notes also helped them to sideline their own interpretations, which put the "self" and all of its assumptions and expectations in greater relief. Although the personal reflections of both groups contained critical reflections on students' assumptions and expectations, the reflections of the two students in group 3 were striking in the degree to which they engaged in a critical examination of self.

FIGURE 4.1.
Three kinds of learning.

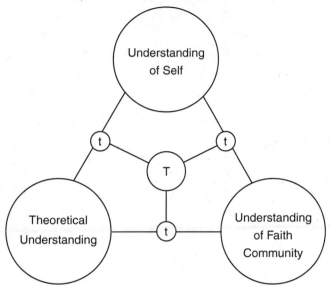

Looking back at the design of the course, we see that there are several ways in which we can increase the likelihood of more students getting to the level of group 3. The diagram in Figure 4.1 conveys the three kinds of learning we focus on throughout the course: understanding of self, theoretical understanding, and an understanding of the faith community students study. Although an understanding of the dynamics among culture, religion, and nationality develops at each point of the triangle, transformations in learning occur when students realize the connections along the sides of the triangle—for example, when students are able to make connections between their own cultural assumptions and notions of nationality, or between Geertz's analysis of the relationship between culture and religion and what they are seeing at their field sites. We are deliberate and attentive to these kinds of associations; in fact, toward the end of the term, we focus on nothing other than these insights and connections.

Writing this chapter, however, has helped us see where we might be more strategic in our focus on the intersections. For example, we could use this diagram with the students so they are (a) better able to understand where we are trying to situate their learning, and (b) better able to intentionally write and reflect at these intersections. We have also come to more clearly distinguish between the "small t" transformations (see Featherston & Kelly, 2007) that occur along the legs of the triangle, and the "capital T" Transformations that occur at the center. We designed the final exam to capture these Transformations, but it is clear now that although we have been very deliberate in asking students to make connections between the conceptual theories in class and their field sites, we have not been as deliberate in asking them to bring their emerging self-understandings into the analysis. We also realize that we have explicit vehicles for students to make connections between theory and field site (field notebooks and reading notes) and between self-understanding and fieldwork (structured reflections), but that we do not have a site for making explicit connections between theoretical understanding and self-understanding. In the future, we will address this by adding an element to the reading notes asking students to explore the ways that their understandings of themselves are connected to their emerging understandings of culture, religion, and nationality.

The second set of conclusions we can draw from the data concern returning juniors and connection or disconnection between the design of the course and where they are as intercultural learners. Returning juniors come to the course having just been through six months of intense intercultural learning in which they have developed a great deal of confidence about their intercultural competence and a sense of self that is tied to that competence. Moreover, they have just returned to the familiarity of home. Quite simply, the design of this course is out of sync with where they are. Although our intention was to provide an opportunity for them to apply their intercultural competence here in the United States, thereby helping them see the transferability and relevance of the knowledge, attitudes, and skills they had developed in a domestic setting, they were clearly not in a place to do this. Their conflation of cultural difference with differences in language and nationality, which made invisible the kinds of cultural challenges they would face in their fieldwork for the class, coupled with the confidence in their intercultural abilities left them unable to see and learn from the intercultural challenges they encountered at their field site. This observation is not a complaint about the juniors; rather, it is an acknowledgment that what they need to process and continue their intercultural learning when they return is not another cross-cultural experience; rather, they need a different kind of course—one that is much more focused on processing and extracting the learning from the experience they just had.

As a result of this analysis and the insights that stemmed from it, we will offer the course as a sophomore seminar in the future. The design of the course, with its emphasis on ethnographic methods, does indeed work for them. The focus on fieldwork connected with a broader conceptual and theoretical understanding of cultural dynamics, along with structured reflection aimed at situating themselves as culturally constructed beings, provides them with the intercultural toolkit necessary to engage in the process of transformative learning while studying abroad. Still to be determined, however, and the subject of another assessment exercise, is the degree to which students actually use this toolkit productively while abroad. Anecdotal evidence from students studying abroad who have had the course suggests that they do. Even without a definitive answer to this last question, however, we can say with certainty that (a) students need to be taught how to learn experientially, and (b) they need a great deal of practice doing it before they become proficient experiential learners.

References

Anderson, B. (2001). Imagined communities: Reflections on the origin and spread of nationalism. In S. Seidman & J. C. Alexander (Eds.), *The new social theory reader: Contemporary debates*. London: Routledge.

Appadurai, A. (2002). Disjuncture and difference in the global cultural economy. In J. X. Inda & R. Rosaldo (Eds.), *The anthropology of globalization: A reader* (pp. 46–63). Chichester, UK: Blackwell. (Original work published 1996.)

Asad, T. (1983, June). Anthropological conceptions of religion: Reflections on Geertz. *Man N.S. 18*(2), 236–59.

Baxter Magolda, M. B. (1992). *Knowing and reasoning in college: Gender related patterns in students' intellectual development*. San Francisco: Jossey-Bass.

Bell, C. (1992). *Ritual theory, ritual practice*. New York: Oxford University Press.

Bourdieu, P. (1984). *Distinction: A social critique of the judgment of taste* (R. Nice Trans.). London: Routledge. (Original work published 1979.)

Cunningham, K., & Grossman, R. (2008). *Continuum of transformational learning*. Unpublished manuscript, Kalamazoo College, Kalamazoo, MI.

Erickson, D. (2007). A developmental re-forming of the phases of meaning in transformational learning. *Adult Education Quarterly, 58*(1), 61–80.

Featherston, B., & Kelly, R. (2007). Conflict resolution and transformative peda-gogy: A grounded theory research project on learning in higher education. *Journal of Transformative Education, 5*(3), 262–285.

Geertz, C. (1973). Religion as a cultural system. In *Interpretation of cultures: Selected essays* (pp. 87–125). New York: Basic Books.

Jurasek, R., Lamson, H., & O'Maley, P. (1996). Ethnographic learning while study-ing abroad. *Frontiers 2*(1), 23–44.

Kegan, R. (1994). *In over our heads: The mental demands of modern life.* Cambridge, MA: Harvard University Press.

Kegan, R. (2000). What "form" transforms? A constructive-developmental approach to transformative learning. In J. Mezirow (Ed.). *Learning in transforma-tion: Critical perspectives on a theory in progress* (pp. 35–69). San Francisco: Jossey-Bass.

Kiely, R. (2005). A transformative learning model for service-learning: A longitudi-nal case study. *Michigan Journal of Community Service Learning 12,* 5–22.

Mezirow, J. (1997). Transformative learning: Theory to practice. *New Directions for Adult and Continuing Education 74,* 5–12.

Ogden, A. (2006). Ethnographic inquiry: Reframing the learning core of education abroad. *Frontiers: The Interdisciplinary Journal of Study Abroad 8,* 87–112.

Pizzolato, J. E. (2007). Assessing self-authorship. *New Directions for Teaching and Learning 109,* 31–42.

Tweed, T. (2006). *Crossing and dwelling: A theory of religion.* Cambridge, MA: Har-vard University Press.

Tweed, T. (1997). *Our Lady of the exile: Diasporic religion at a Cuban Catholic shrine in Miami.* New York: Oxford University Press.

Appendix A: Desired Intercultural Learning Outcomes for Kalamazoo College

Knowledge

- Understand that we are "cultural beings" and our own beliefs and values reflect our own culture
- Knowledge of the student's own culture
- Knowledge of U.S. history, society, and the plurality of U.S. culture
- Knowledge of cultures beyond U.S. borders
- Understand the connections between U.S. history and global histori-cal trajectories

- Knowledge of global economic, technological, and environmental complexity and interdependency, and the ways that these are played out at local, regional, national, and international levels
- Understand the nature of language and how it reflects diverse cultural perspectives (i.e., the way language organizes information and thought processes and reflects culture)
- Understand the ways that the student's own actions have effects nationally and internationally

Skills

- Know how to learn in class and experientially
- Use effective communication, listening, and observation skills to enhance intercultural understanding
- Know the difference between description, interpretation, and evaluation, and be able to initially bracket interpretation and evaluation as "participant observers" in another culture
- Use diverse cultural frames of reference to think critically and creatively solve problems
- Able to interpret U.S. social, political, and economic dynamics from the perspective of residents and nationals of other countries
- Adapt, reinterpret, and restructure behavior when in a new context, recognizing different cultures, values, and norms
- Use coping and resiliency skills in unfamiliar and challenging situations
- Use foreign language to communicate, both orally and in writing
- Use foreign-language skills as a tool for cross-cultural learning and intercultural understanding
- Know how to be an effective and responsible citizen in today's world

Attitudes

- Humble in the face of difference and willing to be in the position of a learner
- Tolerant of ambiguity and unfamiliarity
- Resistant to an "us versus them" attitude
- Sensitive to and respectful of personal and cultural differences
- Empathetic and able to take multiple perspectives

- Open to learning and positively oriented to new opportunities, ideas, and ways of thinking
- Curious about global issues and cultural differences, and willing to seek out international or intercultural opportunities
- Have a sense of efficacy

5

EMBEDDING PREPARATION IN LANGUAGE COURSES

Bonn and Erlangen

Jennifer Redmann

In contrast to most disciplines, study abroad has long occupied a central position within postsecondary foreign language (FL) curricula. Both anecdotal evidence and empirical studies (such as Brecht, Davidson, & Ginsberg, 1995) show that if students are to achieve advanced proficiency in a foreign language, 4 years of college coursework alone do not suffice. Instead, successful FL learners must spend an extended period—at least a semester and ideally a year—immersed in the culture of a country where the target language is spoken. Because study abroad plays this key role in postsecondary FL education, faculty members in the languages tend to advocate, support, and promote study abroad programs: Many take students on short-term trips to target-language countries, serve as resident program directors, help establish and review study abroad programs, run orientation sessions, involve international students in their courses and programs, and actively advertise study abroad opportunities to their students.

In spite of the clear importance of study abroad for the development of FL proficiency among college learners, the experience of studying abroad does not always achieve the goals and expectations set by faculty and students. Although time spent learning the target language in an immersion environment greatly influences the development of student proficiency, students often fail to make significant improvement in their language abilities while abroad (see the study by Magnan & Back, 2007, which I discuss in the following text). One reason for this may be that traditional beginning and intermediate FL courses, with their focus on student mastery of grammatical structures within a controlled language context, do not prepare learners adequately for the challenges of interacting in an immersion environment.

If students are to reap the benefits of an extended period of study in the target culture, FL faculty must work to integrate the study abroad experience—deliberately and systematically, in terms of both linguistic and cultural preparation—into the FL curriculum. This requires a rethinking of the curriculum as a whole to reflect goals for student learning that move beyond language skills training or engagement with literary texts toward a concept of *cultural competence.* Culturally competent learners have developed the knowledge, skills, and attitudes that allow them to negotiate successfully a place within the target-language society. Although there are many possible points of integration for the study abroad experience in the home FL curriculum, I focus in this chapter on a predeparture course at Kalamazoo College that combines intermediate-level language learning with the study of the two German cities—Bonn and Erlangen—that host exchange programs with our college.

During the past decade, the number of American students studying abroad has risen by more than 150% (to more than 200,000 students) (Open Doors, 2007), a fact that one might assume has led to parallel increases in the numbers of students learning and mastering foreign languages. The data, however, reveal the opposite to be true. Fewer colleges now require at least some FL study (73%) than in 1966 (89%), and during the course of the last 40 years, enrollment in language courses as a percentage of total college enrollment dropped steadily from 16% to 8%, where it remains today. Even more disheartening for those who believe in the importance of advanced FL proficiency for the education of effective global citizens, only 15% of U.S. students taking foreign languages in college are enrolled in advanced courses (Bok, 2005).

One reason for the small number of students in advanced FL courses may lie in the nature of the traditional FL curriculum. For years, faculty in the foreign languages have acknowledged a problematic gap between lower-level "skills" courses and upper-level "content" courses (see, for example, Hoffmann & James, 1986; McCarthy, 1998; Rice, 1991). The communicative methods and pedagogical goals of elementary "skills" courses often have little in common with those of advanced "content" courses, and many students struggle to make a successful transition between the two (see Eigler, 2001; Mittman, 1999).

The root of this curricular problem, Kern (2002) argues, lies in the fact that the lower-level language sequence is pragmatic in its focus, aimed at developing students' interpersonal communication skills, whereas the more scholarly upper-level content courses seek to sharpen students' analytic skills, their cultural sensibilities, and their ability to express themselves formally. With these divergent goals come very different pedagogies. Language courses usually focus on social interaction in a warm, supportive, collaborative environment. Topics addressed there tend to be personal in nature and rarely challenge students' thinking. Instructors structure classroom time around new vocabulary items or points of grammar; student speech takes the form of short responses to a clear prompt. In upper-level, "content" courses, by contrast, students are expected to analyze and synthesize material, orally and in writing, using formal discourse and citing textual evidence. The atmosphere tends not to be collaborative or supportive (or "fun," as many language classes are); instead, students listen to lectures and contribute to discussions led by the instructor. Given the different nature of these "skills" and "content" courses, then, it is hardly surprising that many FL programs suffer from poor retention of students from the lower-level to the upper-level sequence.

In spite of the difficulties that many students experience in transitioning from elementary or intermediate to advanced FL courses, one might assume that the pragmatic, "skills" orientation of the traditional elementary FL sequence would at least offer adequate preparation for study abroad. Indeed, the bifurcated FL curriculum described previously was built around the expectation that students spending a semester or year abroad would *automatically* make tremendous gains in their language proficiency. Students' linguistic leaps forward would then allow them, upon returning, to enter advanced FL courses, where they would be able to read and interpret literary texts without difficulty.

Unfortunately, many students spend significant periods studying abroad without seeing measurable improvement in their ability to speak the target language. Magnan and Back (2007) tested the proficiency level of 20 students before and after a semester of study in France; 8 of the 20 (40%) showed no improvement in their French skills after 4 months in an immersion environment. In accounting for why some students improved and others did not, Magnan and Back identified one key common factor: The more language courses students took before studying abroad, the more likely they were to make gains in their proficiency. The authors speculate that those students with more experience learning French likely possessed greater confidence and willingness to communicate with native speakers while abroad, leading to increased improvement in their language abilities. Whether students lived with a French family or in a university dormitory did not affect linguistic gains during the time abroad, although the amount of contact they had with other English speakers did correlate directly with language improvement. Not surprisingly, the less time students spent with their English-speaking peers, the more French they learned.

As this study suggests, successful integration into a foreign culture—one sign of which is improved target-language proficiency—involves a complex interaction between predeparture preparation and in-country experiences. Drawing on a number of statistical studies, Dupuy cites an even wider array of variables affecting study abroad learning, including "age, gender, predeparture L2 [second language] proficiency level, previous language learning and overseas experiences, aptitude, attitude, motivation, and both amount and type of language contact with the target population" (2007, p. 136). As wide-ranging as this list may appear, it can be summarized in terms of three key "axes of adjustment" (Wilkinson, 2005, p. 48) for students abroad: language, culture, and personal identity. Inadequate linguistic and cultural preparation, leading to anxiety about one's lack of skill and a sense of personal failing, may prevent students from making contact with native speakers. Consequently, students may socialize exclusively with fellow English speakers and/or spend large amounts of time communicating with friends and family at home through e-mail, blogs, and social networking sites. In such a context, even an extended stay abroad results in very little linguistic and cultural gain for participants.

Of the three "axes of adjustment" mentioned previously, the typical American college FL curriculum tends to focus primarily on the first, language, although the emphasis most curricula place on discrete points of grammar does not generally serve students well in the uncontrolled abroad environment. Furthermore, in elementary FL courses, study of the target-language *culture* often extends no further than to "food and festivals" or the brief information offered (in English) in the "culture capsule" sidebars of most first-year textbooks. At the intermediate and advanced levels of most

FL curricula, the cultural focus generally shifts to "Big-C" (objective) culture through the study of literature and famous figures. One study abroad participant in France describes her struggles to cope with life in France, even after completing advanced courses at her home university, as follows: "'I didn't know how to ask for a new light bulb in French. I knew the use of light and dark in *Phèdre* reflect her character, the principles of Camus's existentialism, the use of irony and satire in *Candide*'" (Wilkinson, 2007, p. xv). This type of culture learning is very different from intercultural competence, which Deardorff describes as a "dynamic and recursive process" (2007, p. 91). Achieving intercultural competence, Deardorff explains, requires that students "be taught the key process skills throughout the curriculum—the skills for acquiring deep cultural knowledge through listening, observing, interpreting, analyzing, relating, and evaluating" (2007, p. 93). If students are to negotiate effectively the various dimensions of life abroad, they must begin developing complex intercultural and linguistic skills, as well as strategies for overcoming the emotional challenges of living in a foreign country, well *before* studying abroad.

In sum, we must rethink the notion of study abroad as an "event" that will automatically transform beginning and intermediate learners into advanced speakers of the target language. Instead, study abroad should be viewed as a long-term process (Kruse & Brubaker, 2007) that begins in the first days of FL instruction. However, although this call for predeparture preparation and curricular integration may seem perfectly reasonable, it naturally leads to practical considerations regarding the form and substance of such work. Sharon Wilkinson, in her introduction to the volume *Insights From Study Abroad for Language Programs,* poses the following key questions: "What kind of knowledge and skills do students need to gain entry into a target-language community? What kinds of native-speaker reactions should students be prepared to encounter and interpret? How might these differ from typical textbook fare and curricular foci?" (2007, p. xvi). Although one could offer any number of responses to these questions, in the remainder of this chapter, I describe how the German department at my institution, Kalamazoo College, has worked to integrate the study abroad experience into the home curriculum. I will begin by discussing a revamped curricular framework designed to provide students with the linguistic and cultural knowledge and skills that will facilitate their integration into German society. My focus will then shift to one second-year German course that places study abroad preparation at its core.

An Integrated German Curriculum at Home

Kalamazoo College has a 50-year history of sending nearly all of its students to study abroad sites around the world; a majority of the junior class spends September to March in another country. Students of German may study at the universities in Bonn or Erlangen-Nürnberg, and virtually all of Kalamazoo College German majors and minors do so. In spite of how integral study abroad is to the students' experience at Kalamazoo College, however, it has not always been well integrated into the curricula of the various departments at the college, including the languages. Although the FL faculty at Kalamazoo enjoy an enviable situation in which nearly every major and minor spends time abroad, for the reasons cited earlier, students do not always make significant gains in their target-language proficiency.

Prior to a curricular revision process that began in 2002, the German curriculum at Kalamazoo College was structured around the traditional "language-literature split" described previously. In redesigning the curriculum, members of the German department sought to eliminate this split by outlining three broad curricular goals that every course would meet through tasks appropriate to students' developing proficiency: linguistic competence, cultural competence, and critical understanding of the German-speaking world (see Appendix A for a brief description of each goal). The nature of this curricular revision becomes clear when one examines, for example, the catalogue description for beginning German (German 101). Prior to 2002, the description read, "Pronunciation, vocabulary, structural analysis, audio-lingual practice, and selected readings," with no mention of what students would speak, read, and write *about.* The new course description makes the content of the course *explicit,* thereby demonstrating how students' expanding knowledge of the language is reflected in the language *functions* that they will master and the range of *contexts* in which they will be able to use the language. In other words, it is not the language alone that makes up the content of the elementary courses, but the cultural contexts in which that language is employed.

Two intermediate courses build on the foundation of the first beginning courses, and although all four language skills (listening, speaking, reading, and writing) continue to be practiced, one of the courses focuses on developing students' writing skills within the context of issues in contemporary Germany. The second intermediate course emphasizes reading skills within the context of the history of 20th-century Germany. In this way, the intermediate-level courses assist students in making a smooth transition to upper-level courses in which sophisticated reading and writing skills are essential.

The upper-level course offerings in the new curriculum fall into three areas: genre courses, film courses, and thematic courses. By including film courses and both intermediate and advanced courses on contemporary German culture in the revised curriculum, the German faculty sought to emphasize the emergence of new media in the 20th century and how these media have reshaped the nature of German culture. At the same time, several courses continue to focus on literary texts and many take a wider historical view, examining the changing nature of German culture through the lens of a particular genre (such as drama) or theme (such as questions of German-Jewish identity).

Most importantly, in the revised curriculum, it is no longer possible to speak of lower-level "skills" courses and upper-level "content" courses. Instead, the content of every course, as represented by its texts, is made accessible to students at the beginning, intermediate, or advanced level through carefully designed tasks and activities that challenge and develop students' linguistic and cultural competencies. For example, in the third course in the curricular sequence, students (many of whom have had less than 1 year of German instruction) read a full-length youth novel on the subject of Turkish immigrants in Germany. Classroom activities connected to the novel help them acquire the vocabulary and discourse markers they need to discuss, in simple terms, the problems faced by immigrants in both Germany and the United States. At the advanced level, a course on German culture and identity in the 18th and 19th centuries addresses similar questions, but in conjunction with sophisticated texts by authors of that period. Similarly, an advanced course entitled "Contemporary German Culture" deals with many of the same topics as the intermediate courses, but through texts and assignments appropriate to a higher level of proficiency.

In addition to creating a unified German curriculum, one that overcomes the "language-literature" divide, the German faculty at Kalamazoo College also sought better integration of the study abroad experience into the home curriculum. Many of the new initiatives in this area (some of which are still in the planning stages) correspond to recommendations from *Best Practices in Study Abroad: A Primer for Chairs of Departments of Foreign Languages* (2008), published by the Association of Departments of Foreign Languages (ADFL). These include instituting predeparture and reentry courses and developing mechanisms for communication between students at home and students abroad (along with other mechanisms that allow students to maintain contact with the home institution). The ADFL also recommends using students returning from study abroad in on-campus courses and co-curricular events (2008, p. 2). My intermediate course focused on Bonn and Erlangen (described in the following text) serves a number of these functions, because it acts as a predeparture course and requires that students at home exchange e-mails with Kalamazoo College students currently studying at the two German universities. Once they return from Germany, students may enroll in "Contemporary German Culture," a course that offers multiple opportunities for students to reflect on their experiences while abroad. The department also sponsors an annual photo exhibit for returnees from Germany and a panel discussion on the Intercultural Research Program (ICRP) students completed in Germany. One upcoming initiative is the creation of a departmental blog and forum site for students to use while abroad. This site would allow faculty members at home to address questions and offer strategies to students abroad.

Preparing for Study in Bonn and Erlangen

The "Bonn and Erlangen" course began as a second-year, intermediate course focused on developing students' writing skills in various genres. Instead of using a traditional textbook, I put together a collection of readings that included personal portraits, stories, news reports, film reviews, and advertising that reflected aspects of life in Germany today. In addition to reading and analyzing the texts, students learned vocabulary and practiced some of the grammatical structures typical of those genres (for example, when working on personal portraits, students learned terms for describing people and practiced adjective endings). Each section of the course culminated with a writing and/or speaking assessment in each particular genre.

In the new "Bonn and Erlangen" version of the course, students continue to do genre-based reading and writing in German, but the course also serves to prepare them for their study abroad experience in Bonn or Erlangen through readings, assignments, and activities focused on the cities where they might be studying. (See the course description in Appendix B.) The goal of this work is to provide students with practical, cultural, and linguistic preparation prior to their study abroad experience in Germany, or, if they have not settled on whether to study in Germany, to inspire them to do so. In addition, students gain insight into what a "city" is and how it functions as a kind of text (which can be "read" and interpreted) through its physical layout, its geography, its buildings, its history, its industry, its institutions, and its residents, past and present. In this sense, Bonn and Erlangen exist not simply as locations but as multidimensional, multilayered cultural constructs. By approaching these two German cities through various kinds of texts and activities, students come to better understand what it means to *know* a city and feel at home there, as well as how German cities differ from their American counterparts.

The course is structured in three main units, each of which accounts for 3 weeks of the 10-week quarter at Kalamazoo College. We begin with the cities themselves and their universities; texts include color versions of maps of the central sections of the cities of Bonn, Erlangen, and Nürnberg; photos of the cities; and vocabulary for describing buildings and getting from place to place. I divide students into small groups and assign them the task of deciding in which actual university dormitory (either in Bonn or Erlangen) they will "live" for the term. Over the course of 10 weeks, they research their neighborhoods, decorate their rooms, imagine the identities of their neighbors, and role-play various types of interactions, including the resolution of conflicts over noise and the cleanliness of the communal kitchen. Although these activities do not occupy my students for the entire course, they are modeled after project-based "global simulation" FL courses such as *L'Immeuble,* in which learners of French design and play various roles as residents of a virtual apartment building in France. As Dupuy (2007) explains, because global simulations require that students use the target language to accomplish their own particular objectives within an authentic cultural context, such activities can function as a bridge between the classroom and the study abroad environment.

Although the cities Bonn and Erlangen serve as our *content* for the course, I also use them as a meaningful *context* for teaching the German language by designing activities that combine information about the cities with the practice of linguistic structures. For example, when reviewing the comparative and superlative, I provide students with a table that lists the population, area, age, number of hospitals, and so on for Bonn, Erlangen, and Kalamazoo; I then ask students to compare and contrast the three cities (using structures such as "larger than," "less than," and so on). Unlike the work done in most FL classrooms, this serves as more than just "skill practice," for in doing this exercise, students are also connecting with the places where they will later be residents. They are always surprised by how old Bonn is (it was founded by the Romans) and by the fact that Erlangen has so many hospitals (because it is the headquarters of Siemens, a medical technology company). These discoveries lead the class beyond the boundaries of a grammar activity into discussions about the history of Bonn and the economy of Erlangen. In this way, the grammar activity becomes truly content-based, with students focused not simply on a linguistic form, but on the meaning behind it.

The Internet makes it very easy to bring German cities to the home classroom, and when students visit the university websites for Bonn and Erlangen, they are not just visiting a German website, they are discovering resources that they will use for obtaining information when they are actually living in Germany. Students can find out what is being served in the cafeterias in Erlangen on any given day, and because we have exchange students from Bonn and Erlangen working in our department as teaching assistants, they can describe the dishes and how they might compare with what is served in Kalamazoo College's cafeteria. Students also use the Internet to research the dormitory they will "live in" during the course, and in so doing they can learn about the size of the rooms, amenities, and monthly rents. The fact that German dormitories only include single rooms and that the cost of the room is correlated to its size in square meters offers an effective segue to a discussion of the high value placed on private space in a densely populated country.

At the end of the first unit of the course, students do research and give a short presentation on a historical site in Bonn, Erlangen, or Nürnberg, and they also complete a formal essay on a place that is important to them personally. This alternation of focus between Germany and the United States is intended to help students communicate with others during their time abroad by preparing them to reflect on their own lives and hometowns in contrast to German cities and German culture. Before studying abroad, students need to become familiar with German cities, but once they are there, they will need to be able to talk in German about where they come from and their own understanding of American culture.

In the second unit of the course, we move into the past, focusing on famous people and the histories of Bonn and Erlangen. Students work on personal descriptions, as well as on putting together a formal oral presentation on the life of a well-known German. They read short biographical texts and describe portraits of well-known Germans from Bonn (Ludwig van Beethoven, Clara Schumann, Konrad Adenauer) and Nürnberg (Albrecht Dürer), and they do research for a 5-minute PowerPoint presentation on a famous German. This assignment—a formal oral presentation—prepares students for the type of work they will complete in their university courses in Germany. In their presentations, students must be able to speak freely and fluently, using discourse markers appropriate to such an academic setting (such as, "Today I would like to introduce you to one of the best-known residents of Bonn," or "That concludes my presentation. Thank you for your attention.").

In the last third of the course, we move from the past to the present, focusing on leisure-time activities and current events in Bonn and Erlangen. Online newspapers make it easy for the class to stay current with events in the two cities. In this part of the course, students bring news stories from the online Bonn and Erlangen newspapers to class every day; they work on vocabulary and structures related to writing news items; and at the end of the unit, students put together their own news broadcasts from Kalamazoo College. Using online movie listings, we can even find out what movies are currently playing in Bonn and role-play making plans to see a particular film. Class members also exchange e-mails in German with students currently studying in Bonn and Erlangen (both American exchange students and native Germans). Not only does this activity give students a sense of what daily life is like in Germany (and how it differs from life in Kalamazoo), it also raises their awareness of the cultural conventions governing written correspondence in German, including the opening salutation and closing of a letter.

In the final week of the course, we compile the best examples of student writing from the course (place descriptions, stories, film reviews, news items, and advertisements) into a student paper called *Schöner Trick!* (an informal German phrase that translates roughly as "pretty cool") that is distributed to all German students and speakers at the College. The class is always very proud of this collaborative example of its expanding ability to use German effectively in writing.

Although I have focused here on a predeparture course as a means of integrating study abroad into the home curriculum, I will close with a few words about an advanced course, "Contemporary German Culture," that serves as a post-study abroad seminar within the German curriculum at Kalamazoo College. "Contemporary German Culture" complements the Bonn and Erlangen course by addressing similar types of topics, but in a more in-depth and sophisticated way. For example, whereas students prior to studying abroad need to learn about the overall structure of the German university system, returning students are able to discuss current efforts to reform German higher education by instituting tuition and new degree programs. Once students have studied in Germany, they fully understand why reform is necessary and can share their own experiences and opinions. These two courses, in serving as pre- and post-study abroad seminars that integrate the classroom and experiential dimensions of the curriculum at Kalamazoo College, function as an integral part not only of the German program, but also of the college as a whole.

Although pre- and post-study abroad courses can go a long way toward helping students integrate into a foreign environment, we also need broader educational initiatives if Americans are to achieve meaningful levels of proficiency in the languages and cultures of the non-English-speaking world. Integrating the college FL curriculum, with its very different "skills" and "content" courses, is a first step. However, we must also advocate for FL education to begin much earlier (ideally, in elementary school) and for languages to be learned through a continuous, articulated program of study across educational levels and institutions. Only then will American students be able to take fullest advantage of the opportunities presented by the study abroad experience.

References

Association of Departments of Foreign Languages. (2008). *Best practices in study abroad: A primer for chairs of departments of foreign languages.* New York: Author.

Bok, D. (2005). *Our underachieving colleges.* Princeton, NJ: Princeton University.

Brecht, R. D., Davidson, D. E., & Ginsberg, R. B. (1995). Predictors of foreign language gain during study abroad. In B. F. Freed (Ed.), *Second language acquisition in a study abroad context* (pp. 37–66). Amsterdam: John Benjamins.

Deardorff, D. K. (2007). A model of intercultural competence and its implications for the foreign language curriculum. In S. Wilkinson (Ed.), *Insights from study abroad for language programs* (pp. 86–98). Boston: Thomson Heinle.

Dupuy, B. (2007). Global simulation: Experiential learning and preparing students at home for study abroad. In S. Wilkinson (Ed.), *Insights from study abroad for language programs* (pp. 134–156). Boston: Thomson Heinle.

Eigler, F. (2001). Designing a third-year German course for a content-oriented, task-based curriculum. *Die Unterrichtspraxis, 34*(2), 107–118.

Hoffmann, E. F., & James, D. (1986). Toward the integration of foreign language and literature teaching at all levels of the college curriculum. *ADFL Bulletin, 18*(1), 29–33.

Kern, R. (2002). Reconciling the language-literature split through literacy. *ADFL Bulletin, 33*(3), 20–24.

Kruse, J., & Brubaker, C. (2007). Successful study abroad: Tips for student preparation, immersion, and postprocessing. *Die Unterrichtspraxis, 40*(2), 147–152.

Magnan, S. S., & Back, M. (2007). Social interaction and linguistic gain during study abroad. *Foreign Language Annals, 40*(1), 43–61.

McCarthy, J. A. (1998). W(h)ither literature? Reaping the fruit of language study before it's too late. *ADFL Bulletin, 29*(2), 10–17.

Mittman, E. (1999). In search of a coherent curriculum: Integrating the third-year foreign language classroom. *Foreign Language Annals, 32*(4), 480–493.

Open Doors. (2007). *American students studying abroad at record levels: Up 8.5%.* Retrieved July 8, 2008, from http://opendoors.iienetwork.org.

Rice, D. B. (1991). Language proficiency and textual theory: How the twain might meet. *ADFL Bulletin, 22*(3), 12–15.

Wilkinson, S. (2005). Articulating study abroad: The depth dimension. In C. M. Barrette & K. Paesani (Eds.), *Articulation: Developing a theoretical foundation.* Boston: Thomson Heinle.

Wilkinson, S. (2007). Introduction: The view from abroad. In S. Wilkinson (Ed.), *Insights from study abroad for language programs* (pp. xv–xviii). Boston: Thomson Heinle.

Appendix A: Goals of the Kalamazoo College German Program

1. *Linguistic Competence (Production):* Graduates of the Kalamazoo College German program are able to use German to communicate effectively with others and to present information (with grammatical accuracy and using appropriate discourse) in a range of intellectual and professional contexts. They are able to use German creatively to

transform ideas or information into new representations. Students will be empowered to participate actively in German-speaking communities, as both producers and as recipients of discourse and texts in multiple genres. These genres include, but are not limited to, the following:

- Informal and formal conversation (dialogue with familiar and unfamiliar people) in a variety of social situations and cultural contexts
- Formal presentations (lecture, interview, etc.)
- Personal texts, including journals, letters (both formal and informal), and so on
- Journalistic reports
- Academic writing (reviews, argumentative essays, research reports, etc.)
- Creative writing (poetry, short fiction, dialogues, and drama)

2. *Linguistic Competence (Reception):* Graduates of the German program can recognize, interpret, and respond appropriately to sophisticated texts in a variety of genres, including literary, personal, and journalistic reportage (see previous list).

3. *Cultural Competence:* Graduates of the German program demonstrate a rich understanding of modern German-speaking cultures and histories through their ability to read and interpret various cultural products, including texts of all kinds. These include, but are not limited to, visual art, film, music, literature, German history, and drama. Graduates demonstrate not only the ability to read and interpret, but also an understanding of and a sensitivity to the histories of these cultural products.

4. *Critical Understanding of the German-Speaking World:* Graduates of the German program demonstrate a keen awareness of the fact that German culture represents not a monolithic other, but rather a constantly shifting complex of dominant and subdominant cultures, each of which has its own histories and commitments that need to be examined and understood. Successful graduates demonstrate awareness of this complicated reality, and of the critical negotiations that continually take place between the cultural constituents of the German-speaking world. These include, but are not limited to, questions of gender, class, sexuality, avant-garde versus popular culture,

racial and ethnic minority cultures within German-speaking states, and transculturation and its effect upon artistic and cultural production. Graduates have learned to critically examine their own assumptions in light of the German cultural multiplicity, and in so doing learn to value the multiple perspectives that the learning of German affords them.

Appendix B: Syllabus for German 203: Bonn and Erlangen

Required Texts

- German 203 binder with materials
- Rankin and Wells, *Handbuch zur deutschen Grammatik*
- Recommended: *Harper-Collins German Concise Dictionary*

Course Description

In this course, students will deepen their understanding of the German language, culture, and society through a focus on two German cities, Bonn and Erlangen. The renowned universities in these cities are Kalamazoo College's exchange partners with Germany, and in its focus on Bonn and Erlangen, this course is specially designed to assist students planning to study abroad in Germany. This course will orient future study abroad participants to the people, history, and physical environment of the city in which they will be living and will give them the linguistic tools they need to navigate and integrate into German society.

Course Goals

- *Linguistic Competence (Production):* Students in German 203 will use German to communicate effectively with others and present information (with grammatical accuracy and using appropriate discourse) on topics related to life in Germany today and the cities of Bonn and Erlangen in particular. By the end of the course, students will be able to describe people and places, talk about the history of Bonn and Erlangen, describe the lives of people who lived there (past and present), and give information and offer opinions about current political, social, and cultural events in those cities. Students will become familiar with the structures, vocabulary, and discourse markers that characterize language use in a number of genres (see course overview), and they will apply that knowledge creatively in communicating informally with others and in producing their own oral presentations and written texts.

- *Linguistic Competence (Reception):* Students in German 203 will demonstrate their understanding of the texts and topics covered in class through active participation in all class discussions and activities and completion of assignments related to assigned texts.
- *Cultural Competence:* Students in German 203 will develop their understanding of German culture through the example of two German cities, Bonn and Erlangen. Texts in various genres will introduce students to the physical layout of Bonn and Erlangen and everyday life there, as well as past and present events that shape the culture of the cities and the regions of Bavaria and the Rhineland. Students will acquire the vocabulary and discourse markers needed to negotiate communication effectively in a variety of cultural settings.
- *Critical Understanding of the German-Speaking World:* Students in German 203 will begin developing a critical understanding of German culture by examining aspects of contemporary life in Bonn and Erlangen and comparing them with the United States. These will include the history of the cities (including during the Nazi period), education, politics, housing, immigration, and so on.

Course Requirements

Participation, Preparation, Cooperation	20%
Quizzes and Homework	10%
Three essays in multiple drafts	35%
Two oral presentations	20%
Contribution to *Schöner Trick!*	5%
Final oral interview	10%
	100%

Course Overview

Weeks 1–3: Navigating the City and the University

Texts and Topics: Descriptions of Bonn and Erlangen; historical sites; university life

Genres: Travel guides, photographs, maps, city and university websites

Structures: Present tense, adjective endings, prepositions describing location

Vocabulary/Discourse Markers: Describing cities—buildings, public spaces; university life; giving directions

Student Assignments/Assessment: 1. Oral Presentation on a historical site in Bonn or Erlangen; 2. Written description of a place

Weeks 4–6: Residents of Bonn and Erlangen—Past and Present

Texts and Topics: Texts on well-known residents of Bonn (Beethoven) or Erlangen/Nürnberg (Dürer); brief histories of the cities; current residents

Genres: Biography, personal description, historical texts, personal communication

Structures: Past tense, adjective endings, adjectival nouns, word order

Vocabulary/Discourse Markers: Describing appearance and clothing; summarizing biographical information; time expressions; daily routines

Student Assignments/Assessment: 1. Oral presentation on a well-known figure from Bonn or Erlangen; 2. Written communication with resident in Bonn or Erlangen; 3. Written description of a person

Weeks 7–9: Current Events in Bonn and Erlangen

Texts and Topics: Current events in Bonn and Erlangen—political, social, cultural

Genres: Newspaper articles, film and museum programs, films

Structures: Questions words, causal conjunctions, passive voice, relative pronouns

Vocabulary/Discourse Markers: Describing an event; describing a plot; evaluating a film; giving opinions

Student Assignments/Assessment: 1. Written summary or an event taking place in Bonn or Erlangen; 2. Group oral presentation: News broadcast from Kalamazoo College; 3. Written film review

Week 10: Schöner Trick!

Student Assignments/Assessment: 1. Editing and laying out student newspaper (compilation of writing from the course); 2. Final oral interview

6

SEMIOTICS AND THE CITY

Putting Theories of Everyday Life, Literature, and Culture Into Practice

Darren Kelly

Finally the journey leads to the city of Tamara. You penetrate it along streets thick with signboards jutting from the walls. The eye does not see things but images of things that mean other things: pincers point out the tooth-drawer's house . . . signs of what is forbidden and allowed. From the doors of the temples the gods' statues are seen, each portrayed with his attributes so that the worshiper can recognise them and address his prayers correctly. If a building has no signboard or figure, its very form and the position it occupies in the city's order suffice to indicate its function: the palace, the prison, the pythagorean school, the brothel. . . . Your gaze scans the streets as if they were written pages: the city says everything you must think, makes you repeat her discourse.

(Calvino, 1997, pp. 13–14)

As outlined in chapter 1, many study abroad students claim that they learn most outside of the classroom. The aim of this chapter is to illustrate how out-of-class experiences can be mediated through an interdisciplinary academic framework that is linked with and reinforces in-class learning. In essence, I argue that study abroad learning can be particularly effective in breaking down the false dichotomy between classroom and street and between "high" culture and "low" culture.

In Calvino's quote at the beginning of this chapter, newcomers to a city are faced with streets "thick with signboards" and "images of things that mean other things." This chapter outlines how reading the city's architecture and signs as a text provides students with valuable insights about the world beyond the classroom. However, as discussed in chapter 2, many students are not natural explorers; they can fear new places and as a result create comfort zones. Therefore, students must be encouraged to go out and explore their study abroad sites, to wander and wonder. They should learn the city's rhythms by studying its ebb and flow, seek out its hidden spaces, such as courtyards, and "learn the art of seeing" (Sennett, 1974, p. 213).

Students as intentional, critical observers can deconstruct the meaning(s) of their study abroad sites by approaching what they see in a focused and systematic way, through semiotics, the study of signs. I propose that the iconography of cities, which includes monuments and street names, is a means for students to understand the history and cultural context of space and a way of creating a dialogue with the inhabitants of their study abroad sites. According to Hertmans, "The city is the territory of human communication in its most advanced form" (2001, p. 10); therefore to study a city (or any study abroad site) is to study its people, its lifeblood.

The theory underpinning the methodology discussed in this chapter of walking, observing, and critiquing the city borrows from literature and literary theory, cultural geography and cultural studies, ethnography and anthropology, and contemporary French philosophy. It is argued that introducing students to literature and theory will aid the students' abilities to read and understand their study abroad sites. It is hoped that the emphasis on theory and its relationship to study abroad will complement other chapters in this volume that employ methodologies such as participant observation. For example, in this chapter the role of the city walker is related to the concept and practice of *flânerie,* and the role of the observer is related to the ethnographer and anthropologist. Combined, these can be considered *flânography* undertaken by the *flânographer*. Additionally, assignments that encourage students to engage with and learn from their study abroad sites are discussed.

Many of the examples in this chapter of discourse and its relevance to student activities are taken from a course I designed and teach for the Institute for the International Education of Students (IES) to American students studying in Dublin, Ireland, "Communal Irish Identity," referred to in this chapter as "the Dublin course." However, although the term *city* is frequently used in the chapter, the theories, methodologies, and activities can apply to varying degrees to other study abroad sites as well as to home campuses. At Beloit College, a series of curriculum development activities based on some of the work described in the chapter led to the inclusion of similar methodologies in courses now taught in China (see chapter 8), Ecuador, Nicaragua, and Beloit (see chapter 9), and Moscow, as well as courses within the college's first-year seminar program and a travel-writing course.

The chapter is subdivided into three interconnected sections: "Semiotics: Teaching Study Abroad Students How to 'Read' a City," "Walking (Wandering and Wondering) Through the City," and "Returning to Semiotics: Linking the Social Sciences With Literature." Subsections outline the course components and describe exercises illustrating their relevance to particular disciplines and study abroad. Interdisciplinary anthologies such as *The Blackwell City Reader* (Bridge & Watson, 2002) and *The Subcultures Reader* (Thornton & Gelder, 1997) provide particularly useful thematically divided readings relevant to study abroad.

Semiotics: Teaching Study Abroad Students How to "Read" a City

For many students, reading texts about literary and cultural theory can be dense and challenging at best and, at times, close to impenetrable. However, the theory can give them an intentionality for their interactions with their study abroad sites as well as a vocabulary with which to understand them.

In the first session of "Communal Irish Identity," several activities provide students with a basic but functional understanding that semiology can be used to read a city and that cities exist within conurbations of vast and varied symbols (text and visual images) and iconography (architecture, statues, and monuments) with historical, political, and cultural contexts. According to T. Hall, "There have been various frameworks put forward to deconstruct or 'unpack' the meanings inscribed in or attached to urban spaces. Despite their differences these frameworks are all described as being broadly 'semiotic'" (1998, p. 28).

Semiotics in its simplest form is the analysis of the meanings humans derive from signs and symbols, ranging from the written word to architecture. For example, when study abroad students see a building or monument, a signpost above a store, even the styles of clothes worn by the residents of their host site, they derive meanings from them. In effect, they are using semiotics to interpret the world around them. To help make this a conscious practice, the theory of semiotics is made visible in the first session of the course by drawing symbols on a chalkboard.

The students then list and discuss other signs and symbols that they see (read) every day, such as ♀ & ♂ € $ @, and they are asked to consider one symbol at length. I typically use the McDonald's logo, both because it is so pervasive, and because its presence in cities such as Dublin can mask the real cultural differences between Ireland and the United States.

Students' initial responses to the McDonald's logo include fast food, America, obesity, and globalization. They are then asked to consider what the logo might mean in other countries. For example, the logo represents a kind of positive or even elitist status for young Chinese. When the first McDonald's restaurant opened its doors in Moscow in 1990, long queues awaited its opening. The students interpret the meaning of the logo in that context to have meant democracy and freedom for some and a sign of American imperialism for others. The McDonald's logo makes them understand that although the same logo may appear around the world, it has local interpretations. On the other hand, some symbols they may assume are universal are not, such as the Red Cross (Fig. 6.1). Geography and religion led to the creation of the Red Crescent in 1919, but most students fail to recognize the logo, as it falls outside their normal frames of reference. Semiotics does not allow students to be passive receptors of visual information; instead it forces them to actively investigate, decode, and reflect. As Hertmans writes, "You are inclined to think in general terms, so you must look at the small things, the individual, or you will begin to think that you understand the world— the surest way not to understand it" (2001, p. 103).

The Dublin students next are asked to consider what certain well-known buildings and landscapes connote, for example, the Statue of Liberty, the

FIGURE 6.1
Images downloaded from Google images at http://images.google.com.

Golden Gate Bridge, Niagara Falls, and the Grand Canyon. When asked to consider what the site of the "Twin Towers" symbolizes following 9/11, they usually respond with phrases like "horror," "Islamic terrorism," and "an attack on freedom or democracy." The aim of these questions is to illustrate to students how buildings and the natural environment can engender particular emotions and that, in turn, language conveys them.

Nonvisual signs also signify meanings, such as the words that students speak and read. An excerpt from Nobel Laureate Toni Morrison's *The Bluest Eye* (1970) makes them question what they associate with the words *white* and *black*. They respond with snow and purity to the first, and dark, night, and dirt to the second. In the novel, one child internalizes negative associations with the color black and positive with white, whereas the other does the opposite, with implications for both children's self-understanding and actions. The passage elicits an emotional discussion from the students about the ability of language to categorize and stereotype people and create moral panics leading to geographies of exclusion, and shows them how Morrison's work lends itself to postcolonial and feminist readings.

Finally, to connect visual semiotics with linguistic semiotics, I ask the students to consider two identical cities whose main thoroughfares are named respectively "Queen Victoria" and "Karl Marx." As a group, we discuss the possible connotations (historical, political, and sociocultural) a visitor might attribute to each city based on the names of the streets. The students are then asked to discuss the names given to prominent streets or buildings where they live in the United States.

Semiotics and Photo Essays

Photography allows students to test their understanding and practice of semiotics. By sharing their photos in class, students experience firsthand how they interpret images differently. Although students have technical and visual competence, they often make the mistake of taking photographs as a way of remembering the story behind the image instead of visually capturing the story. To make students more intentional or discerning photographers, they are asked to create silent thematic-based PowerPoint photo essays. This forces them to consider why and how to capture an image so that it can speak for itself. Examples of themes include architecture, litter, graffiti, nature, and politics. According to one student evaluation, "The photo essay was great because it forced me to look at Dublin through one specific theme and later to develop that theme into an expanded idea about the city." Another student said, "I really enjoyed this exercise because I could hide behind the camera and screen out what I didn't want to photograph."

In class, we discuss which photographs are most effective as well as how to frame a photograph, such as using a tree as a border or asking people to walk into the frame to naturally "people" the shot. Excerpts from Prosser's *Image-Based Research: A Sourcebook for Qualitative Researchers* (1998), Pink's *Doing Visual Ethnography: Images, Media and Representation in Research* (2001), and *Visual Culture: The Reader*, edited by Evans and Hall (1999) provide background on visual discourse and methodology.

Reading and Decoding Street Names and Monuments in Dublin, Ireland

Readings from Yvonne Whelan's *Reinventing Modern Dublin* (2003) demonstrate how semiotics can help decode or deconstruct Dublin. Whelan researched the historical, sociopolitical, and cultural significance and implications of place names in Dublin following independence from British rule. During this time many street names were changed; for example, the name of the city's main thoroughfare was changed from Sackville Street to O'Connell Street. Analyzing street names is a form of semiotics. A postcolonial reading could focus on their historical context, whereas a feminist reading could take particular notice of the prominence of male names in the streetscape. Students can use the street names to guess when they were constructed; location and architecture of particular streets can also be used to determine date of construction.

As Whelan (2003) documents, not only did street names change, but monuments were removed, destroyed, and relocated. Nations erect monuments to represent themselves and their past; they may remove or change them to signal a departure from the past. If students can read the monuments, that is, understand their cultural and historical context and significance, the monuments can become more than part of the scenery. Whelan cites the case of the history of the highly contentious statue of Queen Victoria. Removed in 1948 from in front of the Irish parliament in Dublin and relocated several times, it eventually was presented to the people of Sydney, Australia, and currently stands in the Bicentennial Plaza in front of Sydney's Town Hall (Whelan, 2003, pp. 195–201).

In the class, we examine the 390-foot, needle-shaped Dublin Spire, the world's largest freestanding sculpture located in the very center of O'Connell Street. Used as a meeting point for many of the city's residents and tourists, it is familiar to all of the students. However, as tall as the Spire is, its history is deeper, revealing to the students, like a piece of historical and sociocultural DNA, an important piece of Ireland's past and collective memory.

On the same site, almost 200 years before the Dublin Spire was installed, an impressive 121-foot pillar was erected in honor of Admiral Nelson. Symbolic of British naval supremacy and the Battle of Trafalgar, in the context of its location the pillar also symbolized colonization and oppression. The pillar was blown up by a splinter group of the IRA in 1966. In 1988, to celebrate Dublin's millennium, a bronze female statue of Anna Livia, a personification of the River Liffey, was placed on the pillar's original site. Referred to locally as "the floozy in the jacuzzi," it was replaced in 2002 by the Dublin Spire, itself contentious, loved by some and loathed by many. Its nickname, "Stiletto in the Ghetto," derives from its close proximity to shops and services owned by and catering to Dublin's newly established immigrant population. Thus the unofficial naming of official places and structures illustrates the power of a populous (and of language) to subvert and change the meaning (label and stereotype) of monuments and places. As Tuan writes, "Naming is power" (1990, p. 688). Cresswell discusses the importance of "inscribing memory in place":

> Monuments, museums, the preservation of particular buildings (and not others), plaques, inscriptions and the promotion of whole neighbourhoods as "heritage zones" are all examples of placing of memory. . . . The connection between place and memory and the contested nature of this connection has been the object of considerable enquiry. (2004, p. 85)

City as Palimpsest: Seeing the Past in the Present

> A city (usually Rome), built on the ruins of its past, with history accumulating but not quite adding up, is a constant analogy for Freud. . . . Ruins, monuments and urban architecture point to an environment where the past continually impinges on the present. . . . And just as psychoanalysis is dedicated to uncovering the power of the past as it acts on the lives of the present, so a study of urban culture must look to understand the power of an urban imagery. (Highmore, 2005, pp. 4–5)

Students in the Dublin course research the historical, political, economic, and sociocultural processes that have given rise to Dublin's current shape and culture, a Highmore-like form of urban psychoanalysis. Understanding the past in the present is important lest we see cities as static, unchanging spaces, rather than sites that physically and culturally morphologize over time. Most notably, cities show their different historical periods through the radical juxtaposition of architecture, such as small houses and skyscrapers. Some of the old architecture—usually the most grandiose—survives; however, as Calvino writes, cities can "follow one another on the same site under the same name, born and dying without knowing themselves" (1997, p. 30).

To uncover and see the past in the present in Dublin, the students study the expansion of the city over five time frames that can be broadly labeled medieval, Georgian, tenement, suburban, and contemporary. The political reasons for each expansion are considered as well as their economic and sociocultural realities. For example, the instatement of a form of self-governance in Dublin, signaled by the arrival of the Duke of Ormond in 1601, put into motion the creation of what is called Georgian Dublin. During the 1700s Dublin became one of the most beautiful and elegant cities in the world. Its large houses were situated around lavish squares and government buildings were constructed in white stone in the neoclassical European tradition. The most prominent squares remain and now are one of Dublin's main tourist attractions. They are also home to some study abroad students, and to appreciate where they live, the students need to look back in time.

Following events such as the failed 1798 rebellion, the Act of Union was passed in 1801, restoring central control and governance of Ireland to London and initiating a rapid fall in Dublin's fortunes. Over a few decades, as the political classes returned to England or moved out from the city to enclaves of prosperity in the suburbs, the inner city imploded because of a lack of taxes to support social services, rural urban migration, and the advent of scrupulous rack-renting by landowners. What emerged was the tenement period, a time of extreme poverty in Dublin. Oral histories and excerpts from the plays of Sean O'Casey show students the period's human dimension.

To track these changes in Dublin through space and time, students view and create maps, either on paper or using Google. The city's expansion over time emerges like the rings of a tree, with the final ring, the M50 motorway, circling it. To develop their understanding of the political, socioeconomic, and cultural realities of a given time, I ask the students to research one and represent it creatively. Students are appreciative of and excel at the creative freedom they are given with this individual or group assignment. They have written fictional letters from family members living in "Tenement Dublin" to relatives living in America, staining and burning the paper to make the letters appear old and crumbling. Others have written poems, songs, or short stories. One student created an illustrated "Medieval Dublin" book for children and another a full-scale game of Georgian monopoly; others have built architectural models. The creative projects are submitted along with a written explanation or rationale for the projects and a bibliography.

Walking (Wandering and Wondering) Through the City

Walking through Dublin is a critical component of the course; it aids the students' understanding of Irish identity and contributes to their intercultural learning. Philosophy (de Certeau in particular), practices (*Flânerie*), sociological theory (the Chicago School), and cultural studies (the Birmingham School) are employed to both give the students different ways to understand and interpret what they are doing and observing, and a vocabulary with which to describe and discuss it.

Flânerie

To learn how to walk and observe the city the students are introduced to *flânerie,* a practice most commonly associated with the 19th-century Parisian male (*flâneur*) who voyeuristically navigated the city by foot and often inhabited cafés to observe the "pageant" of everyday life (Baudelaire, 1965). Despite its negative portrayal as the preserve of the male decadent, over time the theoretical, sociopolitical, and cultural insights provided by *flânerie* were recognized within the social sciences and philosophy and the practice was adopted as a research methodology. Walking and observing in the city has influenced the study of urban space and the patterns and consumption of commodities. In a contemporary context, Carrie Bradshaw in *Sex and the City* can be critiqued as a contemporary *flâneuse.*

The first person to seriously examine the sociological uses of *flânerie* was Walter Benjamin who, with reference to the French poet-*flâneur* Baudelaire, referred to this activity as "botanising the asphalt" (1973, p. 36). Benjamin's use of *flânerie* is most explicitly expressed in his seminal *The Arcades Project,* which explored patterns of consumption and the uses of space in the covered shopping arcades of Paris. *Flânerie* is also associated with the work of sociologist Georg Simmel whose "The Metropolis and Mental Life" (1950), originally published in 1903, discussed the importance and preponderance of "the visual" in cities and what he called the "microscopy" of urban fragments. Both Frisby (1981) and Jencs (1995) maintain that a *flâneur*-like role has relevance in contemporary social sciences through the ability of the *flâneur* or *flâneuse* to walk through the labyrinthine city and observe its rhythms and read its visual clues, to be an insider and outsider simultaneously. To link the concept of *flânerie* with semiotics and the "art of seeing," students visit a website dedicated to *flânerie* and photo essays (www.flaneur.org). They choose one essay to discuss in class and act as a model for their own photo essays. Jenks makes the case for the *flâneur* as psycho-geographer and cartographer with the eye of a photojournalist:

> The walker . . . can playfully and artfully "see" the juxtaposition of the elements that make up the city in new and revealing relationships. . . . All this conceptual re-ordering is open to the imaginative theorising of the wandering cultural critic and yet mostly such techniques have come to be the province of the photo-journalist. (1995, pp. 154–155)

Frisby, linking *flânerie* with investigative journalism, writes that the *flâneur* must not only walk with the crowd but also explore hidden spaces in cities such as "alleyways, courtyards and green spaces" (1994, p. 93). Amin and Thrift write with regard to *flâneur* poet Baudelaire that he "was not a naïve dilettante" but rather, "These were reflexive wanderings underpinned by a particular theorization of urban life, with the demand from theory to reveal the process at work through the eye of a needle" (2002, p. 10).

French Philosophy and Everyday Life

The work of Michel de Certeau helps the students select, order, and interpret their observations, and thus they read "Walking in the City," a chapter from his 1984 book *The Practice of Everyday Life,* which is frequently used in cultural studies and urban studies anthologies. The chapter begins from atop the Twin Towers, the view from which, he argues, is the privileged view of the urban planner and bureaucrat. He argues instead for a way of seeing that ". . . can analyse the microbe-like, singular and plural practices" of the everyday, "which an urbanistic system was supposed to administer or suppress" (de Certeau, 1988, p. 96). De Certeau's Wandersmann has the ability to reappropriate space, or create what I call a "spatial patois." Applied to Dublin, my students understand the patois to represent the different ways in which new communities or ethnic groups use places and spaces, from the rhythm or pace of their movement, to their use of parks and other public spaces, to working practices and business hours. As they walk through Dublin at different times and days the students practice Lefebvre's "rhythmanalysis" (2004), which was inspired by his detailed observations of a Parisian intersection from his hotel window.

When the students act as *flâneurs* and use rhythmanalysis and Jenks's investigative photojournalism, they enter, observe, and critique spaces bustling with businesspeople during the day and empty at night, sections that seem wealthy, poor, or both, and immigrant spaces. Over time, the students can identify the different "urban uniforms" and the uses of space by subcultural groups such as gentrifiers, goths, skateboarders, and tourists.

The Chicago and Birmingham Schools

Seminal essays from the work of the Chicago School of Urban Sociology and the Center for Contemporary Cultural Studies (CCCS), known as the Birmingham School, develop the students' understanding of the links among walking and observation, ordering, and critical analysis. The Chicago School serves as entrée into urban discourse and methodologies such as participant observation. The School saw cityscapes as fluid with immigration and the increasing mechanisation and speed of the city affecting residential space and city growth. The students study this fluidity at work in Dublin, with gentrifiers "invading" small, inner-city neighbourhoods, and learn firsthand the value of combining qualitative and quantitative methods of enquiry. Burgess's seminal concentric ring map of Chicago helps the students appreciate and contextualize their own research and mapping of Dublin's physical morphology through space and time, as well as their mapping of inner-city neighborhoods based on demographics and culture. To quote a Temple University student, "The teaching was very Chicago School. We actually got out into the city to see causes and effects firsthand. . . . [T]he walking tours are the lifeblood of the class; without them it's difficult to grasp the concepts covered in class." Fieldwork thus complements and reinforces in-class learning.

Like the Chicago School, the Birmingham School of the 1970s and 1980s employed observation and analysis of the cultural practices of different sub-cultural groups. In this case, sociologists looked at the effects of immigrant cultures on the host society (England) as well as the political and socioeconomic significance of subcultural movements associated with music and fashion (Hebdige, 1979). Similarly, the Dublin course students are outsiders in their *flânerie* and observation. The following section discusses a self-reflexive process in which they consciously consider their role as outsiders or immigrants to advance their intercultural learning and strengthen their ability to adapt to new cultural environments.

Body Language, Proxemics, and the Meaning of Culture and Style

> In the city emblems are everything . . . the external signs and signals from which I construct the character with whom I am going to deal. . . . (Raban, 1974, p. 29)
>
> All sets of clothes are geared to a known function, to one's place in a hierarchy which is thoroughly and instinctively understood . . . the hierarchy still holds good. . . . the urban uniform, whose sole function is differentiation and arbitrary variety, is an important symptom of that condition of seemingly meaningless flux which Wordsworth diagnosed as the great disease of the city. . . . (Raban, 1974, p. 55)
>
> To be part of the city, you needed a city style—an economic grammar of identity through which you could project yourself. (Raban, 1974, p. 62)

To observe and reflect on the meaning of culture and style in a new environment, students need to consider what their own cultural style and body language means or connotes. We are usually unconscious about our body language and surroundings. As Hertmans writes, "Home is the place where the world around us becomes invisible; that gives us the peace that we need to be able to think about things that are further away. At home, things hide beneath their familiarity" (2001, p. 206). Therefore, once the students trust each other and me, I facilitate drama-based workshops to make them conscious of their unconscious behavior and aid their understanding of the cultural context of human interaction.

In one workshop, I ask the students to walk around the room as they would in familiar, comfortable spaces. Their walks are assigned a number of 5 or 6. They then are asked to walk in the mode of a person who is nervous.

The walk changes; it is usually slower and accompanied by quick looks around the room and receives a number of 3 or 4. When the students walk in the mode of a person who is confident, their walks are faster, authoritative and numbered 7 or 8. I then call out numbers between 1 and 10 and the students change their walks accordingly. Interestingly, most students adopt the same mode when each number is called out, thus illustrating the cultural codes that they consciously and unconsciously adopt.

Edward Hall (1966) gave the term *proxemics* to the distances people keep from each other, depending on whether the spaces are intimate, personal, social, or public. To illustrate Hall's work, I ask the students to enter the room as if attending an interview, shake hands, and then sit down; each has a partner who acts as the interviewer. The students resemble each other in the proxemics they use and how they sit. They have fun silently simulating different scenarios, such as a first date, and mostly know exactly what each person's body language is saying, because they share the same culture. We then talk about how their body language and cultural norms might be "read" quite differently in another culture.

In the mode of *flânerie* and rhythmanalysis, the students are encouraged to slow down when exploring Dublin. They are assigned and choose places to observe such as parks, malls, train stations, pubs, and cafés. For many students this can be difficult because they want to be doing, consuming, and running rather than sitting, watching, and reflecting. Also, compared with the Irish, the students tend to be loud and alienate themselves in public spaces, as in Ireland in general the speakers' volume is only loud enough for their interlocutors to hear. Furthermore, the students fail to notice that Ireland has a high-context culture in which directness can seem rude. That is, they are in a world whose signs are difficult for them to read, and their own behaviors and appearance are being judged based on a set of codes they do not understand:

> The greenhorn lurches forward into myopic destiny. . . . (Raban, 1974, p. 47)
>
> To be initiated, the newcomer must first be stripped of his past; he has to become a child again, innocent of everything except a humbling consciousness of his own innocence and vulnerability. . . . (Raban, 1974, p. 49)
>
> He finds himself in a world of symbols and signals, every one arcane. . . . You become a walking legible code, to be read, and as often

misinterpreted, by strangers . . . a coat stand of symbols . . . my own dim
pallor was a dishonourable badge of my blistering newness in the city.
(Raban, 1974, p. 51)

The students' success in absorbing and applying the lessons of their theoretical studies becomes clear to them when parents and friends come to visit
them in Ireland. They find themselves training their parents in local cus-
toms, such as not talking too loudly, and realize they themselves have gained
the intercultural competence needed to adapt to their Irish surroundings.

Reading Culture and Space

Flânerie and the Chicago School and Birmingham School research methods
shape a number of assignments in the course in which students learn to read
culture and space. For example, a walking tour teaches the students that in
Dublin subcultures that are not popular or "in" but rather culturally "out"
are also spatially "out," that is, located on the periphery. Although this
periphery may be only a few streets away from the most popular streets, students new to the city do not immediately find them. The walking tour therefore follows along a long, winding street that is used by different subcultural
populations. Along the street are second-hand clothes and thrift stores, adult
shops, small casinos, alternative medicine stores, Dublin's largest and iconic
gay bar, nongovernmental organizations, and volunteer organizations.
Through the entrance of a Walter Benjamin-like arcade, the students find
stalls containing memorabilia such as stamps and coins; a fortune teller; an
ear piercing and tattoo service; organic produce; local arts, crafts, and jewelry; as well as secondhand clothing and Asian clothing importers.

Recent changes in cultural classifications of what is "in" and "out" have
turned the street and arcade into a "zone in transition." Secondhand clothes,
vinyl records, alternative medicine, as well as gay bars are now in vogue in
Dublin, affecting the street and arcade as the businesses associated with these
become more expensive and trendy cafés replace the tea and coffee stands.
With this "culturification," fed in part by gentrification, activities now
deemed less desirable are moving farther to the periphery, and rent increases
have forced some of the long-term stall holders to also move. Interviews with
the stall holders about the changes give the students insight into ways in
which Dublin and other cities culturally morphologize over time.

Returning to Semiotics: Linking the Social Sciences With Literature

This chapter began with the theory of semiotics and how students learn to deconstruct physical signs, monuments, and language. To use this tool, the students, as outlined in the second section, are encouraged to walk and observe the city as *flânographers* with the critical insight of social science theory and research methodologies. In essence the students go out of the classroom to scan the streets "as if they were written pages," to return to the Calvino quote opening the chapter (1997, pp. 13–14). The centrality of the city and landscape in literature highlights a connection among literature, social science, and cultural theory. "Just as a book is written by an author and is in turn subject to the critique of the literary critic, similarly the landscape or space is 'written' by a set of agents and is subject to the critique of the geographer" (Whelan, 2003, p. 13).

Humanities and social science texts can aid the students' understanding of the study abroad site and develop their appreciation of different disciplinary lenses and critical thinking skills. For example, a text such as Jonathon Letham's *Fortress of Solitude* (2003) can complement Neil Smith's *The New Urban Frontier: Gentrification and the Revanchist City* (1996). Both discuss inner-city gentrification and the politics of identity, space, and power in New York. Smith's work explicitly discusses the power of language to legitimate expansion by the middle classes into the new "frontier" of the city, in the same ways the "great" western expansion into the American West was legitimated through language. Literature can tap into the emotional, physical, and spiritual realities of a given space in a way that hard science struggles to achieve. Sibley writes that the "oddness of the ordinary, which is examined microscopically by authors and playwrights from Jane Austen to Mike Leigh, [has] been neglected in social geography" (1995, p. xv).

Highmore (2005) and Jenks (1995) argue that the turning by cultural geographers and cultural theorists, particularly the Birmingham School, toward the humanities rather than the sciences increased the pace at which landscape was interpreted as text. In *Cultural Geography*, Crang writes,

> Literary landscapes are best thought of as a combination of literature and landscape, not with literature as a separate lens or mirror reflecting or distorting an outside world. . . . To say it is subjective is to miss a key point. It is a social product. . . . The ideologies and beliefs of peoples and epochs

both shape and are shaped by these texts. . . . Here we may . . . ask whether geographical accounts are so different from literature. We should not see geography and literature as two different orders of knowledge (one imaginative and one factual) but rather as a field of textual genres, in order to highlight both the "worldliness of literary texts and the imaginativeness of geographical texts." (1998, p. 57)

Close readings of excerpts from seminal texts that have an exploration of the city at their core, such as James Joyce's *Ulysses* (1922) and Virginia Woolf's *Mrs. Dalloway* (1925), give the students a concrete understanding of how the city can be read as, and is, a text. In chapter 2, James Joyce's *Ulysses* is cited as an example of a spatial narrative, whereby the route that Leopold Bloom takes on June 16, 1904, provides a major building block for the plot. Joyce's modernist device is similar to that employed by Virginia Woolf in *Mrs. Dalloway,* which follows Clarissa Dalloway's route through London during the course of one day. To quote Crang,

> The plurality of the city is shown where narrative lines relating to different places unexpectedly collide or cross-cut, enacting the rhythm of daily life in the form of the text. Reading the text becomes like walking on the sidewalk itself, not watching someone else do so. In this way the work goes beyond being a text on the city to being a fusion of urban experience and text itself. It stops being a single account and takes into itself the plurality of experiences in the city. (1998, p. 57)

The city of Dublin is not simply the stage upon which Leopold Bloom struts, but becomes the inciting force driving his internal narrative. Indeed, the city is a multitude of signs and symbols, which Bloom observes with the forensic eye of the semiotician. Understanding the relationship between Bloom and the city facilitates the students' self-conscious examination of the sights and sites that drive their understanding of Dublin. A close analysis of literature ranging from Beaudelaire to Joyce makes the students aware of the role (methodology) of walking (*flânerie*) in the city, the use of semiotics and the brilliance of these authors' craft to translate the vibrancy, color, sounds, smells, tastes, and rhythms of the city through language. The texts encourage the students to "read" Dublin with a critical and self-reflective eye and "write" about (show) their experiences with as much life and feeling as possible.

Conclusion

By combining their understanding of semiotics with the practice of photography and *flânerie,* the urban research methods of the Chicago and Birmingham Schools, the philosophy of the production and practice of everyday life and literature, students can not only deconstruct their study abroad site but also construct their own personal city and experience. As Calvino writes, "You take delight not in a city's seven or seventy wonders, but in the answer it gives to a question of yours. . . . Or the question it asks you, forcing you to answer, like Thebes through the mouth of the Sphinx" (1997, p. 44). To quote a student:

> By the end of the semester I gained an understanding of all the different Dublins that existed through space and time but I loved this course most of all because in the end Dublin became my city, based on how I read it, saw it, and experienced it through juxtapositions and semiotics etc :) and I have my maps and photo essay as a great reminder!

References

Amin, A., & Thrift, N. (2002). *Cities: Reimagining the urban.* Cambridge: Polity Press.

Baudelaire, C. (1965). *Art in Paris 1845–62: Salons and other exhibitions.* London: Phaidon Press.

Benjamin, W. (1973). *Charles Baudelaire: A lyric poet in the era of high capitalism.* London: Verso.

Bridge, G., & Watson, S. (Eds.). (2002). *The Blackwell city reader.* Oxford: Blackwell.

Calvino, I. (1997). *Invisible cities.* Weaver, W. (Trans.). London: Vintage, 1997.

Crang, M. (1998). *Cultural geography.* London: Routledge.

Cresswell, T. (2004). *Place: A short introduction.* Oxford: Blackwell.

de Certeau, M. (1988). *The practice of everyday life.* S. Rendall (Trans.). Berkeley: University of California Press. (Original work published 1984.)

Evans, J., & Hall, S. (Eds.). (1999). *Visual culture: The reader.* London: Sage.

Frisby, D. (1981). *Sociological impressionism: A reassessment of Georg Simmel's social theory.* London: Heinemann.

Frisby, D. (1994). The *flâneur* in social theory. In K. Tester (Ed.), *The Flaneur* (pp. 81–110). London: Routledge.

Hall, E. (1966). *The hidden dimension.* Garden City, NY: Doubleday.

Hall, T. (1998). *Urban geography.* London: Routledge.

Hebdige, D. (1979). *Subculture: The meaning of style.* London: Methuen.

Hertmans, S. (2001). *Intercities.* London: Reaktion.

Highmore, B. (2005). *Cityscapes: Cultural readings in the material and symbolic city.* New York: Palgrave Macmillan.

Jenks, C. (Ed.). (1995). *Visual culture.* London: Routledge.

Joyce, J. (1986). *Ulysses.* New York: Vintage. (Original work published 1922)

Lefebvre, H. (2004). *Rhythmanalysis: Space, time and everyday life.* S. Elden & M. Gerald (Trans.). London: Continuum.

Letham, J. (2003). *Fortress of solitude.* New York: Doubleday.

Morrison, T. (1970). *The bluest eye.* London: Vintage.

Pink, S. (2006). *Doing visual ethnography.* London: Sage.

Prosser, J. (Ed.). (1998). *Image-based research.* London: Routledge Falmer.

Raban, J. (1974). *Soft city.* Great Britain: Fontana/Collins.

Sennett, R. (1974). *The fall of public man.* London: Penguin.

Sibley, D. (1995). *Geographies of exclusion.* London: Routledge.

Simmel, G. (1950). The metropolis and mental life. In K. Wolf (Trans.), *The sociology of Georg Simmel.* New York: Free Press. (Original work published 1903)

Smith, N. (1996). *The new urban frontier: Gentrification and the revanchist city.* New York: Routledge.

Thornton, S., & Gelder, K. (1997). *The subcultures reader.* London: Routledge.

Tuan, Yi-Fu. (1990). *Topophilia: A study of environmental perception, attitudes, and values.* New York: Columbia University Press. (Original work published 1974)

Whelan, Y. (2003). *Reinventing modern Dublin: Streetscape, iconography and the politics of identity.* Dublin: University College Dublin Press.

Woolf, V. (1925). *Mrs. Dalloway.* San Diego: Harcourt Brace Jovanovich.

7

COOL CITIES

Kalamazoo and Carthage—The Intersection of Service-Learning and Intercultural Learning

Anne E. Haeckl and Elizabeth A. Manwell

O ne of the challenges of teaching the history, literature, and material culture of the ancient world is the perception among many that the study of antiquity has nothing to say about the modern world and its concerns. As classicists, we believe that ancient texts and remains continue to speak to us in powerful ways about how peoples of varying beliefs, practices, and values can learn from and live with each other. Our own work and careers, in fact, have been shaped by this belief. Elizabeth's research on masculine identity in the Roman Republic initially stemmed from her observation of curiously similar forms of male gender performance that seem to pervade contemporary American culture. Anne's work on sexuality and ethnicity in Roman sculpture and portraiture relies on both the historical contexts in which these works were produced, and on contemporary discussions about ways in which we represent gender, ethnicity, and race. Though our own passion for the ancient world has been sustained and reinforced by the connections we see among these various cultures, students in our courses not infrequently are shocked to find that modern artists and writers consciously or unconsciously respond to ancient artistic and literary motifs. More importantly, students realize as equally compelling and relevant to their own lives the same questions that ancient Greeks and Romans struggled to answer: How does one best manage an empire? How do you know if you are fighting a just war? Can one serve divine and governmental authorities simultaneously? Although we know that the study of classics has much to offer our students as they struggle to grow intellectually and emotionally, and although we have evidence from students who take our courses that the study of the classical world has had a meaningful effect on their lives, we nevertheless must constantly combat the common perception that classics is an irrelevant field except for those with esoteric interests and a passion for the musings of long-dead, white, European men.

In 2005 we began to discuss how we might better respond to this skepticism about the value of classics, and specifically how to draw to our discipline a population we do not typically reach: students whose primary area of study is outside of humanities and foreign languages. In addition, we believed that there were issues that none of our current class offerings were addressing, but that we increasingly believed were critical for our students: incorporating experiential education and structured reflection; integrating study abroad into the curriculum, both before departure and after return; breaking the "Kalamazoo Bubble" (or "K Bubble") by getting students off campus and into other areas of Kalamazoo; and breaking down barriers between upper and lower classes. As a result, we began to consider developing a community-based service-learning course, which seemed ideally suited to achieving our goals. Service-learning is typically defined as a pedagogical approach that "incorporates community work into the curriculum, giving students real-world learning experiences that enhance their academic learning while providing a tangible benefit to the community" (Campus Compact, n.d.). Although service to the community is an integral part of any service-learning experience, the course must also contain a strong intellectual and theoretically grounded component and typically employs structured reflection as a tool for integration of the "intellectual" and "practical" elements (Howard, 2001). Others have had success in bridging the gap between the "intellectual" and the "practical" through service-learning courses in classics, including courses that investigate the connection between ancient and modern urban culture and artistic production (Rosen, 2000).

Although our home institution is a small (approximately 1,340 students), modestly endowed, private liberal arts college, Kalamazoo College does offer one rare resource to faculty interested in developing new service-learning courses or class projects. This is the privately funded Mary Jane Underwood Stryker Institute for Service-Learning, which annually awards LaPlante

Grants to faculty service-learning proposals; its dynamic director, Alison Geist, also provides invaluable assistance in identifying and liaising with off-campus community partners. After our initial deliberations, we met with Alison and concluded that we could craft a course unique among the offerings in our department, and unlike most of those on campus. Indeed, offering a service-learning course provided at least three distinct advantages to us and to the college. First, we could structure our course in consultation with Alison, who was particularly interested in soliciting service-learning proposals that would explore "town/gown" collaborations beyond what had become the standard Underwood Stryker Institute model of college students working on enrichment programs in Kalamazoo public schools. In addition, because the college recognizes that service-learning courses are labor-intensive, we, a philologist (Elizabeth) and an archaeologist (Anne), had our first chance to team-teach a course that would combine our specializations and demonstrate to our students the value of integrating classical literature and material culture. Finally, we were energized by the same challenges we planned to pose to our students, popping the "K Bubble" of academic isolation, and venturing beyond the safe boundaries of scholarly expertise to deepen our sense of belonging and contribute to the city where we live.

As the subject for our service-learning course, we chose "Cool Cities Ancient and Modern: Carthage and Kalamazoo" for topical, local, and curricular reasons beyond its catchy alliterative title. Michigan Governor Jennifer Granholm's Cool Cities Initiative was our inspiration. This statewide program funds community projects aimed at making Michigan's economically depressed, rust-belt towns more attractive places for talented, idealistic, and educated young people (exactly the profile of our Kalamazoo College students) to settle, in the hope of reversing Michigan's long-term trends toward demographic and urban decline. Kalamazoo boasts several recipients of Cool Cities grants, the first of which became one of our community partners. "Cool Cities" was also a sound addition to our classics curriculum, which lacked the kind of Ancient Cities course that has proven edifying and popular at many other schools.

The academic lens through which we address the question of "what makes a city cool?" is the archaeological and philological exploration of Carthage, a great North African metropolis of Near Eastern origin and heritage that tends to get short shrift in classics departments. The reasons for this neglect are complex, but remain rooted in an Orientalist bias for which tradi-tional classical scholarship has recently been criticized. Because compara-tively little Punic literature, art, and architecture have survived, the Phoenician founders of Carthage have effectively gotten no respect from most classicists. By making Carthage the centerpiece of our investigations into urban "cool," we fill a curricular gap with the study of a multicultural Mediterranean city that was the site of an ancient "clash of civilizations" between East and West and therefore confronted urban tensions that remain contemporary today.

Implementation: The First Cool Cities Course

Cool Cities has no prerequisites and is open to students at all levels; its debut in winter quarter 2006 attracted a varied group of 24 students who ranged from first-years to seniors and from classics majors to those who had never taken a classics course. Several students were veterans of prior service-learn-ing courses; they became valued collaborators in our neophyte venture into the pedagogy. The primary class format alternates lectures with class discus-sion aimed at explicitly relating Carthaginian material to our own city of Kalamazoo. As the term progresses and student service projects get under-way, community-based, off-campus fieldwork occupies some scheduled class periods. Writing assignments are predominantly descriptive or reflective, although every service project includes a significant research component. The course culminates in a symposium-like forum, in which student groups present their service-learning projects to an audience that includes class-mates, current and prospective community partners, Underwood Stryker Institute staff, and invited faculty members.

Arranging appropriately course-specific service placements for our 24 Cool Cities students was not easy. New partners in the community and city government took some convincing that working with groups of students for a 10-week quarter, a period universally considered too short to complete use-ful projects, would be a worthwhile time and benefit investment. Because no partner was willing to supervise more than four or five students, we had to coordinate five separate service projects, with attendant administrative, logis-tical, and personnel challenges. Yet, despite initial skepticism, some bumpy but instructive negotiations between academic and corporate supervisory styles, and a few radical midterm project redefinitions, all our service groups produced solid final products that satisfied community partners. Everyone was willing to work with us again; positive evaluations expressed such sentiments as, "It was phenomenal that the students could get so much done"; "I had expected to do a lot of hand-holding, but they held our hands"; "It warmed my heart that students, at the end of their PowerPoint presentation, said it was an honor to be part of this."

Our five service projects were a varied lot. Although all contributed to the course goal of making Kalamazoo a cooler city and college town, it was a constant challenge to find common threads among them, not to mention meaningful reflective connections to ancient Carthage. One group worked with local artist Holly Fisher, who received Kalamazoo's first Cool Cities grant to establish the Smartshop, a multipurpose art studio, gallery, and metalworking school, on the city's impoverished and largely minority north side. Holly envisioned the Smartshop's artistic resources and outreach programs as a tipping point for neighborhood improvements, but felt isolated and frustrated by a local tendency to regard the Smartshop as an elitist enclave largely irrelevant to surrounding residents and businesses. Our students worked on breaking down the barriers of preconception by building relationships with influential neighborhood organizations like African American churches and designing promotional materials and fun, art-related events to attract neighborhood families to the Smartshop's first fair-like outdoor River Arts Market in summer 2006.

Mitzi and Julie DeLuca, a mother-and-daughter team, led the Burr Oak Court Lighting Project, a grassroots effort to promote neighborhood solidarity, deter vandalism, and increase security in a historic but rundown, crackhouse infested, and graffiti-festooned cul-de-sac in downtown Kalamazoo. Students left their collegiate comfort zone to work the neighborhood, persistently knocking on doors and getting to know residents to gauge support for the installation of a street-wide lighting system and security cameras. They tracked down absentee landlords to create a database of property owners, enlisted electricians to provide estimates for street and porch lights, and developed a proposal that included community clean-up and landscaping improvements. The DeLucas have since used the proposal to request Burr Oak Court funding from the Vine Street Neighborhood Association and the City of Kalamazoo.

The Empty Bowls project was a huge collaboration that involved a second college service-learning class (Ceramics Hand Building), a shared student's Senior Individualized Project and a whole network of community partners: artists, charities, schools, and restaurants. Empty Bowls is a national organization that combines the creation of handmade ceramics with the fight against hunger. Ceramic bowls made by artists, students, and needy citizens are the centerpieces of fundraising events that heighten awareness of and alleviate urban poverty. To contextualize Kalamazoo College's first Empty Bowls event, our students researched hunger and homelessness in Kalamazoo, as well as the ethics of philanthropy. They presented their shocking statistics (for example, 25% of Kalamazoo's residents fall below the federal poverty line) and strategies for sustainable solutions in several venues, leading discussions in the Hand Building class and creating informational poster displays for the event itself. The group was also responsible for securing donations of soup, bread, and saleable ceramics from public-spirited local restaurants and professional artists. Our Empty Bowls event was a moving community gathering and a gratifying financial success; $5,000 was raised for Kalamazoo Loaves and Fishes and Heifer International.

Two projects partnered students with City of Kalamazoo administrators. The River West Sculpture Trail group accomplished tasks involved in opening a new city park where commissioned public art will take center stage. Students researched policies and procedures for the installation and maintenance of open-air works of art; they also organized and hosted a community meeting in which representatives of the city, county, Downtown Development Authority, Kalamazoo Public Schools, the Smartshop, Western Michigan University, Kalamazoo College, and the lakeshore cities of St. Joseph and Saugatuck gathered to share ideas and experience. The Planning Commission group grappled with ways to make the all-volunteer Kalamazoo Planning Commission, traditionally the preserve of prosperous, retired, White folks, a more inclusive body that better reflects the city's demographics. Students organized and hosted the first Planning Commission retreat ever held on the Kalamazoo College campus and presented a proposal to allow student representatives of the city's three institutions of higher learning (Kalamazoo College, Western Michigan University, and Kalamazoo Valley Community College) to serve on the board in a nonvoting capacity.

In addition to logistical difficulties and occasional glitches in working with community partners, our greatest challenge was integrating the various aspects of the course. Both students and faculty were called upon to integrate three very different kinds of knowledge—the history and culture of ancient Carthage, contemporary political and urban planning problems in Kalamazoo, and the concrete knowledge that they gained through their service projects. Though there was satisfaction with these individual elements of the course, students consistently cited the disparate kinds of information they were asked to synthesize and the huge differences between ancient Carthage and modern Kalamazoo as the two greatest impediments to seeing the class as a unified whole, rather than two or three mini-classes.

To help students integrate the various kinds of information they were learning, we asked them to engage in very structured reflective exercises. The essay prompts asked students to analyze some of the big concepts of the class (for example, what makes a city cool?) by using all the multifarious evidence at their disposal. Because the reflective essay is by definition personal and individual, students were free to—and frequently did—express their uncertainty about how the information fit together, how their attitudes changed throughout the term, and whether their work in the community was truly beneficial to others or themselves. By identifying student unease and common questions in a series of essays, we were able to think more deeply about their concerns and respond to them promptly. Students also engaged with fundamental course problems early on and in a sustained way throughout the quarter. As a result, most students' final reflective essays showed a development in their thought and ultimately a successful synthesis of all their experiences.

The second issue was thornier. Even we had to acknowledge that in many ways Carthage was a very different kind of city than Kalamazoo. Two issues, however, did continue to reappear in our discussions of both cities— the plight and invisibility of the poor and the role of public art in promoting civic identity and pride. Our students correctly recognized that many of the issues that they addressed in their projects—hunger, economic disenfranchisement, and public safety—are perennial urban problems. Moreover, just as the poor of Carthage left little trace of their existence, so too is it difficult to hear the voices and concerns of the disenfranchised in Kalamazoo. Two of the most successful projects looked to remedy this invisibility by using community art and public spectacle to raise their visibility. Both the Empty Bowls and the River Arts Market groups met with multiple constituencies to create public events that responded to the needs and desires of the "invisible" by bringing people from all walks of life together to share in food and art.

Revision: The Second Time Around

As we prepared to teach the course a second time, we desired to address the specific difficulties we encountered in the course's first iteration, as well as some pedagogical issues that we had not attempted to incorporate the first time. First, as stated previously, the coherence of the course was an obvious problem. We thought we might tackle this problem in a number of ways. Because we had had such success in focusing on issues of urban poverty and invisibility and on the role of public art, we decided to foreground these topics as we introduced material and readings. Likewise, because students seemed to benefit from the opportunity to reflect on their experiences, we offered them more opportunities to engage in structured reflection, increasing the number of required essays from two to three. In addition, we believed that in part the lack of coherence stemmed from the fact that the five groups had little common ground. For the second offering we attempted to design five projects that all shared a common theme or project.

In the midst of our revisions, two distinct but related activities on campus motivated our consideration of another role this course might fulfill. In September 2006 we were invited to participate in a workshop sponsored by the American Council on Education and directed by the editors of this volume, Elizabeth Brewer, Director of International Education at Beloit College; and Kiran Cunningham, Professor of Anthropology at Kalamazoo College. The workshop facilitated conversations, brainstorming, and sharing of ideas and methods to transform a course into a vehicle for preparing students for foreign study or to help them integrate their experiences more effectively upon their return. Soon after our participation in the workshop, Kalamazoo College embarked on a discussion of how best to revise our general education curriculum. A recurring theme in these discussions was the need to better prepare our students for their study abroad experiences and to offer them opportunities upon their return to process what they had gained from their time away. Both the workshop and the sustained conversations on campus led us as a department to examine our curriculum, and we concluded that Cool Cities, with its focus on Orientalism, "otherness," and the

Roman response to Carthaginian exoticism might be an ideal vehicle to prepare students not only before they travel abroad (because the course focuses
so intensely upon the perception of Carthage from the outside, and requires
students to interpret the evidence we have from multiple cultural perspectives) but also upon their return (because the focus on the pleasures and
problems in a large urban environment are some of the most striking and
enduring memories our students relate post-study abroad). Thus, the version
of the course that we offered in winter 2008 looked somewhat different from
its predecessor, given our previous experiences and our interest in preparing
students for and giving them a chance to process the cognitive or "high-
intensity" dissonance that results from foreign study (Brewer & Cunningham, chapter 1 of this volume; Kiely, 2005).

This time 31 students enrolled, again composed of first-years through
seniors, a handful of classics majors, and some students with service-learning
experience. We devoted much of the first week of class to having students
describe their experiences of cities: Specifically, what makes a city cool? And
what could make Kalamazoo cooler? Here we are careful to ask them to write
about and discuss with us and other students any experiences of foreign cities
that they have had. In particular this offers juniors and seniors the opportunity to talk about study abroad as something that provided them with valuable knowledge (a very important first step, because a complaint often heard
from students is the lack of interest in or acknowledgment of expertise of
those who have recently returned). This also encourages underclassmen to
reflect on their experiences of cities—in their home environments and in
travel within and outside of the United States—and early on plants a seed
that study abroad might offer unforeseen and important insights to them as
well.

Likewise we added other activities that compel students to learn more of
the city in which they currently reside. They are required to complete four
"fieldwork" assignments: a visit to a "cool," independently owned local business; a religious service one would not normally attend; an entertainment
venue, a museum, or a neighborhood new to them; and participation in a
community-service project off campus. Students must then describe the
experience, provide their reactions, and attempt to integrate it with the academic course content. Students report that these experiences have given
them increased comfort in navigating Kalamazoo, have led them to discover
parts of the city they never knew about, and forced them to do things that

initially made them feel extremely uncomfortable. We believe these field-work assignments can assist students in experiencing cultural dissonance of a kind that they will meet on study abroad, but in a more familiar environment. It also gives them a template for how they might process these experiences.

Students divide into small groups to engage in two projects. For the first, students build upon their study of the political motivations for Carthage's conflicting foundation legends by researching and rewriting the foundation legend of Kalamazoo. We hope that this allows students to realize that most cities have a rich, interesting, and contested past. The second assignment asks students to proceed in groups from campus in a different cardinal direction. Students walk a path laid out by the professors and map their journeys using photographs, notes, thought maps, or any other kind of mapping system they want. When students present their maps to the class, many find significant differences between their previous experiences of these areas and the actual maps that they create. Indeed, several groups were startled by what they found; their reactions (fear, delight, apprehension) to the neighborhoods they found themselves in were all the more jarring when they realized how close these locales are to the campus that they consider familiar and safe. We believe that this experience may make them more attentive, both to their physical surroundings and to the borders between areas in cities, and may encourage them to venture outside their comfort zones while on study abroad.

The bulk of the students' work, however, remains their engagement in service-learning group projects in the community. In 2008 we paid special attention to the composition of these groups—the few classics students in the course were separated, so that they could provide historical context to as many groups as possible, and we strove to distribute the seniors and those students who are natives of other countries throughout the groups, so that each group might have students whose foreign study experience could facilitate their negotiation of the city. In addition, we have observed that those groups that had some upperclassmen provided leadership to the group and gave them opportunities to mentor the younger students—and not just in the project. One first-year student, for example, confided that he had not intended to participate in study abroad, but a senior in his group kept encouraging him to, and at this writing he thinks that he will.

All of the service-learning groups (with one exception) focused on a single project: the preparation and beautification of a new park at the eastern edge of the Kalamazoo College campus, to be known as College Park. The area the park encompasses, previously a parking lot and an overgrown field bordering a small creek and the railroad tracks beyond, had nominally been considered public space, but, because of the wildness of the area and its lack of amenities, it was perpetually deserted. Though in a sad state, the site boasted one developed feature, a large-scale statue by artist David Black titled "The New Arcadia," which would become a focal point for the new park. An association of community members (the self-titled Gateway Coalition) worked for more than 10 years to secure funding for improvements to the area and the creation of a public park. Financial support was ultimately donated by city, state, and private entities, including donations from Kalamazoo College and Western Michigan University, the two colleges bordering the park's north and south edges. Although the Gateway Coalition was thrilled that the park was soon to be a reality, there were various ancillary projects that required additional research, and our students were divided into groups to investigate these specific issues. We hoped that by focusing our efforts on a single location we might not only reduce logistical headaches and create greater coherence in the course, but also encourage students to think more intentionally about the borders of their own campus environment. If students began to view the boundaries of the campus as a part of their own community and began to interact with other members of that community, our reasoning went, we might be able to encourage a sense of ownership of and responsibility for public spaces, a willingness to explore beyond the borders of campus, and a sensitivity to other community members that could have a positive effect on Kalamazoo, those venturing on study abroad, and ultimately into the world after college.

The projects themselves also allowed for a tremendous amount of personal initiative. As part of the official celebration of its 175th birthday, Kalamazoo College planned a day of community service, the Day of Gracious Giving, for Saturday, May 17, 2008, with the goal of involving at least 175 volunteers from Kalamazoo College and the City of Kalamazoo in three different projects, including a beautification and planting program in College Park. This group project worked with the college's architect for the event, Jim VanSweden, of the college's Facilities Management Office, who is also a neighborhood resident, and with Gateway Coalition member Bill Snyder to formulate an organizational plan for the volunteer event. In consultation with their partners, the group determined what sort of plantings would be most appropriate and inviting for College Park, located the best and most affordable source for the plantings, researched the feasibility of cleaning College Park's New Arcadia sculpture as one of the day's activities, and explored the viability of building a small patio area in the park to be used for events.

A second group explored the restrictions and possibilities of installing public art in Kalamazoo, with an eye to the installation of works created by Kalamazoo College art students in College Park. This is a complicated process involving city government, civic art and philanthropic organizations, and local and state funding agencies. The group, therefore, worked with ceramicist and professor Sarah Lindley; Vibbert Scholar Julia Gartrell, whose mission is to promote civic engagement and activism through art; and community artists to collect and compile information on how to finance and implement public art projects in Kalamazoo. Their end product was a manual that professors and students in the art department can now consult as they begin the process of gaining permission to add additional pieces to the park.

The Gateway Coalition strongly believed that College Park deserved a kick-off celebration, both to celebrate its completion and to welcome the residential, commercial, and college communities to the new park. Thus it was the job of another group to organize an inauguration event for the official dedication and opening of College Park. The group approached local businesses (both to request donations and to draw their attention to the new park), liaised with city agencies to determine what permissions they would need to hold the celebration, found entertainment from both the community and the colleges, and made recommendations about the timing of the event, so that it would draw the largest possible crowd and have the greatest visibility. Though delays in the completion of the park meant that the June date for the inauguration that the group envisioned was not feasible, they did create a handbook for use by those who may plan such an event at a subsequent date.

Part of the original plan for College Park was to provide attractive historical markers at key points, which would offer information about the history of the neighborhood, including the location of former businesses and descriptions of notable architecture. Because of budgetary constraints, these markers are no longer part of the plan, but members of the Gateway Coalition still believe they are important to the project; they would give park users opportunities to pause and reflect, and to create connections between residents and the history of their community. Therefore, a group reviewed the accuracy of the historical research that has been done to date and devised an additional marker for the New Arcadia sculpture. In addition, they determined the best type of signage for the area, priced such markers, and searched for sources of possible funding to support the endeavor.

A final group worked on a project not directly connected to College Park. The Downtown Retailers Association (DRA), chaired by local businessman Bill Van Dis, wants to work toward making Kalamazoo "greener," both through projects to assist business owners in recycling their waste more easily and effectively, and by providing recycling facilities to customers and patrons. A recycling campaign such as this offers a crucial step in maintaining the aesthetic appeal of our business districts, raising awareness of issues of the environment in our community, and could provide a model for other areas in and around the city. This group researched a number of issues related to the development of a recycling plan for the DRA. Members attended meetings of the city's Environmental Concerns Committee to assess civic ideas about and commitment to the project; developed, administered, and analyzed data from a survey that determined the recycling issues that are most pressing to local businesses; and created brochures for distribution to downtown retailers on why and how to recycle their waste.

As students completed work on their final projects, we requested that the two senior classics majors in the class, Katie Coaster and Alanna Muto, fulfill a departmental graduation requirement by reflecting on connections they perceived among study abroad, their experiences as students in Kalamazoo, and the ancient city of Carthage. They agreed and offered a presentation to the class during the last week of the term. Based on their experience they detailed four distinct periods when one is on study abroad: (a) trying to define an identity, (b) increasing comfort with oneself and one's surroundings, (c) a broadening of horizons, and (d) a sense of the end approaching in which one relishes one's final experiences and begins to reflect on the experience. Katie and Alanna found that these phases likewise correlate to the 4 years of a college experience (especially when the third year contains a study away component), in which students undergo the same emotional and intellectual challenges, though over a longer time frame. In addition, the students found that these periods of development applied more broadly to the time-line of the city of Carthage, in which distinct phases of occupation (Punic, Roman, Christian, and Modern) showed continued development, though all the while relying on and being shaped by the past. The women's work was provocative, and no doubt underutilized by us, because the presentation was given on the final day of class. However, this certainly gives us ideas about how we might use their work or a similar presentation in the future. Linking life phases of cities to human life cycles, and encouraging students to think about the critical moments when confusion gives way to clarity in their own lives, the lives of others, and the lives of the cities we study offer opportunities for students to realize that their course experiences may serve as real preparation for challenges in life and likewise provide chances for them to reflect upon how far they have come in their journey. In the next iteration of this course, we hope to introduce these concepts a little earlier and find a way for students to collaborate and grapple with them in a hands-on way.

Continuing Challenges and Conclusions

Although some of the modifications we made to the course offered substantial improvements, things did not necessarily work out the way we had planned. In an attempt to address problems with the coherence of the course and to diminish the logistical challenges of managing so many projects, we believed that having a single project would alleviate some of our earlier troubles. In theory this might have worked well, but the particular project we chose was so very closely tied to the college—its location bordered campus, community partners for four of the projects included Kalamazoo College faculty or staff, and the project seemingly would have a direct effect on the campus—that students did not really have the sense that they were working within the community and expanding their borders. In fact, in our attempt to fashion the course as a study abroad preparatory course, projects that encourage students to work with new communities in unfamiliar areas would seem to have a greater resonance and effect, so the proximity of the project to the campus community actually diminished our effect in this area as well. Likewise, although focusing on a single project might offer increased coherence, there were also problems attendant with this. Groups frequently overlapped their work (e.g., researching David Black's New Arcadia sculpture), resulting in complaints from community members who had been requested to provide information on the same topic to three different groups. Moreover, although the project dealt explicitly with urban improvements and public art (two foci of the class), the problem of invisibility of the city's poor and disenfranchised was not a part of any project. This had been the aspect of the projects in 2006 that had had the greatest effect and allowed for the greatest connections among the three parts of the class. Furthermore, though the groups largely focused on one discrete project, the amount of logistical oversight was not significantly diminished. Finally, as advisors, we perhaps saw a greater unity to all the projects, but this was not necessarily the case for the students, who largely focused on their own particular piece of the plan. In the future, we will opt instead, when possible, for community-based assignments that encourage students to work away from campus with communities unlike those they are familiar with and that put them in situations that create the kind of dissonance that facilitates deeper reflective connections (Kiely, 2005; Mezirow, 1997).

A second problem had to do with the composition of the class itself. As Kalamazoo College increases the size of its student body, caps on certain classes have been raised. Whereas we had 24 students enrolled in 2006, in 2008 the class size increased to 31. The consequences of this were troublesome—the students had less interaction with each other, inhibiting their ability to become a cohesive group. In addition, the service-learning groups mushroomed from four or five members to six or seven. It was much easier for members of certain groups to shirk their responsibilities, or for work not to be equitably distributed. Problems within individual groups were much more prevalent this time than they were in 2006. In addition, most students who enrolled in the course had no idea that it was a service-learning course, much less that the service-learning component was quite significant. Thus, several students noted in their course evaluations that this was not at all the kind of course they were hoping for.

On the positive side, our attempts to foreground invisibility and public art did help set the tone and focus the in-class portion of the course in a way that highlighted issues of importance to both Carthage and Kalamazoo. Additionally, the new emphasis on study abroad was quite successful. Although students felt that the service-learning projects were too closely tied to the college, their reflections on their fieldwork and other two group exercises revealed an increased engagement and awareness of the city of Kalamazoo and the environs immediately around campus. We believe that if we could pair these experiences more explicitly with a service-learning component, we could develop a course that might allow both departing and returning students to respond in a more thoughtful and critically engaged way to their foreign study experiences.

Finally, despite our desires to be all things to all people, we realize that if this course is to integrate study abroad experiences successfully, we will need to be more explicit about that goal, as well as be willing to sacrifice some of the other course content. Although this course remains very much a work in progress, we still believe that a community-based service-learning course, bridging the ancient and modern worlds, may still serve as an effective vehicle for reflection and integration of intercultural dissonance.

References

Campus Compact. (n.d.). Service-Learning. Retrieved July 15, 2008, from http://www.compact.org/initiatives/service-learning.

Howard, J. (Ed.). (2001, Summer). Service-learning course design workbook. *Michigan Journal of Community Service Learning.*

Kiely, R. (2005). A transformative learning model for service-learning: A longitudinal case study. *Michigan Journal of Community Service Learning, 12,* 5–22.

Mezirow, J. (1997). Transformative learning: Theory to practice. *New Directions for Adult and Continuing Education, 74,* 5–12.

Rosen, R. (2000). Classical studies and the search for community. In I. Harkavy & B. Donovan (Eds.), *Connecting past and present: Concepts and models for service-learning in history* (pp. 173–187). Sterling, VA: Stylus.

8

CHINESE CITIES IN TRANSITION

The City as Classroom

Daniel Youd

I t is a stiflingly hot day in late August 2007 about a week before classes resume at China's Henan University. Although not yet formally enrolled in the Chinese university's program for international students, a handful of Beloit College students, as participants in the college's Chinese Cities in Transition course, have already begun a crucial part of their study abroad experience. As one of these students later records in a field-note writing assignment, walking through the university's imposing, Chinese-style southern gate, she leaves behind the relative tranquility of the university campus and emerges onto Minglun Road, a bustling urban thoroughfare. Jostled by a sea of humanity and somewhat taken aback by the chaotic mix of bicycles, motorcycles, and automobiles weaving up and down the street, she realizes that, although but a provincial city, Kaifeng, the home of Henan University, is nevertheless bursting with energy and industry. On assignment to engage a willing local in a discussion about life in modern-day Kaifeng, the student passes by any number of street vendors, cheap noodle shops, and businesses, many of which cater to the local university population, until she catches sight of the driver of a *sanlúnche* (literally a "three-wheeled vehicle")—a large motorized tricycle with covered seating behind the driver, used by many as an inexpensive alternative to a taxi. In her own words, she remembers:

Not sure of how to approach . . . the driver, I just stood in an alley opening across from him until he made eye contact with me, probably wondering if I needed a ride. This was my chance: I introduced myself as an international student and asked if I could question him about his life as a three-wheeled-vehicle driver. He immediately broke into a smile and welcomed me with words and arm motions to a shadier spot where we could talk. While he sat in the driver's seat and I stood next to him, he told me about himself. I had a list of questions all ready to be answered, but as I asked them, I realized the story he wanted to tell didn't come from the practical questions I asked about. . . .

Superficially, perhaps, this American student's encounter with a Chinese three-wheeled-vehicle driver may appear unremarkable. Such encounters, many faculty members and administrators at U.S. colleges and universities assume, must happen all the time: Why else, after all, are we sending our students abroad in ever greater numbers, if not to immerse them in the everyday realities of unfamiliar environments? Yet, as former president of Harvard University Derek Bok writes:

> Whatever the country chosen, opportunities to study abroad often fail to give students a deep engagement with a different culture. Like other pieces in the mosaic of international studies, such programs are seldom closely coordinated with other parts of the curriculum that might prepare participants to make the most of their overseas experience. More than one third of the undergraduates who go abroad have never studied the language of their host country. . . . Most have never studied [its] history, politics, or culture. . . . With such skimpy preparation, only a minority of enterprising students truly immerse themselves in the local society. (2006, p. 237)

Thus, as Elizabeth Brewer and Kiran Cunningham explain in chapter 1, it is not unusual for students to return from a period abroad with a sense of unfulfilled expectations and missed opportunity. Indeed, a common thread tying together all of the contributions to this volume is that success in study abroad is, for the majority of students, not something that happens spontaneously, but is rather the intentional product of carefully structured programs—programs that not only create opportunities for thoughtful, engaged learning while abroad but also integrate this learning into the broader college curriculum both prior to students' departure and after their return.

As a contribution to the ongoing conversation concerning the design and assessment of college-level study abroad programs in the United States, then, this chapter outlines the learning goals and structure of the Chinese Cities in Transition course at Beloit College. Although designed to respond to the particular, present-day demands of study abroad in the People's Republic of China, the course may nevertheless serve as a model for other off-campus programs, both abroad and domestic, insofar as it shares its interdisciplinary approach to teaching and learning with other Beloit College Cities in Transition courses: for example, those taught in Quito, Ecuador; Dakar, Senegal; Moscow, Russia; Managua, Nicaragua; and Beloit, Wisconsin, itself. The process that led to the development of these courses is briefly described in the following text.

Knowing and Growing: Identifying Learning Goals and Defining Success

The collaborative work on improving international education at Beloit College, which has resulted in the development of the shared teaching methodology and overlapping learning goals of the Cities in Transition rubric, began with two simple questions: What constitutes a *successful* study abroad experience? And, how can we as college and university educators and administrators maximize the chances that students will meet with such success while studying abroad?

For Beloit College faculty and staff these questions and the answers that we have formulated in response to them relate directly to our college's emphasis on student exchange programs as a primary means of internationalizing undergraduate education. Not only do such programs diversify the student body and curriculum of the college through the enrollment of students from partner universities, but they also provide Beloit College students themselves the opportunity to study at institutions with different educational philosophies and pedagogies. As noted in chapters 1 and 3 of this volume, however, direct enrollment in universities abroad does not always lead to an increase in students' disciplinary knowledge, nor does it necessarily ensure meaningful engagement with the culture of the host country. Several years ago, an assessment of learning outcomes from several of Beloit College's exchange programs led faculty members and administrators to conclude that students' language skills had not advanced as much as desired, nor were students returning home with substantially more cultural knowledge than before their departure. Furthermore, although students responded that they had returned home with greater maturity and self-confidence, they regretted that their study abroad failed to integrate more meaningfully with their academic pursuits on the Beloit College campus. Not wanting to abandon the exchange program model because of its positive rewards and potential, Beloit College faculty and staff embarked on a project to enhance the curriculum offered by its partner universities.

Certainly, it would be impossible to formulate any universally valid template for addressing these problems. Nevertheless, building on recent trends in the field of international education, student feedback, and our own personal experiences as teachers, we at Beloit College, in developing the Cities in Transition model, have realized the benefit of consciously integrating both the content-based and developmental learning goals. As Pablo Toral illustrates in chapter 11 in this volume on the senior thesis, these goals define contemporary expectations—whether students', parents', or educators'—of study abroad: Students enrolled in Cities in Transition courses at Beloit College encounter academically challenging material aimed at furnishing them with a depth of knowledge of their host country's culture and society *within* an instructional framework that demands a high level of initiative and maturity.

Put another way, Cities in Transition courses engage students beyond the international-student classroom with the environment in which they live during their time abroad. They also encourage active coordination between students' studies abroad and the overall trajectory of their liberal arts educations. Much of this coordination can be accomplished through both predeparture courses and post-return seminars, as discussed in detail in chapter 3. In this way the goal of "knowing"—mastering specific content and acquiring actual skills (e.g., language proficiency)—is attained through a decidedly individualized process of "growing," whereby students develop heightened awareness of the difficulties of ethical action in a morally ambiguous world. Additionally, it is important to remember that Beloit College students, as participants in college-run exchange programs, do not receive the "mediation" that students in third-party-provider programs do. We have come to realize that if no one on site can help students make sense of their experiences, observations, and day-to-day lives when abroad, then we have to teach them how to do this for themselves. Thus the development of specific observational skills—and the means to process these observations—are a central feature of Cities in Transition pedagogy.

Those familiar with study abroad conditions in mainland China will immediately recognize the desirability of these goals for a number of reasons: (a) despite recent attempts to integrate international students more fully into their Chinese host institutions, foreigners are still regularly housed in separate dormitories in out-of-the-way parts of Chinese university campuses; (b) because of their need for basic Chinese language instruction, most international students do not enroll in regular university classes, but instead attend language classes offered to foreigners like themselves; (c) the growing cosmopolitanism of China's big cities allows international students access to expatriate communities, many of which remain highly isolated from the Chinese society around them; and (d) with in-room Internet access and cyber cafés on just about every corner, students have difficulty disconnecting—even for short periods—from friends and family back home. Given these conditions, educators must work particularly diligently to avoid their students returning from China with the sense that they were barely even there.

Language

Normally, Beloit College students who study abroad in China have completed two years of study of Modern Standard Chinese (*putonghuà*). Moreover, progress toward fluency in the language is one of the major goals that students cite in making the decision to study in China. For this reason, well-taught language classes for international students are essential. Beloit College is fortunate, therefore, that its two Chinese partner institutions provide quality instruction in this regard. Beloit's Chinese Cities in Transition course does not seek to replace these basic courses. Rather, one of our main objectives is to encourage students to put into practice in real-life settings the linguistic competence that they are developing in the language classroom.

It is significant, therefore, that almost all of the work that students do for the Chinese Cities in Transition course requires substantial engagement with the Chinese language. In the excerpt of student writing cited at the beginning of this chapter, for example, the student prepared her questions in Chinese and used Chinese as the medium of communication with the three-wheeled-vehicle driver. Her field notes, although written in English, included an appendix of key vocabulary and phrases used and learned through the assignment.

Yet the assignment was not centered on language learning per se. Instead, through the process of talking with a Kaifeng local about his life, language became for the student a means of active, independent communication. In the course of the assignment, the student quickly realized that to engage another human being in real and revealing dialogue, she must be willing to move beyond scripted, classroom-based material. In fact, the true significance of the student's field notes lies in her realization that the "story [the three-wheeled-vehicle driver] wanted to tell didn't come from [the questions she had prepared]."

Independence

Crucially, years of experience in international education have demonstrated that moments such as this—when a student moves from the artificial, albeit reassuring, environment of the international student classroom to the complexity of real world experience (here exemplified by the city)—do not happen often enough. To cite Derek Bok again, U.S. study abroad programs "tend to be . . . too isolated from the surrounding society" (2006, p. 247). In such cases necessary support structures (i.e., international student classes) may actually constrain learning, as well as enable it. To remedy this situation Bok advocates creating "programs of education abroad . . . to put participants in as much contact with the local society as their level of preparation permits."

Of course, creating the conditions under which such contact may occur is no easy matter, not least because many U.S. students when abroad are quite reluctant and unsure how to act independently—their youthful bravado notwithstanding. Certainly it is revealing that in recounting her conversation with the three-wheeled-vehicle driver, the student structured her field notes around a sense of uncertainty—"[n]ot sure of how to approach . . . the driver"—which she conquered—"[t]his was my chance"—in large part because she was "on assignment." Not coincidently, the Beloit College Cities in Transition model is designed to *teach* independence.

This means, at a most basic level, that students must acquire skills to map and interpret unknown environments. To that end, as Darren Kelly discusses in more detail (both practical and theoretical) in his chapters, students enrolled in Cities in Transition courses learn how people delimit, navigate, and inhabit space. By asking what boundaries define (in their experience and that of others) various, primarily urban environments, students begin to think how they might responsibly push beyond them. Students moreover must undertake most of their urban explorations on their own. Without the distractions of even a single peer companion, students are far more likely to interact meaningfully with the environment through which they pass, registering its sights, sounds, and smells, and taking note of the diverse array of human expression—artistic, economic, political, religious, and so on—that creates the fabric of life in their temporary home.

Nuts and Bolts: About the Course

Overview

To participate in such an ambitious program, Beloit students who enroll in the Chinese Cities in Transition course ideally plan ahead. They learn Chinese; they take courses related to Chinese history, literature, politics, philosophy, religion, and so on; and they develop a disciplinary focus through their major that may well guide their studies once they are in China. Additionally, during the semester before their departure, many students elect a modular course that prepares them to draw upon the breadth and depth of their liberal arts training in experiencing their semester abroad. This course introduces students—through various observational and mapping exercises conducted in the city of Beloit itself—to the idea of using the city as a classroom (i.e., as a place for disciplinary, as well as interdisciplinary, inquiry and analysis). Once abroad, students are expected to employ these newly acquired observational skills to complete, during the course of a semester, a significant work of independent research that focuses on a specific aspect of life in their chosen city of residence. Finally, upon their return, students may continue the process of integrative learning by refining research done abroad, presenting their work at Beloit College's International Symposium, and/or incorporating this research with the guidance of their major advisor into a senior thesis or project.

The City as Classroom

Like Beloit students enrolled in Cities in Transition courses in Ecuador, Senegal, and Russia, students studying abroad in China find themselves in the midst of complex, vibrant urban spaces. (The focus of the Cities in Transition program on urban, rather than rural, phenomena is largely a result of this fact. We do not wish to suggest, therefore, that rural areas and rural problems are any less significant. In fact, the connections between the urban and the rural are often a major theme in class discussions and student projects.) Because of their very complexity, moreover, these urban spaces invite multiple forms of engagement and lend themselves to various forms of analysis. Indeed, Beloit College's Cities in Transition pedagogy is premised on the idea that urban phenomena are ideal objects of investigation in study abroad courses precisely because they allow students with varied disciplinary interests—economics, political science, history, public health, and others—to carry on discussions of a common topic: the city. As Ash Amin and Nigel Thrift write: "The city is everywhere and in everything" (2002, p. 1).

In the case of China, moreover, the topic of urban transformation is of particular importance. Throughout its history China has produced remarkable examples of urban culture. One need only think of the Shang dynasty ritual center of Anyang (14th century BCE), the Tang dynasty (618–907) in Chang'an, and the various cities of the Yangtze delta that defined the commercial and cultural centers of 16th- to 18th-century Chinese life. Currently, the People's Republic—which in 1970 had about 200 cities and now has roughly 700—is urbanizing faster than any other society in human history (Campanella, 2008).

Through partnership agreements with two institutions of higher education—Henan University in the city of Kaifeng, Henan Province; and Shandong University, in the city of Ji'nan, Shandong Province—Beloit College has ties to two of these cities. Although students opt to study for a semester in either one or the other, they have the opportunity to visit both. The semester begins in August with an intensive 2-week seminar in Kaifeng; students reconvene in October in Ji'nan, at which time they make preliminary reports on their site-based research. The Beloit College faculty instructor is on site during the two weeks in August and one week in October. Otherwise, students maintain contact with the course instructor and submit class assignments electronically.

Kaifeng and Ji'nan are both ancient cities in states of rapid transformation. The very visible, and sometimes incongruous, juxtaposition of old and new prompts a host of questions: What were these cities like 20 years ago? One hundred years ago? One thousand? What are they like now? And what will they be like in the future? Allowing students to study in two different cities—one from China's wealthier east coast (Ji'nan), and one from the less prosperous central part of the country (Kaifeng)—provides an additional comparative dimension to their inquiry: Are there regional differences in the rate and quality of urban change in China? What are the opportunities associated with this change? What are the costs? And, how do particular cultural values shape the speed and direction of change?

Site-Based Learning

To answer questions such as these, students are instructed to look closely, read widely, and discuss regularly with their fellow classmates and, via the Internet, with their instructor. Moreover, throughout the semester, students work toward the completion of what we call a "site-based participant-observation project" that focuses on one aspect of urban transition in contemporary China. (See the appendix to this chapter for a model assignment sheet for the site-based participant-observation project.) Whereas group activities in August and October and assigned reading and distance-learning exercises throughout the semester provide students with a broad overview of key course themes, the site-based learning project gives them an opportunity to develop skills of observation and analysis in a more in-depth fashion.

Typical early assignments (carried out in the August seminar) include:

1. **Mapping.** Shortly after arriving at the campus of Henan University in Kaifeng, before they begin course readings, students are asked by their instructors to map their environment. Students typically are given several hours during one morning to reconnoiter, marking down in their notebooks what strikes their interest, where they go, and what they observe. They may write, sketch, or take pictures to incorporate into their maps, which need not be literal street maps. (In the last year, we have experimented with using Internet mapping technology—for example, Google maps—as part of this assignment.) In the afternoon, students are given time to create their maps in the medium of their choosing, which they then present and interpret to their classmates. The questions and observations that arise from this exercise set the basic parameters for classroom discussion of the following week to ten days. (Elsewhere in this volume, Nancy Krusko [chapter 9] and Darren Kelly [chapter 2] describe similar mapping

exercises, and Appendix A in chapter 3 contains a sample mapping assignment from Elizabeth Brewer's study abroad preparatory course.)

2. **Navigating.** After completing the mapping assignment, students generally have begun to familiarize themselves with the university and its surrounding neighborhoods. The next assignment aims to expand their view of the city to include a sense of its current diversity and historical meaning. Students receive the name in Chinese of a site of historical or cultural interest in the city. It is their job to navigate, by any means but taxi, to that site, uncover its significance, and record their observations. Not only should they learn about their destination (and how to get there using the same transportation local citizens do), but they also should begin to make use of their developing ethnographic skills to record what they see along the way.

3. **Interviewing.** Building on assignments such as those discussed previously, students are finally directed to interview a willing resident of the city. (The passage of student writing quoted at the beginning of this chapter comes from this assignment.) Students may go anywhere they like and interview anyone they wish, as long as they observe the ethical guidelines we discuss in class. They prepare questions in advance, record the content of their conversations, and practice writing up their reflections on their experiences in field-note form.

After these early exercises navigating the city and engaging with its inhabitants, students are ready to delve more deeply into its complexity. The structure of the Chinese Cities in Transition course encourages this development by requiring students to pursue specialized urban research projects. Thus, under the guidance of the course instructor and after exploring a number of sites in the assignments described previously, students define, observe, and research a particular site in either Kaifeng or Ji'nan. In choosing their sites, students are advised to be creative but also practical. A feasible site must be capable of holding the student's interest over the course of the semester. It must also be suitable to the assignment, which requires repeated visits over a series of months. In the past, students have chosen, among other sites, restaurants, cricket markets, construction sites, public parks, temples, churches, Internet cafés, and museums.

Once students have chosen their sites, they must immerse themselves in them. They should visit them at different times of the week, at different times of the day, under different weather conditions, and even in different styles of dress, to observe their many facets. Additionally, if possible, they should participate in activities that take place at these sites. They should talk casually to some participants and more formally interview others.

Writing and Ethics

Immersion itself, however, is not enough. Writing—whether as journal entries, field notes, or the end-of-semester research paper—is a central aspect of the site-based participant-observation project from start to finish. While working on their projects, students are expected to use writing and rewriting to document, process, and reflect upon their experiences. Students are encouraged to keep detailed, organized notes on all of their project-related activities. Obviously, the more material they generate during the earlier stages of the project, the better. In this way, their learning will be enhanced, and they will have plenty of data and ideas for their final papers or creative projects.

While observing and writing, students use many of the techniques, reminders, and warnings presented in *Writing Ethnographic Fieldnotes* by Robert M. Emerson, Rachel I. Fretz, and Linda L. Shaw (1995). *Writing Ethnographic Fieldnotes* is especially important in defining the ethical complexity entailed in undertaking a project such as the one expected of students in the Chinese Cities in Transition course. Prompted by this text, students discuss how and when outside observers may appropriately introduce themselves into the activities of a site. They also address the ways in which preconceptions and prejudices may impede one's ability to approach the meaning of a given site. As the authors of *Writing Ethnographic Fieldnotes* note, "The object of [participant-observation] is ultimately to get close to those studied as a way of understanding what their experiences and activities *mean to them*" (Emerson, Fretz, & Shaw, 1995, pp. 12–13). At the same time, the authors recognize that participant-observation is by definition "polyvocal," blending both "outsider" and "insider" views of a site or activity. They state, "[W]hile fieldnotes are about others, their concerns and doings gleaned through empathetic immersion, they necessarily reflect and convey the ethnographer's understanding of these concerns and doings."

In addition to guidelines provided by the technically focused *Writing Ethnographic Fieldnotes,* instructors of the Chinese Cities in Transition course have found it useful to expose students to models of writings of a more popular orientation. The works of two authors—Peter Hessler and Rod Gifford—have seemed particularly appropriate to the goals of the course. Hessler's *River Town* (2001) is an ethnographically sensitive account of his 2-year experience living and teaching English in a remote Sichuanese town. Gifford's *China Road* (2007), which is more journalistic in style (as befits the author's status as former Beijing correspondent for National Public Radio), chronicles a 6-week road trip across the length of China. Both books rely heavily on careful observation, recorded conversations, and interviews to tell their stories. Additionally, they weave personal reflection with objective analysis in a way that mirrors the Chinese Cities in Transition goal of advancing students' knowledge of China while at the same time enabling personal growth. Finally, both books demonstrate how nonacademic writing may be engagingly written, humorous, anecdotal, yet culturally and historically informed.

Student Work

As should be apparent by now, Chinese Cities in Transition is a demanding course. When students begin the semester they are often unsure of their ability to complete the work required of them, and they are especially intimidated by the scope of the site-based participant-observation project. Although the texts cited previously provide guidance and reasonable models for the kind of thinking and writing that they should aspire to produce, nothing is more inspiring to students than the ability to read and discuss the work of others who, like themselves, have completed the course before them. Produced by undergraduates with similar levels of preparation, exemplary research demonstrates what it is possible to learn and achieve in the length of one semester abroad.

Indeed, in the four years that the Chinese Cities in Transition course has run at Beloit College, quite a number of students have completed noteworthy projects. A summary of two of the most exceptional projects follows.

Urban Construction and Migrant Labor

An economics major and 2007 graduate of Beloit College participated in the Chinese Cities in Transition course in China in the fall of 2005. During his semester abroad, he conducted an innovative study of migrant laborers at a shopping mall construction site in Shanghai, China. (In 2005 Beloit College's China exchange program was located in Shanghai.) The student combined his passion for economics with course methodologies to complete a nuanced analysis of the lives of these workers and their employers. His research combined analysis of the broad social forces that shape the migrant labor markets of China's fast-developing cities with an anthropologically sophisticated depiction of daily life at the construction site and in the workers' dormitories. Much of the enlivening anecdotal material in his final course paper derived from the hours of conversation he had with workers and members of the site's management team.

The student is quick to admit that participation in the Chinese Cities in Transition course made his semester in China tremendously rewarding, as it allowed him opportunities both to enhance his Chinese language abilities and to increase his understanding of modern Chinese society. What he did not realize, however, was the effect his participation in the course would have on the direction of his life when he returned to the United States. Although he thoroughly enjoyed the work he did in China for his Cities in Transition project, he nevertheless questioned what this research had to do with the study of economics he engaged in back at Beloit. Not until he returned to Beloit and continued his research on migrant labor did the connections become more apparent.

Indeed, the skills the student began developing for his Cities in Transition project have continued to serve him well. In the summer of 2006, he served as an assistant in post-Katrina reconstruction and rebuilding research led by Beloit College economics professor Emily Chamlee-Wright. His ability to carry out this work hinged not only on his economic research skills, but also on his experiences in China interviewing people very different from himself. As part of this research, he conducted interviews, not unlike those he conducted in China, with residents of various New Orleans communities. Following his graduation, he subsequently was hired to manage the teams continuing to interview New Orleans residents. This work allowed him to continue to explore the link between economics and anthropology that he first discovered in China. For the academic year of 2008–2009, the student once again returned to China, this time in Wuhan with Fulbright funding, to continue and deepen the research on migrant labor that he started in the Chinese Cities in Transition course.

The Night Markets of Kaifeng

An East Asian languages and cultures major and 2006 graduate of Beloit College participated in the Chinese Cities in Transition course in China in the fall of 2006. His site-based participant-observation project evolved into a semester-length study of the vibrant and fascinating night markets of Kaifeng. Like the economics student, this student used Cities in Transition skills to conduct innumerable interviews in Chinese with his informants: street-stall owners, regular night-market customers, and Chinese tourists, among others. In addition, he documented his visits to the city's night markets with a series of stunning photographs. His final written project consisted of a photographic essay, in which striking and deeply human images were glossed by telling anecdotes and insightful analysis of the complex patterns and rhythms of life of Kaifeng's various night markets.

In addition to conducting interviews, the student worked closely with local informants to gather information on the history and present functioning of the markets. He learned how, after a period of prohibition under Mao Zedong, the markets revived in the 1980s; he learned about the procedures necessary to become a licensed vendor in the markets; and he learned how the market vendors both compete and cooperate. His work also led him to consider the effects of class, ethnic, and religious difference in modern Chinese society. He credits much of his success in advancing his study of Chinese and Chinese culture during his semester abroad to the Cities in Transition project. At present he is planning on entering graduate school, most likely in an East Asian Studies program.

Conclusion

To have students produce such research is obviously highly gratifying. We should remember, however, that not all students need to succeed at the level of the students discussed here to realize the learning goals of the Chinese Cities in Transition course. Most students who write final papers and produce final projects of more modest scope will, by virtue of earnest participation, make marked progress in a number of areas. Their use of the city as a classroom will stretch their language skills, their knowledge of modern Chinese urban life will expand, and they will develop the confidence to act independently and ethically in unfamiliar surroundings. Most importantly, they will return from their time abroad with the skills to integrate the experience abroad into the broader context of their liberal arts education.

During the four years that the Chinese Cities in Transition course has been a part of the Beloit College curriculum, course instructors have discovered that students thrive on the independence provided by the course. Students also respond well to the course's high expectations of them. Nevertheless, experience has demonstrated that most students are still in need of explicit directions to complete most projects to satisfaction, and thus from year to year, the course instructors have created more structured assignments.

Finally, from a faculty perspective, implementation of the Chinese Cities in Transition course has been as rewarding as it has been challenging. Even with good cooperation from partner institutions, most of the work has had to be done by Beloit College faculty and staff. Extremely beneficial to the development of the course have been a number of faculty trips—including Asianists as well as specialists in other disciplines—to assist in designing the course. In many ways, these trips served as test runs for the course itself, as participants did course readings, carried out model assignments, and critiqued methodology and results. Above all, the varied interests of non-Asianist faculty participants helped us imagine how students could frame their experiences in China using the skills they have acquired through their liberal arts training.

*   *   *

Note: Major participants in the development of the Cities in Transition courses at Beloit College include all of the contributors to this volume, especially Elizabeth Brewer, Marion Fass, Darren Kelly, and Nancy Krusko. Donna Oliver, professor of Russian and associate dean of Beloit College, has also contributed much to the development of the Cities in Transition idea. With particular reference to Chinese Cities in Transition, Carsey Yee and Natalie Gummer, both of whom have taught the course, deserve special mention, as does Rob LaFleur, who is a professor of history and anthropology at Beloit, an instructor of the course in its earliest incarnations, and a pioneer of many of the course's innovative pedagogical ideas.

References

Amin, A., & Thrift, N. (2002). *Cities: Reimagining the urban.* Cambridge, England: Polity.

Bok, D. (2006). *Our underachieving colleges: A candid look at how much students learn and why they should be learning more.* Princeton, NJ: Princeton University Press.

Campanella, T. J. (2008). *The concrete dragon: China's urban revolution and what it means for the world.* Princeton, NJ: Princeton Architectural Press.

Emerson, R. M., Fretz, R., & Shaw, L. (1995). *Writing ethnographic fieldnotes.* Chicago: University of Chicago Press.

Gifford, R. (2007). *China road: A journey into the future of a rising power.* New York: Random House.

Hessler, P. (2001). *River town: Two years on the Yangtze.* New York: HarperCollins.

Appendix: Assignment Sheet for Site-Based Learning Participant-Observation Project, Final Paper/Project

The assignment consists of two parts:

A. A site-based participant-observation project that you will conduct throughout your semester in either Kaifeng or Ji'nan.

B. A final academic paper (or suitable alternative, if approved by me) that will be based on the observations you make and the themes and issues that emerge from your site-based observation activities.

A. Site-Based Participant-Observation Project

Choosing Your Site

In Kaifeng in August you practiced mapping the city, honing your observational skills, and pushing yourselves to move beyond the usual foreign student hangouts and environment. You observed the many layers of experience (historical, social, environmental, etc.) that contribute to the sense of modern Chinese urban life.

Now it is time for you to choose a location that will serve as the focus of your site-based participant-observation project. If you have not already done so, visit several possible sites over the next weeks. Then:

• Make your final site decision and have it approved by me by October __.

• Remember, you will make a presentation about your site to me and a visiting Beloit faculty member on October __.

B. *Final Paper/Project*

Your paper or project should reflect your interests. To complete the assignment successfully, you must be both self-directed and self-disciplined. Remember, however, the project is not only an independent research project. You will also need to maintain regular e-mail and Web contact with me and make weekly Web postings on your activities.

Unless otherwise arranged, your final paper should consist of 10 to 15 double-spaced pages of careful observation and analysis of your chosen site. You must also include the following:

1. A detailed log (formal record) of all of your site visits, including dates, times, and duration of each visit.

2. A glossary of Chinese terms from your site, including Chinese characters, pinyin pronunciation with tone marks, English translation, and optional usage notes.

3. Documentation of your verbal interactions with Chinese people at your site. List and describe at least three conversations (or formal interviews) that you had on three separate occasions with three different Chinese people. Indicate the date, time, and duration of each conversation, and whether you spoke in Chinese or English. Provide excerpts from your field notes, full transcripts (if available) or summaries of the specific content and/or general gist of these conversations, as well as your reflections on these interactions.

4. A bibliography or list of sources. Proper citation is required throughout your paper, whether you are referring to published academic sources or your own data.

5. Digital photographs and/or maps of your site. (You may omit these if you decide to intersperse this material throughout the body of your paper.)

9

HEALTH AND MICROCREDIT

Beloit as a Laboratory for Understanding Nicaragua

Nancy Krusko

In January of 2004, I spent one week traveling in Nicaragua, witnessing how various forms of microcredit transformed people's lives. Ultimately, the visit would lead to the development of a course in which both microcredit and Nicaragua would be major focuses, along with health and the city of Beloit, Wisconsin, the home of Beloit College where I teach. The course in turn would serve as an example of how faculty/student collaboration and faculty development activities can lead to curricular innovations and facilitate the integration of study abroad into the curriculum.

Why was I in Nicaragua? One of my students, Amanda Mehl, had challenged me to join her on a travel seminar sponsored by the Wisconsin Coordinating Council on Nicaragua (WCCN) so that I could learn firsthand about microcredit programs there. Amanda, who had traveled to Nicaragua twice before, once with her church and once with the WCCN, had taken a medical anthropology course with me. Many of the topics we covered resonated with her experiences in Nicaragua. For example, students read Paul Farmer's book *Infections and Inequalities: The Modern Plagues* (1999). Using Haiti as a case study, Farmer illustrates how racism, sexism, and political economy lead to forms of structural violence, which constrain individual agency (p. 79). Those lacking agency are usually impoverished, live in unclean environments, and lack adequate nutrition. Because poverty is a pathogen, these conditions lead to poor health outcomes. Along with the Farmer book, students read an article by Thomas McKeown, who presents data suggesting that health improvements during the last two centuries are due to better food, sanitation, and birth control rather than to medical advances (1978, p. 60). Thus, by eradicating conditions associated with poverty, health can improve. In the course, we therefore examine how micro-credit can provide a mechanism for people living in poverty to improve their health.

As Amanda and I traveled in Nicaragua with the other seminar members, we became more and more excited about collaborating in the design of a course that would enable other Beloit students to learn from Nicaragua's example in the ways we were learning on the trip. No study abroad site is inherently aligned with any one discipline, although some might be associated with one more than another (for example, Athens with classical Greece, or the Galapagos with marine biology). Nicaragua seemed to demand knowledge from multiple fields to unpack its complex and interconnected lessons, and thus Amanda's and my work led to the creation of an interdisciplinary course drawing on the humanities, social sciences, and natural sciences that is based in Beloit but includes travel for one week to Nicaragua. Amanda's contributions included her knowledge of Spanish and women's and gender studies along with her firsthand experiences in Nicaragua and with travel seminars, whereas as a medical anthropologist, I brought to the project expertise in the sciences and social sciences.

However, in creating the course I also stretched myself to acquire new knowledge and skills. Eventually, I took several semesters of Spanish to increase my proficiency in the language. I realized my ability to teach the course would be greatly enhanced if I could communicate directly with people in Nicaragua during that portion of the course. I also contacted colleagues in various disciplines at Beloit College to acquire background knowledge and sources on Nicaragua (history, economics, politics, geology, geography); I also drew on the suggestions of the WCCN and the Augsburg College Center for Global Education (CGE). Their perspectives added to my own knowledge of Nicaragua, and enabled me to provide a richer context about Nicaragua for my students. In turn, some of the faculty looked to my course to enrich Beloit's Latin American Studies program and as a model for courses they might create. Additionally, I took advantage of several of the on- and off-campus faculty development activities discussed in chapter 12 of this volume to both create the course and prepare to teach it. In particular, the faculty development activities allowed me to experiment with different experiential learning methods and to think through their connection to the subject matter of the course.

This chapter, then, tells the story of how "Nicaragua in Transition: Health and Microcredit" was born, and offers lessons for other faculty who might similarly want to connect study abroad to their teaching and scholarship.

Pedagogical Philosophy and Course Design

While in Nicaragua, Amanda and I realized it would be impossible to make arrangements for the week-long seminar from Beloit. We did not have established contacts with people or institutions in Nicaragua, nor did we know how to make the international travel arrangements or find places to stay while in Nicaragua. Fortuitously, our translator in Nicaragua suggested that the Nicaraguan offices of Augsburg College's CGE might be able to help. We therefore met with a CGE employee who handles short-term seminars, and she helped us design the itinerary for a week-long seminar; staff in the Minnesota office provided logistical support at a low cost. The partnership worked well, as the CGE and I share similar pedagogical philosophies. Our approach to education is intercultural, experiential, and transformative. Learning is a lifelong process; it is ingrained in our experience and allows us to become responsible global citizens capable of action. Knowledge doesn't flow from teacher to student; instead the teacher and student share a learning community. Each member of the community must draw his or her own conclusions. We both employ Paulo Freire's (1973) circle of praxis as a model, and the model helped me build the syllabus for the course and helped the CGE to shape the week spent in Nicaragua. The steps in Freire's circle of praxis include acquisition of new information and experiences, reflection and analysis; additional experience, information gathering, and reflection; and analysis and reflection, evaluation, and celebration.

The course, "Nicaragua in Transition: Health and Microcredit," ultimately took advantage of Beloit College's academic calendar, which includes a week-long midterm break halfway through the 14-week schedule, to take advantage of Augsburg College's facilities and staff in Nicaragua. Thus, during the midterm break, the class of 12 to 14 students travels to Nicaragua to study firsthand topics they have discussed in class. The first part of the semester is spent in preparation for the visit, and the last part devoted to reflection and integration. Each of the parts of the course in turn corresponds to different aspects of Freire's circle of praxis.

Part 1: Preparation—Acquisition of New Information and Experiences, and Reflection and Analysis

During the first week of class, we share previous experiences as related to course topics. This allows us to practice intercultural communication skills and to establish a learning community by listening, discussing, and seeing how we can learn and gain new insights from people with different backgrounds. In the next six weeks, in preparation for the week in Nicaragua we study the Nicaraguan context as well as microcredit and health, and practice skills that will be helpful for our stay in Nicaragua.

The Nicaraguan Context

A general understanding of the Nicaraguan context helps students appreciate the intersection between health and microcredit in this particular locale and reinforces the notion of informed inquiry. Currently, Nicaragua is the second poorest country in Latin America. Since the time of European contact, political, economic, and natural factors have conspired to economically suppress most Nicaraguans. We begin with history and politics so students can understand Nicaragua's place both locally and globally. Internal and external political strife have played a major role in economically suppressing Nicaraguans. Since Nicaragua's independence from Spain, the United States has intervened in a variety of ways to wreak havoc on political and economic stability. Additionally, Nicaragua's geography and geology shape the realities of Nicaraguans' lives. Situated in the southern portion of Central America, Nicaragua's land mass is part of the Caribbean plate. This region of the plate is geologically active with volcanic eruptions and earthquakes occurring from time to time. In both 1931 and 1972, large-scale earthquakes devastated the capital city of Managua, leaving many people dead or injured and destroying city infrastructure. Nicaragua is tectonically active because of its volcanoes and position on the Caribbean plate (Kott & Streiffert, 2005). For example, during a 10-day period in 2009, 14 earthquakes were detected by the Nicaraguan Dirreción de Sismologíca (n.d.). Although most of these quakes are not of high magnitude or horribly destructive, a number of high-magnitude quakes have hit Nicaragua in the past 75 years, destroying infrastructure and taking lives in a nation-state that has few resources. Earthquakes are not the only geologic forces wreaking havoc in Nicaragua. Maps of Nicaragua show a string of eleven volcanoes (one extinct, five dormant, and five active) running along the western side of the country from the northern to the southern border. When active volcanoes erupt, they often devastate and destroy the villages and cities beneath them.

Weather also creates its fair share of problems for many Nicaraguans. Geographically, Nicaragua is located in the Caribbean's tropical storm/hurricane lane, which is active from June 1 to November 30 each year. Many of these storms travel inland, dumping excessive moisture on the land below. Perhaps one of the most severe hurricanes on record, Mitch, roared through Nicaragua in October 1998, leaving approximately 50 inches of rain in its wake. The water flooded fields, created massive mudslides, and turned rivers into lakes. Transportation was affected as roads and bridges were knocked out, power lines and sewage systems were damaged, and more than 400,000 people were displaced as the result of flooding. In fact, our travel seminar visits several of the settlements created by the government for displaced Nicaraguans. Almost ten years after Mitch, these communities still lack basic infrastructure.

To provide students with information on the Nicaraguan context, my search for sources included consultations with the CGE and colleagues at Beloit College. Thomas Walker's (2003) informative book on Nicaraguan history, politics, economics, and culture of the country has proved particularly valuable. The students become familiar with Nicaragua's geography through a mapping assignment, and a weekly assignment to track and report news published in two of Nicaragua's newspapers informs them about current events.

Understanding Microcredit and Health, Developing Skills

Because we study the intersection of health and microcredit or microfinance, it is vital for students to understand what microcredit is, how it works, and who it serves. To this end, I supply a number of readings about Muhammad Yunus, the Bangladeshi economist considered the "father" of the microcredit industry. We examine the pros and cons of the microfinance industry and learn about its applications in Nicaragua. In many Latin American countries, microcredit is provided mostly to urban entrepreneurs; however, Nicaragua is unique in providing microcredit loans for agriculture and livestock

(Arenas, 2006). Given Nicaragua's status as the second poorest nation in Central America, it is not a surprise to discover that most Nicaraguans lack access to financial services offered by commercial banks. Establishing a bank account requires a minimum balance far greater than most Nicaraguans have, and most of them lack the collateral necessary to take out loans. This means most Nicaraguans rely on cash or barter transactions and the services of various nongovernmental organizations (NGOs) that provide access to financial services. Since 1980, many of these NGOs have become versed in the area of microfinance and this industry has thrived in many Central American countries, including Nicaragua. In fact, Nicaragua has the largest number of borrowers among regulated and nonregulated microfinance organizations in Central America (Arenas, 2006).

We also examine what it means to be healthy. What is the definition of health? What are the determinants of health? How can one qualitatively or quantitatively determine if an individual, neighborhood, or community is healthy? I provide readings from public health, social science, and scientific journals to help us examine the determinants of health. Because the students come from a wide variety of majors, they provide insights from their own disciplines. We spend a great deal of time discussing these topics and how one might qualitatively and quantitatively examine health cross-culturally.

Several exercises require students to make observations in the city of Beloit and gather information on the health of our local community. This teaches them how to learn experientially, and thus when they get to Nicaragua and undertake similar exercises, they are prepared and able to transfer what they learned in Beloit to Nicaragua. Thus Beloit becomes a laboratory for studying Nicaragua.

For example, to examine if neighborhoods are healthy, I send the students into various areas in Beloit to make observations and take photos. While walking through the neighborhood, they record observations on infrastructure. What are the buildings like? what are they made of? what is their condition? How might they have been used in the past? What are the roads, sidewalks, or paths like? Are yards and streets tidy and free of trash? They also look at the natural world. Are yards pleasant? Are recreation areas available? How much of the natural world is visible? Are plant and natural animal life noticeable? How does the area smell? What can you hear or feel? Are animals present? If so, are they pets or part of the natural world? I ask them to observe human activity. Who occupies the spaces along the route and how? Do the people live here? Are the homes owned by the occupants or are they rented? How old are the people living in the neighborhood? Is the neighborhood residential or are business properties interspersed? In addition to indicating something about the health of the neighborhoods, the observations also teach students how people use space, and what is considered private and public. Such distinctions vary between cultures. For example, in the United States our yards belong to us; however, in Moscow, yards between apartment buildings are semipublic. Discussions about such questions help the students sharpen both their observation skills and their ability to make sense of what they observe.

To complete the assignment, the students bring ten photos to class to tell the story of their Beloit neighborhood's health. They complete a similar assignment while in Managua to reveal the cultural differences between the two cities, and modify their conceptions of what constitutes a neighborhood and how to assess its health. We also can discuss whether the differences in neighborhoods are based on culture or economic conditions.

Grocery stores and marketplaces provide a great deal of cultural and nutritional information about a group of people and therefore their health, as populations and individuals with adequate nutrition are usually healthy. Thus a structured observation project is undertaken in both Beloit and Managua. In Beloit, the students observe purchasing behavior in local grocery stores. Who is shopping? How old is the shopper? What purchases are made? How nutritious might the purchase be? How much does the shopper spend and how might this be related to the shopper's income? After collecting the data, the students analyze it both qualitatively and quantitatively. In Managua, the students collect and analyze data from a large market, and then compare these with the results of their Beloit research to better understand how the two populations relate in their access and consumption of nutrition.

For qualitative data collection, I also teach students to take field notes and keep a journal. Field notes are the most common method used by anthropologists engaged in participant-observation research to collect data, and are based on detailed observations. The students learn about the difference between taking field notes, which they have not yet done, and keeping a journal, which is familiar to most. Journals contain information that often relates to personal experiences and may be value-laden. Field notes, on the other hand, are an objective record of observations. The ethnographer can't record everything, so he or she concentrates on particular behaviors and interactions. Because humans are visual animals, I ask them to remember to record, in addition to what they see, what they hear, smell, and taste, along with any tactile information associated with the field site. Two class periods are devoted to learning how to take field notes, after which the students select a "field site" in Beloit based on their interest. To date, they have attended a city council meeting, a church service, a baseball game, a student senate meeting, an academic senate meeting, and so on. Their field notes and a short essay explaining their findings serve as the basis for evaluation. When they get to Nicaragua, however, I ask them to both take field notes during our visits to the various organizations and communities and keep a journal, so that they can record and reflect on their emotional and intellectual reactions to the visits.

Approximately half of the students taking "Nicaragua in Transition" have not traveled outside the United States. Some have not experienced significant cultural differences, and most have not witnessed people who live in poverty as they do in Nicaragua. According to the 2000 census, 12.5% of Beloit's population lives below the poverty level. Furthermore, in 2007–2008, 62% of schoolchildren were eligible for subsidized lunches. However, the outward signs of poverty are different from those seen in developing countries, and, therefore, it is difficult for students studying in Beloit to experience the "culture" of poverty before traveling to Nicaragua. As Farmer (1999) suggests, people often conflate cultural differences with poverty when confronted by them in another country. In other words, in some places what we see as "culture" is actually a response to living in poverty and lacking agency to make changes. Therefore, I want my students to try to evaluate how poverty may contribute to the culture shock they experience in Nicaragua. This is why the study of history is so important. It allows us to gain some insight into local "cultural norms." If these are not familiar, perhaps lack of access to resources may be playing a role.

To facilitate their cultural learning, I use a "cultural bubble" assignment so they will experience culture differences before going to Nicaragua. How culture is defined often depends on the context in which the word is used. For this course, I define culture as "shared, learned behavior passed down from generation to generation." For the cultural bubble, I ask students to visit and interact with a place or take part in an activity outside of their comfort zone. Thus they have played bingo at the senior center, visited a nursing home, eaten at the VFW or local diner, shopped in a Hispanic market or clothing store, played in or attended a Hispanic soccer club match, attended a church service of another denomination, and so on. They then prepare a three- to five-page report on their experiences and their personal reflections on them, the lessons they learned, and how these will help them in Nicaragua.

Part 2: Nicaragua Field Explorations—New Experience and Information Gathering, Reflection

By the time we leave for Nicaragua, students have formed a learning community and gained new information on Nicaragua. They have acquired new tools and skills to study the intersection of health and microcredit, and can position their knowledge in a particular locale, Nicaragua. Additionally, they have acquired the skills to operate in a foreign country where daily life is quite different from what they know. They are ready to travel, have new experiences, and learn from the experiences of others (both their classmates and Nicaraguans). They also are prepared to engage in critical analysis of the different perspectives they will hear as they meet Nicaraguans.

The week-long travel seminar is based in Managua, but we spend two to three days in cities or villages where microfinance institutions operate. The course focus on the intersection of health and microcredit takes us primarily to organizations concerned with health issues. In Managua, we visit Dos Generaciones, an NGO in operation since 1991, founded to promote human rights of children and adults who live and scavenge to make their living in La Chureca, Managua's municipal dump. We visit with Eddy Perez, one of the organization's founders, who outlines this NGO's mission to (a) advocate for people of the dump and let their voices be heard, (b) stop and prevent physical and sexual violence, and (c) make it possible for children to attend community school programs by paying their parents the sum their children normally would earn in the dump (personal communication, March 7, 2007). Perez then takes us to the dump to witness the squalid, smoky conditions his clients live and work in. Parts of the dump are always burning to make space for more material, while adults and children with bandanas over their noses and mouths root through the cooler remnants looking for steel, plastic, and other recyclable materials to sell to middlemen. They also compete with circling birds for anything edible. The main health issues in the community reflect the conditions, and include respiratory and skin infections, eye problems, and malnutrition.

We also visit Ciudad Sandino, the poorest city in Nicaragua and home to more than 150,000 people. Located just north of Managua, Ciudad Sandino was established in the late 1960s when the Nicaraguan government relocated people whose communities had been destroyed by floods. Since that time, Ciudad Sandino has become home for a number of other people whose communities were destroyed by the 1972 earthquake and Hurricane Mitch. The students are quite surprised to discover that a government can make people leave their former homes to move to a new location. This leads to a discussion of property rights in Nicaragua. The students assume people own or rent the land their homes are built on; however, this is not the case for many neighborhoods in Nicaragua (or in other parts of Latin America for that matter). In Ciudad Sandino we stop in Nueva Vida, where families were issued land allotments 10 yards by 15 yards, but were not provided with building materials, water, electricity, or sewage disposal. As the families built homes from scratch, they received help from a number of NGOs and church groups, one of which we visit, Jubilee House. Jubilee House is an arm of the Center for Development in Central America, an NGO that seeks to help communities become self-sufficient and sustainable. To this end, Jubilee House facilitated training in business and industrial sewing for 50 women seeking to form a sewing cooperative in 1999. They were also helped in accessing microcredit to raise start-up funds, as banks would not extend loans to them. It took two years to begin operations, but now the cooperative has 52 employees and is the first worker-owned free-trade zone in the world, sewing organic and fair-trade cotton clothing for export to the United States and Europe (J. Zulemay, personal communication, March 5, 2007). Other residents used microcredit loans to start a brick-making business, a biodiesel fuel-processing business using cooking oil to power vehicles, and a small plant that fashions terra cotta pots to filter microorganisms out of water to make it potable. Microcredit loans have enabled residents to improve their living conditions, send their children to school, and use the clinic that Jubilee House runs in their neighborhood. Their stories illustrate for the students the way microcredit loans ultimately can improve health in families and neighborhoods.

In other areas of Ciudad Sandino, Promujer, a microfinance institution, has branches that provide loans and training for approximately 2,500 women. First, loans of $100 are given to a collective of 15 to 20 women. Repayment gives them access to another $200 after four months. Promujer provides training for women in these collectives, and they report a default rate of only 6%. Promujer is also proactive in combining lending with health promotion. Its clinics screen for cancer, take care of infections, and teach women how to work against violence, as these constitute the most common health problems in Ciudad Sandino. Promujer loan officers, who live in the same neighborhoods as their clients, report that the women who receive loans gain self-confidence and feel validated by Promujer (M. E. Martinez, personal communication, March 5, 2007).

Other visits take us to microfinance operations that focus on economic sustainability as well as health. In March 2007, we went to Matagalpa, located high in the mountains in the northern part of the country, and known as Nicaragua's coffee capital because its cool, mountain climate is excellent for growing shade coffee. There we visited the local offices of the Society for the Promotion of Social and Economic Development of Individual Women Producers (SACPROA), which provides microcredit, health initiatives, literacy programs, and marketing strategies for women growers in the Matagalpa vicinity. Fidelina Andino and Maryel Mercado, local directors of SACPROA, talked about their successes and challenges and took us to visit women members who farm high in the mountains outside of Matagalpa. This gave the students the opportunity to see the interconnectedness of individuals, their families, and communities served by microcredit organizations and how these, in turn, have multiple, interconnected agendas and effects. For example, we ate lunch at the Santos farm where Doña Santos told us about her organic certified coffee-growing operation and the microloan she had recently secured from SACPROA to build a pond to raise tilapia fish to sell in the marketplace along with plantains, bananas, cacao, and other root crops. Doña Santos' husband works in town as a mechanic, and her children attend the local school; however, they help her tend the crops and go to market when they are home. Doña Santos is a municipal government representative and a member of the Rainbow Committee, which cares for the sick, weighs and measures children, and refers the ill to clinics or hospitals. In addition, she spearheads local health campaigns on hygiene and prevention, conducting workshops for parents and children on proper water-filtering and hand-washing methods, and making sure women take their children to the village when the immunization van comes (M. Santos, personal communication, March 8, 2007). Riding back to Managua in the bus the afternoon after visiting with Doña Santos, the students remarked on the interconnected relationships of Nicaraguans in that the productivity of the Santos farm is both a family and, perhaps to some extent, even a community effort; Nicaraguans seemed less individualistic than U.S. Americans to them. The three-hour bus ride gave us an opportunity to discuss the similarities and differences in our cultures and how we might learn a great deal from Nicaraguans.

When we return to Managua, we try to put what we have observed into the larger Nicaraguan context. To this end, we meet with a variety of individuals to gain different perspectives on the relationship between poverty and health. For example, we meet with a representative from the ministry of health to gain the government's perspective on the health of its citizens. We visit a public hospital and learn about health care from the perspective of the director and senior nurse. We also visit the Women's Center of Acahualinca. Acahualinca is the city north of Managua just outside La Chureca, the municipal dump. In Acahualinca, 70% of the population is unemployed. The economy is precarious, and some of the inhabitants travel to the dump on a daily basis to make a living; many of the women work as prostitutes. At the clinic, the directors provide workshops for sex workers to prevent and treat sexually transmitted disease, and screen for cervical cancer and HIV. Additionally, the clinic provides legal assistance to clients dealing with divorce, child support, worker violence issues, and child abuse. They also have workshops on family violence prevention and how to raise self-esteem (Villalta & Bonilla, personal communication, 2007). We also meet with Elizabeth Campos, the subdirector of Nitlaplan, a research and development institute of the Central American University providing microcredit loans in rural areas and promoting reforestation, land access, and property rights. The meetings allow the students to see how poverty limits people's ability to live in safe environments, have access to clean water and/or trash removal, and provide adequate nutrition for their families.

Every few evenings our group meets to share our thoughts and reflect on our experiences. The meetings with resource people, members of organizations, and members of various communities constitute the "experience" component of Freire's circle of praxis. We discover that individual members of the group react to the experiences differently. Each of us has our own particular ways of "seeing" the world and these lenses color the way we inter-pret what we see. Given the impoverished conditions we experienced, these meetings are often emotional and create strong bonds among the members of our group. For example, in 2005 one young man was distressed that adult men were often not considered reliable beneficiaries of microcredit loans. He saw this as a form of reverse sexism. Other students were distressed by the level of poverty they were witnessing. They saw people living in worse condi-tions than many animals do in the United States. This troubling insight led to a variety of emotional responses: extreme sorrow, anger, and guilt. I and Suyen Barahona, who accompanies our group on behalf of the CGE, are vigilant about monitoring the students' emotional states and do our best to check in with each of them to see how they are coping.

Because health and microcredit are the topics of scrutiny, our discussion centers on these. However, our meetings with resource people from a variety of sectors (government, academics, NGOs, local co-op members) reveal very different understandings and analysis of the issues. For example, the Director of Health Services in the Ministry of Health interprets crucial health issues quite differently than the directors of the Women's Center in Acahualinca. We spend a great deal of time processing these differences and coming to our own conclusions about the intersection of health and microcredit in Nicara-gua. The students also realize their Nicaraguan "informants" know a great deal more about United States politics and policy than they do. At first they are surprised, but in time they begin to see how much influence the U.S. government exercises even at very local levels in Nicaragua, to the extent that knowledge of U.S. politics and policies becomes a survival strategy.

On our last night in Nicaragua, we hold a final group reflection. On a macro-level, the students talk about how globalization increases income disparities and the tremendous influence of foreign governments, such as the United States, on Nicaragua. A number of the students comment on prob-lems associated with machismo and how gender inequity contributes to pov-erty. However, they note that many microcredit organizations lend primarily to women; this functions as a way to evenly distribute the power in a rela-tionship. The students also discuss how Nicaraguans' value system differs from their own. For example, Nicaraguans may have few resources, but can still be happy, proud people. They value their families and community and work collectively to improve them. The students see that people organizing at the grassroots level can create change. This is a very powerful experience for them.

Part 3: Analysis and Reflection, Evaluation and Celebration

On our return to Beloit, we spend several class periods analyzing and reflecting on the Nicaraguan experience. We talk about who the power holders were, which people's voices were given validity and why. We talk about how the students' perspectives on Nicaragua have changed as a result of the visit. For instance, prior to the visit, many of the students believed the poorest of the poor would benefit from microcredit lending; however, many of the microfinance organizations we visited do not provide loans to the poorest people, as microcredit at this level is ineffective. The realization that some populations are hard to help is difficult. We discuss the contradictions we saw, such as the disparities between local and government outlooks on health. Then we discuss the factors that might explain the contradictions. Government officials, for example, may not want to discuss increases in HIV/AIDS cases in the country, for fear this will negatively affect the foreign aid they receive.

In Freire's circle of praxis, the next critical stage is action. As a class and on an individual basis, we began to develop strategies for action learned in Nicaragua. Many of the students are able to think more critically and concretely about the intersection of microcredit and health, and thus choose to conduct further research on the scholarship related to this. This is one form of action related to Freire's model. Others investigate how microcredit programs might be implemented in poorer areas of the United States. Still others begin the study of Spanish, or use the course as preparation for semester-long study abroad in another variation of action in Freire's model.

The final step in Freire's circle of praxis involves evaluation and celebration. Back in Beloit the students spend time individually evaluating their experiences. Additionally, the class as a group devotes time to sharing our thoughts and the lessons we learned. Although individual reflection and group discussion are extremely valuable and a cause for celebration, we also believe in the importance of sharing our experience with the Beloit campus community. I have taught this course two times and each time I have allowed the students to decide how they wanted to share what they had experienced and learned with others on campus. The first year, the students decided to use the campus coffeehouse to re-create a Nicaraguan marketplace on a Sunday evening, when the campus dining commons is not open and students must forage for their Sunday dinner on their own. To lure people to the marketplace, the students therefore served *gallo pinto* (the national rice and beans dish of Nicaragua), fried plantains, and chocolate milk made with Nicaraguan cacao. Each member of the class sat at a "stall" in the marketplace with a poster presentation outlining a pertinent aspect of the visit to Nicaragua. In the 2 1/2 hours the marketplace was "open," it was visited by more than 150 members of the campus community. The students were exhilarated by sharing their experiences with others.

The second time the class was offered, the students created a photography exhibit that was displayed for two weeks. Each student selected two or three photos from their collection and wrote text describing how the photos demonstrated the connection between health and microcredit. The students also hosted a two-hour opening on a Sunday evening, again serving Nicaraguan food. We had a wonderful turnout, and the response to the event was positive. Many students saw how some of their coursework resonated with what the students were presenting, and there was much discussion of interdisciplinary topics and their relationship to students' experiences on the ground. Additionally, each year several students have used their classmates' photos to create a PowerPoint presentation as both celebration and evidence of their learning. Such celebration and sharing were extremely important to the students as it helped them focus their reflection and evaluation as well as connect these to the experiences of others in the campus community. Many students feel disconnected on return from an overseas experience and this celebratory sharing can be instrumental in helping them reconnect on return. Further, as Downey (2005) suggests, it is important to avoid closure that returns students to the predeparture stage. Instead, the post-study abroad experience should encourage activities, such as continued research and discussion, that will teach students that learning is not compartmentalized, but rather is a lifelong process.

"Nicaragua in Transition: Microcredit and Health" has made lasting impressions and spurred many of the students to think and act differently as global citizens. For example, some have gone on to public health programs focusing on international health issues; others have decided to work for NGOs in the United States focused on economic sustainability among local populations. Others have decided to go into medicine or nursing to work with underserved populations. Those who will not pursue careers directly related to the course topics also have been affected. For example, one young man interested in pursuing a career in photojournalism reports he now follows international politics more closely and will make more of an effort to vote responsibly.

All of the students spent significant time reflecting on the course as a means for furthering their educational goals and made specific connections to their academic fields of study. For example, several of the students in environmental studies were interested in the sustainability projects run by several of the microfinance institutions in Nicaragua; until now microcredit's role in sustainability had been invisible to them. Health and society majors think about poverty as a pathogen and microfinance as providing resources and agency to improve health. Our trip to La Chureca, the municipal dump in Managua, made a lasting impression on all of us. As Eddy Perez said, "The people live here, grow up here, fall in love here, and die here." This is a valuable lesson for students of social change: Impoverished people can lead lives of value and be happy.

Conclusion

The course "Nicaragua in Transition: Microcredit and Health" offers students a powerful learning and life-altering experience. Because the study abroad component of the course is short, considerable attention is paid to structured preparation and follow-up, so that the week in Nicaragua can succeed as a vehicle for learning (see, for example, Selby, 2008). The first time I taught the course, students earned two semester credits. I realized the amount of time I spent with the students was not sufficient to prepare them and, as Bennett (2008) suggests, create intervention strategies so students could learn from the short experience. Therefore, the next time I taught the course, it was offered as a full four-credit course, giving me the time to prepare the students for the short overseas experience and allowing them more time to process the experience upon return to campus (Vande Berg, 2007). This change has greatly enhanced the richness of the course.

Another important aspect of the course design is its transferability. Although I focus on the intersection of health and microcredit in Nicaragua, one could easily design a similar short travel seminar anywhere in the world, even in the United States. The key for success in designing the travel component is having the proper connections in the host country to implement the logistics of travel with experiential pedagogy. In my case, the CGE has worked with me to create a sound educational experience, and it has done this at a price that is right. The observational skills and recording methods are transferable to a number of sites as are many of the pretravel exercises. An instructor would simply have to alter the content of the preparatory readings to ensure students are adequately prepared. With proper planning, short travel seminars embedded in courses taught on campus are an effective means to educate global citizens.

References

Arenas, C. (2006). Microfinance in Central America: Nicaragua's place in the industry. *Nicaraguan Developments, 22,* 2.

Bennett, J. M. (2008). On becoming a global soul: A path to engagement during study abroad. In V. Savicki (Ed.), *Developing intercultural competence and transformation: Theory, research and application in international education* (pp. 13–31). Sterling, VA: Stylus.

Downey, G. (2005). From personal reflection to social investigation: Undergraduate research as an antidote to autobiographical cliché. In L. C. Anderson (Ed.), *Internationalizing undergraduate education: Integrating study abroad into the curriculum* (pp. 117–121). Minneapolis: University of Minnesota Press.

Farmer, P. (1999). *Infections and inequalities: The modern plagues.* Berkeley: University of California Press.

Freire, P. (1973). *Pedagogy of the oppressed.* New York: Seabury Press.

Kott, J., & Streiffert, K. (2005). *Cultures of the world series: Nicaragua* (2nd ed.). Tarrytown, NY: Marshall Cavendish Corporation.

McKeown, T. (1978). Determinants of health. *Human Nature, 1,* 60–67.

Nicaraguan Dirreción de Sismologíca. (n.d.). Monitor de Sismos en Nicaragua. Retrieved July 2, 2009, from http://www.ineter.gob.ni/geofisica/sis/monitor.html.

Selby, R. (2008). Designing transformation in international education. In V. Savicki (Ed.), *Developing intercultural competence and transformation: Theory, research and application in international education* (pp. 1–10). Sterling, VA: Stylus.

Vande Berg, M. (2007). Intervening in the learning of U.S. students study abroad. *Journal of Studies in International Education, 11*(3/4), 392–399.

Walker, T. (2003). *Nicaragua: Living in the shadow of the eagle* (4th ed.). Boulder, CO: Westview.

10

BUILDING GLOBAL AWARENESS THROUGH BIOLOGY, PUBLIC HEALTH, AND STUDY ABROAD

How Science Study Can Prepare Students for Study Abroad, and How Study Abroad Can Prepare Scientists for Citizenship

Marion Field Fass and Ann M. Fraser

M uch as a map of the city influences how we move through it, our educational background shapes what we see and how we interpret it. On an interdisciplinary faculty trip to Moscow and its monuments, one of us (Fass) focused on the public toilets next to the monuments, rather than the monuments themselves, and took photos that juxtaposed the toilets and the city around them. The omnipresent public toilets illustrated a new effort in post-Soviet Moscow to improve sanitation and public health, much as the viewing platforms in Red Square were evidence of former Soviet power. A picture of the toilets and the older woman who took care of them became a symbol to the faculty group of how different ways of seeing can shape the study abroad experience, open up new questions for students as they map the city, and work to make sense of new environments, cultures, and governmental policies.

Science as a "way of knowing" constructs meaning by developing and testing ideas or hypotheses using information gathered through observation and measurement. Inferences drawn from data lead to the rejection or further refinement and testing of hypotheses. In this way, scientists progress from a state of speculation to one of greater understanding and certainty about the natural world. In many ways, the study abroad experience for students emulates this process, as preconceptions and assumptions about oneself and the larger world are tested through experience and reflection, both abroad and upon return.

All students, not just science majors, can benefit from seeing the world through a scientific lens. With planning, biology and other classes in the sciences can support international study by giving all students additional perspectives and tools for viewing and analyzing the new worlds they will encounter. Science classes can also serve as forums for helping students to process and build upon their experiences abroad. If we return to the influence of maps on how we explore and navigate our world, we might imagine geographic information system (GIS)-type maps created by students who bring perspectives from environmental studies and public health to the study of societal issues abroad or at home. The maps are anchored not only by streets and monuments, but also by habitats, elevations, food and water resources, and health facilities. They may be maps that look at species distributions in small parks or at opportunities for building alternative energy sources. Exposure to science education and an empirically based way of knowing enriches the map from which knowledge and understanding about our world emerges.

The experience of an international relations student from Beloit College on a summer service-learning project in Zambia speaks to the value of science preparation. In the spring of her second year, she enrolled in a course, "Biological Issues: Emerging Infectious Diseases," to fulfill her science requirement. The following summer, she traveled with a group from a different university to a small village in Zambia where previous groups had started to build a library. Upon arriving at the village, the group found a community with needs far greater than the library alone. The villagers had suffered from drought and consequent malnutrition because of lack of fish in the dry lake, and they were located in an area with a high incidence of HIV/AIDS. The community members asked the students to help with nutrition projects and with an HIV/AIDS awareness and testing day. The Beloit College student, who had learned about HIV/AIDS in her "Emerging Infectious Diseases" course, was able to educate her peers about the public health problems facing the community, and in so doing provide them with the background necessary to help the community. Her presentation in Beloit College's International Symposium, titled "No More Fish to Fry Where the Water Meets the

Sky" (Helling, 2007), highlights how the student was able to apply her science education from Beloit College to a hands-on problem of HIV/AIDS education in Africa, and how this experience led to deeper reflection on the challenges of short-term "mission" trips.

In this chapter, we describe how science courses for majors and nonmajors can help provide students with the tools and skills needed to explore new environments and cultures, and to begin to make sense of how these elements affect broader societal issues. In the first two sections, we focus on (a) how science methods and content can help prepare students for study abroad, and (b) how science courses and independent studies can help students construct meaning from their experiences abroad. In the latter sections we address two key questions associated with science and study abroad, namely (c) what motivates science students to study abroad and what they gain from the experience, and (d) how we can encourage science students to study abroad at the same rate as students from other disciplines. As biologists, many of the examples and lessons we describe are related to biology, conservation, and public health. However, other science disciplines are mentioned, and we believe the lessons from biology also apply to the other natural sciences.

Preparing Students for Study Abroad: Seeing the World Through a Scientific Lens

Science classes, particularly those that address biodiversity and conservation, ecology and the environment, and disease and public health, provide important frameworks with which study abroad students can make connections between classroom "theory" and local realities, be they economic, political, social, or scientific. Students who have taken science classes structured intentionally to enhance study abroad tend to look systematically at the environment, at the weather and the water, and at the behavior of animals and people, in addition to museums and marketplaces. Just as courses in language, history, and culture provide new lenses through which students see their worlds, the tools of epidemiology and of environmental and ecological analysis help students develop important perspectives on the new situations they encounter.

Skills of scientific observation and hypothesis testing, and the content that supports these skills, are learned in science courses and can enrich students' study abroad experiences. By learning about the relationships of living organisms and their environments, students learn to value contributions that science can make to our understanding of human ecology. Many students study in areas of rapid urbanization, such as Quito or Dakar, or in areas of social and environmental change, like Moscow, and their understanding of environment and ecology enables them to begin to assess the effects of the changes not only on culture but also on land use, biodiversity, water quality, and health. Studies of ecology and conservation biology provide context for observing invasive species and endangered species, agriculture and the food supply, and the effects of changing lifestyles on the environment. In Moscow, the alert student may notice the relative absence of babies, whereas in Cuernavaca she may see the plastic bags and tiny puddles of water that accumulate in the deep ravines around the city where recent migrants live. These simple observations are keys to understanding the population and public health of the city, such as the falling birth rate and increasing number of elderly in need of support in Moscow, or the effects of migration and trash on the mosquito-breeding environment in Cuernavaca. These analyses are important to students learning about a new city or country.

All science classes seek to instill fundamental skills of careful observation and accurate documentation. These skills are frequently taught through hands-on exercises in the laboratory, for example, through examination of live or preserved material, or through manipulative, controlled experiments designed to test cause and effect. Observation and documentation skills can also be taught using selected course readings. For example, "Organism Diversity," a required sophomore course for biology majors at Kalamazoo College, uses selected chapters from *Biophilia* by Edward O. Wilson (1984) for this purpose. The first two chapters of this book offer excellent examples of the acute observational and descriptive skills of a field biologist as Wilson explores the South American jungle and describes the intricate relationships between organisms that are literally under our noses, but that go unnoticed by the unsuspecting and untrained eye. This reading is followed by a field exercise in which students spend one laboratory period collecting invertebrates from different habitats at the college's field station and a subsequent period in the lab identifying and cataloging the organisms. This exercise is designed to expose students to hypothesis testing in a field setting and to introduce them to various invertebrate sampling techniques. In addition, however, the exercise is designed to hone the observational and inquiry skills of the students and to open their eyes to the array of invertebrate diversity that exists in a seemingly vacant field. In this way, it demonstrates how careful observation and probing can reveal a hidden world, not unlike the one that may lie ahead for students studying abroad.

In addition to uncovering hidden worlds, the observational skills taught in biology and other science classes also translate well to other disciplines and can be particularly helpful when studying culture in situations in which an individual's language proficiency is limited. For example, observational skills acquired in science courses complement ethnographical methods such as those used in "Chinese Cities in Transition," described in chapter 8 in this volume by Daniel Youd of Beloit College, and in "Culture, Religion, and Nationality," described in chapter 4 by Carol Anderson and Kiran Cunningham of Kalamazoo College. Keen observational skills can also enhance an individual's own reflective skills, leading to a deeper, more meaningful study abroad experience.

At Beloit College, efforts have been made across the curriculum to intentionally prepare students for study abroad. A biology course designed primarily for nonmajors, "Biological Issues: Emerging Infectious Diseases," addresses "place" as an important variable in disease emergence and encourages students to look systematically at health and development data to understand the emergence of disease (Fass, 2000, 2008). Students read a Kenyan scholar's book, *The African and the AIDS Holocaust* (Thairu, 2003), in which the author presents a compelling interpretation of the emergence of AIDS that differs from that of Western scholars. Comparison of the two perspectives encourages students to consider that phenomena they see as "fact" can be explained differently. Students also learn to analyze disease as not just a pathological event caused by an encounter with a microbe, but rather as a complex interaction among the host who contracts the disease, the characteristics of the agent of disease, and the environment in which they meet.

Assignments in the "Emerging Infectious Diseases" course encourage students to think comparatively and quantitatively about the environment, development and health, and to test hypotheses with data. As they progress through the course, students develop a set of epidemiological tools that can be applied to a variety of problems and contexts. For example, students analyze problems of identification and control of disease outbreaks, and investigate relationships between variables such as access to clean water, women's education, or fertility rates and life expectancy in countries they select. They use statistical software to graph and analyze the strength of the relationships and then ask why they can predict the outcome in some countries but not others. These exercises introduce students to important data sets collected by the United Nations and expose them to the complexity of factors that affect health. Using the sophisticated tools at Gapminder World (www.gapminder .org), students investigate changes in health and development indicators over time. Students are challenged to develop questions and contrast findings for specific countries, and to bring in additional resources to explain relationships they discover. For example, two students investigating their study abroad sites, Tunisia and Argentina, extracted data on various measures of development, education, and mortality, and compared results from their respective countries. The differences they discovered motivated them to investigate more closely the history, economics, and social structures of their two countries. As this example illustrates, exercises of this type can help prepare students for study abroad by getting them to think about issues from a multidisciplinary perspective.

Courses similar to "Biological Issues: Emerging Infectious Diseases" are being offered at many universities in the United States. These courses aim to help students develop scientific skills and cross-cultural sensitivities (Meacham, Kosal, & Fernandes, 2008), and in some cases to explicitly prepare them for social-justice projects in international and domestic settings (Broverman, 2008).

At Kalamazoo College, an "Organism Diversity" course includes several exercises that integrate upcoming study abroad experiences with course material. In the field exercise on invertebrate diversity described previously, students hone their skills of observation and inquiry so they can apply these to their explorations abroad. In the conservation portion of the course, students research various aspects of biological diversity and conservation in their intended study abroad country (most will apply to a specific program the following term) and present their findings informally in groups to the class. This exercise, which requires part of one class period to initiate and one to two class periods for presentations, also provides students with the opportunity to get to know other students intending to study in the same country.

Using primarily Web-based sources such as the International Union for the Conservation of Nature Red List (http://www.iucnredlist.org) and Conservation International's Biodiversity Hotspots site (http://www.biodiversityhotspots.org), students in "Organism Diversity" investigate whether their countries host notably rich or endemic taxa, and whether they contain any formally designated biodiversity hotspots. They also seek information on threatened taxa in the host country and the underlying causes for biodiversity declines. Finally, they are asked to investigate what conservation organizations or efforts (e.g., programs, preserves) are in place—locally, nationally, or internationally—to help conserve biodiversity. Although many Kalamazoo College students do not participate in science-focused programs while abroad, this type of exercise raises awareness about issues of biodiversity and conservation in host countries and may encourage students to explore further the underlying causes of these issues while abroad. Exploration of this type could be intentionally encouraged by expanding the current conservation biology exercise to include more detailed investigations of underlying ecological, economic, political, and social factors that contribute to biodiversity patterns in the region, as is done in Beloit College's "Biological Issues: Emerging Infectious Diseases" course.

Case studies adapted to global questions can be used creatively in many science courses that are not explicitly international. In introductory human biology or introductory genetics courses, students learn about variation and genetic disease. Focus on sickle cell anemia and other hemoglobin diseases can introduce concepts of environment and adaptation. Recent work on the emergence of lactose tolerance in different environments can also be used as an example of human evolution and provide examples of the interaction among genotype, phenotype, and survival. Equally relevant are plant and animal examples from around the globe that illustrate the evolution of analogous traits among distantly related taxa. Some classic examples of convergent evolution, in which environment creates similar selection pressures in different regions, are plant members of the Cactaceae and Euphorbiaceae, and marsupial and placental mammals. Ethical concerns can be introduced as well, contrasting the aversion to genetically engineered foods in the European Union to the general lack of concern over this issue in the United States, and the enthusiastic welcome of drought- and pest-resistant crops in many parts of Africa and Asia.

Finally, courses in all scientific disciplines can explicitly introduce students to the importance of international collaborations, and to the different perspectives these collaborations bring to scientific research. Discussion of these collaborations in many science courses can encourage students to think about how culture and environment influence the questions scientists ask and sensitize science students to the importance of study abroad.

How the Science Curriculum Can Help Students Construct Meaning From Their Experiences Abroad

Study abroad students have amazing adventures with intense experiences. When they come home, they have changed dramatically. Our challenges as professors are both to give them time to reflect on the emotional and cultural aspects of their travels, and also to connect them to academic literature that addresses issues they engaged with while abroad. This academic exploration gives them the opportunity to see that others have made similar observations and to enter into conversation with scholars.

Students who are not science majors often return from study abroad with the realization that they need to understand epidemiological or environmental realities to comprehend what they encountered. A student who recently studied in Kenya completed a study of the acceptance of bed nets for malaria prevention in a Maasai village. He learned that many villagers did not adopt bed nets because they believed that malaria was transmitted by polluted water in the community and not spread by mosquitoes. To understand the efficacy of the "common-sense models of disease" adopted by the Maasai, he found himself integrating information about groundwater and weather patterns, mosquito life cycles, and the pathology of malaria. Another student interning with a nongovernmental organization (NGO) in India found it important to learn more about HIV prevention and treatment as he worked to reflect on his experience and its meaning. Following their experiences abroad, these students took additional science courses to enhance their understanding. Science students at Beloit College also use the process of preparing a senior paper or a presentation for the college's International and Student Research Symposia as a springboard for developing in-depth knowledge to support observations and investigations started on study abroad.

At Beloit, the International Symposium also serves as an important medium through which students analyze and organize their experiences to share with others. Classes are cancelled for the day, and students present research they have done while abroad, or examine cross-cultural issues that they have continued to explore after returning to campus. Instructors of first-year seminars, in particular, design assignments around the Symposium to expose their students to the study abroad experiences of older students. The first-year students see what can be learned through a foreign study experience and are encouraged to begin mapping their own educational paths, including study abroad.

At Kalamazoo College, student reflection on study abroad is not integrated into a formal symposium. Instead, faculty members are encouraged to include reflection time in their courses. In the biology department, a portion of the spring senior seminar course, "Functioning as a Biologist," is designed to help students process their study abroad experiences and to share these experiences with others. Both senior and junior majors participate in the seminar, and most juniors have just returned to Kalamazoo College from a 6-month study abroad program. The first one or two weeks of the seminar are used for juniors to relate their experiences abroad to their junior peers, senior classmates, and biology faculty, and for seniors to reflect on their senior thesis research experience. An interview method, developed by anthropology professor Kiran Cunningham and modified by biology professor Paul Sotherland, has been used for the past two years for this activity and has been particularly effective in providing students with an outlet for a sustained conversation about their experiences abroad and in the research laboratory. In small groups, junior and senior biology majors interview one another using a list of guiding questions. For example, seniors might ask juniors questions such as:

- What are some of the reasons for choosing the study abroad program you did?
- Describe a situation in which your morals and values were in contrast to those of your host culture. How did you deal with this? What did you learn?
- In what ways have you changed since going on study abroad? How would you describe yourself before? After? How has your identity changed?
- What plans do you have to reconnect with friends at Kalamazoo College?

Juniors, in turn, have the opportunity to ask their senior colleagues about the senior thesis research experience. Juniors come to recognize that the problem-solving skills and self-confidence they acquired while abroad are attributes that will serve them well during their senior thesis research. The written notes from interviews are collected and summarized by the faculty seminar convener for the benefit of students and faculty. Not only do the interviews yield insights into transformative moments during students' experiences abroad and at home, but they also provide students with opportunities for sustained, meaningful conversation about their experiences and how these have influenced their perceptions of themselves and others, their education, and their career path.

As discussed so far, study abroad can be a powerful, transformative experience for students, and education in scientific methods can enrich and enlarge this experience by sharpening an individual's observational and analytical skills, and by heightening his or her awareness of the natural world. But what motivates science students to study abroad, and what do they gain from the experience? In the remaining sections of this chapter we turn our attention to these issues and to some key challenges and solutions to making study abroad a reality for science students.

What Motivates Science Students to Study Abroad, and What Do They Gain From It?

When science students choose to study abroad, they do so for a variety of reasons, many of which may not be unique to them. First and foremost may be a general desire to enhance their knowledge and view of the world. This can occur within the classroom, for example, when studying energy in Denmark, where the resources and perspectives on this issue are different from those in the United States, or through homestays and living experiences. Science students may also be motivated to study abroad by a desire for personal challenges through immersion in a foreign language and culture. Through interactions with host families, peers, and the larger community, students encounter daily challenges that may be unique to living in a foreign country. As a result, they gain self-confidence and return from abroad with a greater sense of themselves and their home countries. Moreover, they inevitably come away with new perspectives and a greater sense of awareness of world events, regardless of the program in which they participate.

Many students realize the value of place and hands-on experience in the process of learning, and may seek out study abroad opportunities that contribute directly to their futures as scientists, educators, and health professionals. Few experiences can compare with studying evolution and environment on the Galapagos Islands of Ecuador, as students from both Beloit and Kalamazoo Colleges do. Similarly, students who study immunology may only appreciate the need to develop vaccines that are stable without refrigeration when they realize the gaps in the "cold chain" in many developing countries. Many of the 6-month Kalamazoo College programs include a 1-month Integrative Cultural Research Program (ICRP) component, during which students choose some aspect of the host culture to research in a more direct, experiential manner. Science students frequently develop projects that combine their interests in science, education, medicine, or conservation with cultural exploration. Examples include teaching science in local schools in Spain, Thailand, and India; assisting with care or educational programs at local zoos, conservation organizations, and health clinics in Kenya, Thailand, Australia, and Ecuador; and working in university research laboratories in France and Spain. These community service opportunities challenge students personally and professionally and help them better define their career aspirations. For medically inclined students they also offer a valuable opportunity to compare firsthand the U.S. health care system with that of another country.

The importance of cultural sensitivity and cultural competency for health professionals is well recognized (Weiner, 1997) and students going on to careers in this area should be motivated to study abroad for this reason, among others. Beloit College's "Nicaragua in Transition: Health and Microcredit," described in chapter 9 of this volume by Nancy Krusko, offers an example of how study abroad enhances the preparation of health professionals by bringing students into contact with a different culture. Small-scale health assessment studies in Maasai communities done by Beloit College students in an evolution and ecology program in Tanzania demonstrate the valuable questions that students can ask, and answer, with the aid of perceptive cultural understanding skills. For example, one student found that pregnant women developed the strategy of not eating during the last trimester of pregnancy to avoid childbirth complications and related hospitalization. This finding, never before described in the medical literature, has been important to local public health professionals (Neils, 2003).

For science students going on to careers in research, study abroad is equally relevant because of the importance of international collaboration to scientific research today. This is evident in science journal publications as well as at professional meetings such as the American Society of Micro-biology, where the most prestigious and groundbreaking presentations summarize the work of 20 or more researchers from five or six universities in as many countries. Traveling abroad to study science can show students that problems may be framed in different ways by scientists with different back-grounds, and demonstrate that despite different questions, the processes of science remain the same. For example, a biochemistry major from Beloit College who studied biotechnology in Denmark reported that he learned to recognize different assumptions made while doing science in a small, social-ist, European country like Denmark. He found that researchers were less likely to do research for the sake of knowing, but rather asked, "What will understanding these amino acids do for Denmark?" Through study abroad, our students benefit from seeing how scientists in other cultures interact and collaborate, and how they approach and structure research. When we leave science students home while their peers study abroad, we are minimizing the importance of their contributions to our global society.

Finally, for some students, study abroad provides the opportunity to study topics that are beyond the scope of our small liberal arts colleges. For example, a biology major interested in paleontology at Kalamazoo College chose to study abroad in Wollongong, Australia, in order to take geology courses not offered at his home institution. In doing so, he furthered his career goal of becoming a professional paleontologist (he is now in a graduate program in paleontology) and successfully combined his studies with the opportunity to travel and investigate other cultures.

Whereas myriad factors motivate science students to study abroad, all students stand to benefit significantly from the experience, both personally and professionally. They return with a greater understanding of themselves, other countries, and other cultures. They also bring back new perspectives on old issues and new ways to approach novel problems. Students who choose to study science in college graduate not only as scientists and health care professionals, but also as journalists, teachers, lawyers, or businesspeo-ple. The importance of international and intercultural competency skills applies equally to all job sectors now as our community becomes increasingly globalized. They are on their way to becoming global citizens, regardless of the career path they follow. Given the obvious benefits of study abroad, one might wonder why science students historically have low participation rates in study abroad programs, and what can be done to change this.

How to Get Science Students Abroad

Students majoring in the sciences often participate in study abroad at lower rates than do students from other disciplines (Wang, 2006). This may be due to the structure of science programs, in which sequenced courses and additional cognate requirements increase the need to plan ahead for study abroad. Moreover, students intending to go on to graduate or professional programs after college may need additional courses on top of their major and general education requirements, making it even more difficult to "fit in" study abroad. Another reason that science students may be less likely to study abroad is that the experience does not seem relevant to their intended career path or area of interest. If our institutions are truly committed to being interdisciplinary, experiential, and international in our educational offerings, then we have the responsibility to structure academic programs to meet the needs of students studying science, and to help them see how study abroad can help them prepare for their future careers. Change does appear to be in the air, however. Participation in study abroad by science students is on the rise (Wang, 2006).

Various study abroad providers are recognizing that science students do not want to be left out and are building programs to attract young scientists and help them expand their horizons, scientifically and socially. The Danish International Study (DIS) Program offers programs in medical practice and policy, and biology and biotechnology that serve science students well by allowing them to pursue studies related to their majors, continue to prepare for exams such as the Medical College Admission Test, and learn about and from Danish culture. The TransAtlantic Science Student Exchange Program, composed of a consortium of member universities from the European Union, the United States, and Canada, offers students in the physical and life sciences an opportunity to continue their science studies abroad through 1-year exchange programs.

To enhance participation rates in study abroad among science students, science departments at Beloit College and Kalamazoo College have a strong tradition of making study abroad a priority for their students, just as it is for students in other disciplines. This requires careful planning and flexibility in scheduling on the part of faculty and students, and a science-heavy course load for first-year and sophomore students, especially for those planning to attend medical school right after college. But as a result, some students expressly seek out our institutions because of the ability to combine study abroad with a science major.

Carving out time for study abroad in science programs is important because it creates the *expectation* that science students will go abroad. At Kalamazoo College, more than 80% of the students spend three to nine months studying in another country, most commonly six months. Because course sequences for majors in the sciences are built around a presumed 6-month study abroad experience during the junior year, science majors participate at the same rates, and in the case of biology majors, slightly higher rates, as students majoring in other fields. For many science students at Kalamazoo College, and at other institutions, study abroad serves as a way to fulfill general education requirements, thereby creating room in the home institution schedule for additional courses needed for postgraduate programs. Nevertheless, students with interests in biology, environmental studies, or the health professions can choose from programs in Australia, Costa Rica, Ecuador, Kenya, Scotland, or Thailand that offer courses in one or more of these disciplinary areas. Students with an interest in complex systems and computational neuroscience can study in Hungary.

At Beloit College, approximately 50% of the student body, and 40% of students in the sciences, study abroad through exchange programs administered by the college, direct enrollment in universities abroad, and programs offered by study abroad organizations. Students in the new interdisciplinary majors of health and society and environmental studies are virtually students of the world, with 80% of them studying abroad. Beloit science students most commonly choose programs that enhance perspectives on their major. For example, students interested in environmental sciences may study in the Galapagos Islands, Tanzania, Australia, New Zealand, or other countries. Physics and mathematics students participate in programs in Hungary and in Australia. Students majoring in health and society or in environmental studies may take "Health and Microcredit" in Nicaragua, and then study environmental and health issues in Ecuador, Brazil, or Kenya. Others enroll in the DIS Medical Practice Program; School for International Training programs with a public health focus in South Africa, Thailand, and Argentina; or the International Honors Program that travels between South Africa,

India, and China in one semester. Students focused on a goal of medical school or graduate school may be hesitant to stray too far from the laboratory, or to engage in international study. These are the students, however, with the most to gain from study abroad. Carefully selected programs can benefit them by enhancing their scientific knowledge and enabling them to stretch culturally by living with host families, learning new languages, and engaging in cross-cultural experiences. Anecdotal evidence suggests that study abroad also increases the competitiveness of their postgraduate applications, as applicants to medical school who are conversant about health care in South Africa or environmental risks in Costa Rica can attest.

Conclusion

Regardless of the focus of the program abroad, making the study abroad experience a meaningful and connected part of students' education and career development is paramount. This can begin before students leave for study abroad and continue to build and develop while abroad and upon return. Many alumni from Beloit College and Kalamazoo College report that the real effects of their study abroad experiences did not become clear to them until five or more years after graduation.

With planning, science classes can give students additional perspectives for viewing the new worlds they will encounter. Science classes provide tools to look at ecology and agriculture, to explore culture in different environments, or to look at the effects of rapid urbanization not only from the social perspective, but also in terms of biological changes and health effects. These new perspectives may show up in the photos students take. They begin to notice the slabs of fat for sale in countries with high levels of heart disease, the posters on the sides of buildings advising how to minimize mosquito breeding places, or street children at risk of disease. They take pictures of interesting plants and insects, of standing water, or of cash crops growing in resource-poor countries as they work to make sense of the differences between their "home" and the new world they encounter while abroad.

Building a tradition of sharing experiences and constructing meaning from these experiences helps all students see that study abroad can be an enriching and rewarding experience regardless of academic discipline. Kalamazoo College has built a strong culture of study abroad that encourages student involvement and that links the study abroad experience to the personal and professional development of its students. Efforts at Beloit College to increase the effect of study abroad on the institution as a whole resulted in an annual International Symposium that gives students the opportunity to reflect on their experiences and to share these with others.

As we write this chapter, issues about science in an international context fill the news. We worry about drilling for more oil in the United States and its environmental effects, and about potential contamination of vegetables imported from Mexico. We read about the changes in China brought about by the Three Gorges Dam, and the concern about pollution in Beijing during the 2008 summer Olympic Games. Clearly, educated citizens will need scientific and international perspectives to engage responsibly in the democracies of the future, as argued recently by *New York Times* columnist Tom Friedman in his book *Hot, Flat and Crowded* (2008). Study abroad has the potential to enable students to observe carefully, to bring in varied perspectives, and see the issues of the future in a broad, multidisciplinary context. Our challenge is to develop the courses and activities, similar to ones described here, to enable students to accomplish these goals.

References

Broverman, S. (2008). AIDS research: Global understanding & engagement. *Science Education for New Civic Engagements and Responsibilities.* Retrieved May 4, 2009, from http://serc.Carleton.edu/sencer/aids_research/index.html.

Fass, M. F. (2000). Teaching emerging diseases: A strategy for succeeding with non-majors. *Microbiology Education, 1,* 20–25.

Fass, M. F. (2008). Syllabus and activities for "Biological issues: Emerging infectious diseases." Retrieved May 4, 2009, from http://www.beloit.edu/health/heal_pdfs/HEALeidsyl2008edit.pdf.

Friedman, T. L. (2008). *Hot, flat and crowded: Why we need a green revolution and how it can renew America.* New York: Farrar, Straus and Giroux.

Helling, M. (2007). No more fish to fry where the water meets the sky. *Sixth Annual International Symposium Abstracts.* Beloit, WI: Beloit College.

Meacham, J. A., Kosal, E., & Fernandes, P. (2008). Life science in context: Sub-Saharan Africa and HIV/AIDS. *Science Education for New Civic Engagement and Responsibilities.* Retrieved May 4, 2009, from http://serc.carleton.edu/sencer/africa_aids/sub-sahara_africa_hivaids.html.

Neils, A. A. (2003). Doing it right: Research and ethics in Tanzania. *Second Annual International Symposium Abstracts.* Beloit, WI: Beloit College.

Thairu, K. (2003). *The African and the AIDS holocaust.* Nairobi: Phoenix Publishers.

Wang, L. (2006). Passport to science: Once outnumbered by humanities majors, science students are now studying abroad in force. *Chemical & Engineering News, 84*(36), 96–98. Retrieved May 4, 2009, from http://pubs.acs.org/cen/education/84/8436education3.html.

Weiner, T. S. (1997). An international perspective on health care: The case for terms abroad for future physicians. *Frontiers, 3.* Retrieved May 4, 2009, from http://www.frontiersjournal.com/issues/vol3/vol3-15_Weiner.htm.

Wilson, E. O. (1984). *Biophilia.* Cambridge, MA: Harvard University Press.

II

SYNTHESIS AND CAREER PREPARATION
The International Relations Senior Thesis

Pablo Toral

I n an article published in 2000, Jane Edwards warns of a growing gap in perceptions among policy makers, parents, and students on the value of study abroad. Policy makers believe the ultimate goal of study abroad is to create more productive workers. They see study abroad as an instrument that can teach skills useful for the marketplace, including foreign language competency. Parents and students see study abroad more as an opportunity for individual self-maturation and attainment of greater self-confidence (Edwards, 2000). The implications of these divergent understandings are serious, because these perceptions shape the way in which our scarce resources are invested. This chapter does not seek to settle this debate, but it addresses an area—undergraduate research—that can help bridge the gap between both perspectives. Although the chapter focuses on international relations in particular, its examples can be applied to other disciplines as well.

Surprisingly, the website of the International Studies Association (ISA), the professional organization for international relations, does not have a single link devoted to the teaching of international relations, although three of the sections address aspects of pedagogy, namely active learning, comparative interdisciplinary studies, and international education. None of the three address the role of study abroad in international relations education; instead they emphasize research and serve as meeting places for researchers who share similar interests. ISA's sister association, the American Political Science Association (APSA), does a little better. It has a section on pedagogy, but there is no statement or even a mention of the role of study abroad in political science education. Fortunately, the American Council on Education (ACE) invited APSA in 2005 to participate in a debate on how to internationalize the American undergraduate curriculum. As a result of this invitation, APSA commissioned a report in 2006 to evaluate the internationalization of the undergraduate curriculum in political science at American colleges and universities.

With this report, APSA sought to increase cross-cultural awareness and identify best practices for teaching sensitivity to the demands of globalization. The report concluded that political science undergraduates' knowledge and understanding of political systems outside the United States is weak and underdeveloped. The report went on to affirm that this is especially troublesome in an era when decisions that profoundly affect the United States are made in other countries and international regimes. To remedy this, the committee recommends a set of goals that include the development of cultural competency and empathy to encourage us to see the world through the eyes of others, recognize the interconnectedness of the world, and be able to discern similarities and differences across peoples and cultures (Ingebritsen, Cassell, Lamy, Martin, & Mason, 2006, pp. 2–3). Interestingly, the report only refers to study abroad indirectly when it recommends scholarships for international research and development of long-standing relationships with universities outside the United States. However, it does not give a single thought to integration of international research into the curriculum.

ISA's omission may reflect the perception by ISA's members that study abroad is so obviously critical to the teaching of international relations that there is no need to address the topic. APSA's report also largely assumes that "content" is the way to achieve cross-cultural and international learning, and ignores the affective and experiential learning that many consider critical to actually being able to apply one's content knowledge in real-world settings (Ingebritsen et al., 2006). The report also ignores the need to help students develop cross-cultural skills before departure and the need to push students to reflect upon their study abroad experience, as well as the possibility of building international research into the students' curriculum. This chapter therefore explains how study abroad can be integrated into the international relations curriculum and provides some strategies, including undergraduate research, that could be adapted to other disciplines.

Integrating Study Abroad Into the International Relations Curriculum

Faculty and staff at Beloit College like to describe Beloit's educational philosophy as a three-legged stool. The three legs on which we build our programs are international, interdisciplinary, and experiential. Study abroad is an important part of the international relations major because it brings the students in contact with the geographic region and the subject of study in which they choose to specialize, and it incorporates all three legs of the stool simultaneously.

Interdisciplinary learning seeks to understand how knowledge is constructed and continually reconstructed. In international relations, this is achieved in part by requiring students to take courses in several different fields: four in modern languages (or two beyond intermediate level), three in economics, three in political science (in addition to "International Politics," which serves as the gateway course for the major), and three electives outside of the previous fields. The students choose their courses on the basis of their area of specialization, which could be a region such as East Asia or a theme such as development. Further, students are strongly encouraged (but not required) to spend at least one semester abroad. During their last semester they take a senior seminar to write their senior thesis. Infusing an international approach into an interdisciplinary degree gives the students ethnographic tools to learn about the process of knowledge construction and disciplinary development of each field. Because the language of instruction abroad is often the vernacular, study abroad helps the students improve their foreign language skills, often after two or more years of study of the same language at the college. By the time they go abroad, they have already fulfilled most of their requirements in economics, modern languages, and political science, so they have freedom to find internationally oriented elective courses in other disciplines. In some countries where Beloit College administers its own programs (see chapter 8), they can take courses that have been designed for them with an interdisciplinary focus.

Reflection on and integration of disciplinary knowledge is central to interdisciplinary studies. Many scholars trained in a more disciplinary fashion might regard this type of education as "lacking in rigor" or as a hiatus in the student's process of disciplinary growth. However, disciplinary learning in a different cultural context can connect culturally ingrained research biases and can also lead to a demonstration of the application of previously gained disciplinary knowledge in a new context (Bollen & Martin, 2005). Lindsey Green was a Beloit international relations major. She participated in Beloit College's program in Senegal in the spring of 2006 and the School for International Training's program in Uganda in the spring of 2007. After finishing the program she remained in Uganda in the summer to conduct an internship at a local nongovernmental organization (NGO), Human Rights Network Uganda (HURINET-U), for 3 1/2 months. Working with HURINET's advocacy officer, the national coordinator, and the Uganda Coalition for the International Criminal Court (UCICC), she attended a number of conferences, workshops, and meetings, and prepared a paradigms paper on the interdisciplinary tension between NGOs focused on human rights and those focused on conflict resolution. The courses she took in Uganda and her experience at the NGO enabled her "to gain a holistic understanding of the human rights environment in Uganda and to understand the multifaceted nature of the causes (political, economic, social, and environmental) that lead to human rights abuses" (L. Green, personal communication, August 23, 2008). When she returned to the college, she wrote a thesis in which she analyzed the response of the international community to internally displaced people in Africa.

The experiential component of the major also allows the students to see the practical side of their studies, and gives them new insights into their areas of interest and expertise. Beloit programs and some non-Beloit programs help the students find volunteer and internship opportunities related to their area of specialization, so that they can give an experiential character to their stay abroad. They can understand the economic, political, and social context of social justice at home and elsewhere in which institutions and practices developed, and reexamine their values, attitudes, and responsibilities for global and local citizenship. This is what the students normally refer to as "life-changing experiences" and what experts define as a "state of developmental readiness" (Olson, Evans, & Shoenberg, 2007; Pusch & Merrill, 2008). One of Beloit's international relations majors, Bobby Harris, said about his stay in India:

> Not only did I receive inside information by being there, I was inspired to make sure that the thesis I wrote was true to the place and people [who]

so graciously showed me their world. I interviewed people on their death-bed, while their families wiped them with cool rags and their doctors were giving them IVs. You can't get that obligation from reading a book. That made my thesis better. I really tried to emphasize not losing the level of commitment that I held when I was in India. I did not want to forget who and what I was writing for. So I stayed involved in learning about it. (B. Harris, personal communication, August 12, 2008)

Study abroad also helps students achieve a goal set out in the college's mission statement that is not explicitly captured by the three-legged stool, namely personal development. Applied to study abroad, personal growth is understood by many scholars to involve emotions stemming from disorientation (Bennett, 2008; Olson, et al., 2007; Selby, 2008). Bobby spent the summer of 2007 working in India as a volunteer, helping to educate poor urban citizens on how to prevent the spread of HIV/AIDS. Upon returning, he wrote a thesis comparing Brazil's and India's HIV/AIDS policies. He stressed how study abroad helped him give meaning to his studies:

> My time in India inspired me to work abroad and try to make this world a better place. I love the roller coaster of emotions that we all deal with in a foreign country, especially a developing one. It was a test of mental and physical determination, focus, and passion, and I loved it. It was the truest thing I have ever done. I got to be a part of improving people's lives on a daily basis. I got to meet people from all walks of life, and they all changed my life. (B. Harris, personal communication, August 12, 2008)

Although study abroad is not a requirement at Beloit, the share of international relations majors spending at least a semester abroad is around 80%, and those not going abroad are almost always foreign students, who consider Beloit as their study abroad. One of the reasons for this high rate is that many of the students who apply to Beloit are attracted by its reputation in international education and already intend to go abroad. Another reason is advising. The advisors in the Office of International Education, as well as faculty who advise for the major, spend a great deal of time with the students working out their area of specialization and helping them choose study abroad programs that will allow them to strengthen their area of focus and both supplement and complement the Beloit curriculum. These measures ensure that the courses they take abroad will count toward the international relations major or toward their other graduation requirements. More importantly, their study abroad is likely to add value to their Beloit studies.

Getting Ready for Study Abroad

Colleges and universities devote a lot of energy to discussions on how to integrate study abroad options into the college experience and academic curricula for students of all majors. Chapter 3 in this volume on study abroad preparatory courses discusses the kinds of learning that students need to have for study abroad: content, experiential, intercultural, and foreign language. The focus of this chapter is on how we can help students integrate study abroad into most if not all disciplines through courses and assignments before and after study abroad, culminating in research in the senior year. (Interestingly, undergraduate research is not often mentioned as a means for study abroad integration. See, for example, NAFSA: Association of International Educators, 2008).

Most Beloit international relations majors choose to spend half or all of their junior year abroad, although there are some who go during their sophomore year and some during their senior year. This depends on the time they take to fulfill the college's requirements for study abroad (distribution requirements and foreign language requirements mainly). Prior to departure, we start working with the students when they declare the major in international relations to help them define their area of focus, on the basis of which they plan their course selection. In turn, this will shape their choice of study abroad program. To help the students be prepared for study abroad, they take foundation courses, including at least one course that focuses on the region where they are going and/or the themes that they will study there. Before going to India, Bobby took courses that focused on economic development, health care, and political representation. Before going to Senegal and Uganda, Lindsey took classes that focused on Africa, economic development and human rights, as well as language courses. She writes,

> The courses were helpful in giving me general frames/points of reference (historical, political) for what I would experience and observe when I was actually abroad. Additionally, most of the courses I took provided me the opportunity to do more specific in-depth research on particular issues in the country I was going to study in. (L. Green, personal communication, August 23, 2008)

Nick Stuber was a political science major who spent a semester in Costa Rica through the program run by the Associated Colleges of the Midwest (ACM) and subsequently wrote a thesis on the Costa Rican discourse of democracy and equality. Before going abroad, he took courses in Spanish language and on Latin American civilization; in one of these he conducted research and wrote on Costa Rican history, politics, economy, and society (N. Stuber, personal communication, August 12, 2008).

When Beloit College does not offer courses directly related to the study abroad site, the students are required to write research papers on those topics and regions in the context of other courses they are taking, or as an independent project directed by a faculty member. Because most courses we teach involve a research component, relating study abroad to a specific course can be most easily achieved by relating the research papers assigned in a course to the research the students are going to conduct or have conducted abroad. For example, an environmental studies major going to India took my course on international political economy and focused his research papers for the course on environmental political economy in India. The professor and the advisor in the major normally coordinate these types of research projects. Students going abroad also need to meet the language requirements of the program. As Beloit teaches six modern foreign languages, many will have had at least two years of study in the target language. In addition to language instruction, students are exposed to culture and civilization in language courses to acquaint them with the culture of the host country. Some of the assignments also require the students to become familiar with our partner institution abroad, as well as with the host city and host countries. This allows them to develop some basic knowledge of how to navigate the city and the host institution. They are also encouraged to take courses other than language courses with a focus on the country or region. When the college does not offer courses in the country they are going to, they are encouraged to complete assignments in courses based on the target country. In some cases the language courses the students take prior to departure give them a strong basis for successful research abroad: "The French classes I took before going to Senegal gave me the 'advanced' basics but my French improved innumerably [*sic*] while I was abroad," affirms Lindsey. But even when the college does not offer the language the students will need abroad, taking a foreign language can help them learn a new language when they get there.

Bobby argues that "although Spanish was not very useful in India, my foreign language training at school gave me the ability to pick up some basic Hindi and Marathi in India."

Conducting Research Abroad

The November 2005 issue of *Frontiers* provided a compilation of noteworthy research conducted by undergraduates abroad. In one of the essays by faculty members, David Macey regrets that few educators take advantage of the opportunity afforded by a junior year abroad to push the students to use the resources and materials available in their host country. In addition to the emotional disorientation discussed previously, Macey notes the excitement the students feel when their academic studies come alive for the first time because of the physical proximity they have to their subjects. He argues that when students conduct research abroad and then complete a senior thesis at home with the appropriate literature, this represents the epitome of the liberal arts experience, "integrating" in the most complete way the student's time abroad with the home school curriculum (Macey, 2005).

Beloit students are advised to start thinking about a topic for their thesis while they are abroad. We encourage them to write an independent research project with an advisor or to write a few papers in the context of their courses on topics that they might want to continue to explore when they return home. Having a committed research director abroad can help the students narrow their areas of interest so they can start conducting research. First, Nick worked very closely with the director of the program in Costa Rica, who helped him find the focus of his research and pointed him in the direction of many useful resources and individuals. Second, his host family was a direct conduit into the cultural, economic, and political precepts he wanted to target in his research. He spoke with them many times regarding aspects of Costa Rican culture and history. This grounded his research topic into concrete examples from which he could extrapolate. And finally, the curriculum in Costa Rica was interdisciplinary and gave a good overview of all aspects of Costa Rica, allowing him to plunge deeper into specific aspects that he found interesting.

While interning at HURINET-U, Lindsey completed a large final practicum paper on transitional justice in northern Uganda. In the course of this research, she became familiar with the concept of internally displaced persons (IDPs) in northern Uganda, on which she wrote her senior thesis. "Though the paper touched on IDPs only as it related to the achievement of justice, it definitely sparked my interest in pursuing the topic of internal displacement more thoroughly" (L. Green, personal communication, August 23, 2008). After completing the paper, she was able to learn more about IDPs in northern Uganda specifically during the remainder of her internship, which included traveling to the region and completing two focus group discussions with IDPs.

> In Uganda I learned equally as much about the conflict that had affected northern Uganda when speaking to the guard at the gate to my house as when speaking to well-educated, gainfully employed members of civil society organizations. The guard, originally from northern Uganda, had moved to Kampala in his teens after most of his family was killed or disappeared; he taught me from first-hand experience. The NGO and CSO [civil society organization] staff, on the other hand, had intimate knowledge of justice methods. Therefore, all aspects of the international experience, conducting formal research and living everyday life, can provide an opportunity for learning and personal growth. Upon returning from Uganda I found that it was difficult for me to feel academically satisfied by merely going to class, doing my reading, and writing papers. I wanted more engagement with the subjects I was studying; I yearned for the passion found from connecting somewhat sterile academic subjects with people's everyday lives, something which is fundamental and essential in international educational experiences. (Green, 2008)

Reflections Upon Return

Some experts recommend a reentry course in the context of which the students can achieve some "closure"; that is, they can think about what they experienced abroad and retain what they have learned (Selby, 2008). Other scholars, however, caution against defining reentry as closure, as this can bring the process of reflection to a close and return the students to the point of predeparture. Rather, reentry should spark a lifelong learning perspective through which the students unfreeze long-standing, unexamined understandings and think critically about alternative careers (Downey, 2005).

Writing a thesis on a topic "discovered" abroad is one of the most important ways in which the international relations major at Beloit encourages students to continue to think about their experience abroad. Because most of them go abroad during their junior year and they will not defend their thesis until they take the senior seminar in the spring semester of their senior year, they have a whole year to write the thesis after they return to campus. However, several options get the students started as soon as they get back to campus: They can write papers for their courses based on the topic of their thesis, they can present a paper based on their study abroad at the International Symposium (a campus-wide student conference at which returning students present the research they conducted abroad), and they can take a unit of independent research with an advisor to start drafting the thesis. Most students choose the first two options.

When Bobby returned from India, he enrolled in courses on health, human rights, and economic development. He also took an independent study with a professor to begin writing his thesis. Through this independent project he started to look at the connections between economic development and the increased spread of HIV in impoverished communities. He wrote a paper and prepared a presentation that he gave at the student symposium in November. He also participated in global HIV/AIDS discussions on campus. When Nick returned, he contacted the director of the Costa Rica program and refined portions of the research paper he wrote there, which ultimately became the foundation for his senior thesis. He also spoke with his advisors to narrow down his approach, wrote a proposal, and researched questions he had regarding his topic. When Lindsey returned, she continued to familiarize herself with the issue of internal displacement and sought opportunities within her courses to look at internal displacement resulting from other African conflicts around the continent: "Therefore when it was time to come up with my thesis topic I already felt fairly familiar with the issue and had an idea of which conflicts would provide the best case studies" (L. Green, personal communication, August 23, 2008).

Senior Thesis and Senior Seminar

On average, between 50% and 75% of the students in the senior seminar write their thesis on a topic they began researching abroad. For example, out of the 16 students who graduated from the international relations program in 2007–2008, 11 based their theses on their study abroad research. Of the other five, two did not study abroad, and personal circumstances led two others to postpone their sojourns abroad until after graduation. However, these two wrote their theses on the topic they had planned to research abroad. The remaining student spent a semester in Africa, but was also interested in the Middle East. Because he was applying for positions with NGOs in both regions, he decided he would increase his chances if he wrote his thesis on the Middle East.

Theses based on the research conducted abroad are normally the best, because by the time they are finished, the students have spent a considerable amount of time working on them and they are informed by on-the-ground experience. Some students might have started brainstorming for topics early in their junior year (or even before). As discussed previously, they refine the topic while abroad, where they start conducting research, and continue to write and reflect upon the topic of their thesis through their senior year until they get to the senior seminar, during which they have to give the thesis its final shape.

The students write their thesis in the senior seminar in International Relations, which is taught with four main goals in mind: (a) empower the students so that they become critical readers, (b) make them feel comfortable as researchers, (c) give them a capstone experience, and (d) give them a taste of graduate school. The three-hour seminar meets weekly for discussion of a set of assigned readings, moderated by two of the seminar students. Questions and comments based on the readings are circulated beforehand for consideration by the rest of the students. In class the moderators organize a discussion in which they summarize and discuss the main arguments of the reading, make linkages between the week's reading and other books or articles they read in previous weeks or courses, and relate the reading to their own theses. In the first two-thirds of the semester we read and discuss a book. During the last one-third of the semester we discuss the students' drafts.

The senior seminar is probably the only course the seniors will take together. Therefore, it plays an important role in providing a venue in which they can discuss what they have done in four years at the college. The students enjoy learning about each other's areas of expertise, the study abroad programs they have done, the research they have conducted abroad, their career goals, the courses they have taken on and off campus, and so on. They exchange ideas and give each other advice. During the discussions based on the readings, each student develops a preference for some readings and becomes expert in these. Over the weeks, they refer the other students to their approach or author of preference in which they have expertise, and they experience a sense of accomplishment. They feel they have mastered difficult books and they feel confident to critique them. They respect and value the input they receive from the others as well. As the semester goes along, we spend more time discussing their theses. The students bring drafts to class for peer review and are required to provide periodic updates. They become very engaged as they try to emulate the hard work of the scholars we have been reading since the beginning of the semester. They realize they are capable of original research. The expectation from the professor is higher than in the other courses and we make this clear to them. We tell them that the amount of reading and the quality of the research they have to do in the course will be evaluated as if the seminar were a real graduate course. Although at first they feel a bit intimidated, over the weeks they appreciate the trust and responsibility we give them and try hard to meet our expectations. This approach also makes them realize how much they have learned and also that they can do graduate-level work. The wide spectrum of experiences and research topics gives them a sense of accomplishment, individually and as a group.

The senior thesis is a critical part of the seminar because it is the longest original research assignment the students have had to conduct in their lives. For this reason, we encourage them to write on a topic they feel passionate about, and, preferably, a topic they researched during study abroad. We ask the students to write a thesis that is both professional and personal. By "professional," we mean that they have to demonstrate their ability to write a review of the literature, conduct an original research project, use sound methodology, make a clear thesis and arguments, use appropriate and professional citations, and so on. By "personal," we mean not only that they are passionate about it, but that the topic is original because they have had access to primary sources (oral or written), have been to the area on which their research is based, or the research is related to their potential future professional career. As Macey (2005) argues, this makes their academic experience come to life.

The senior seminar is the venue in which all of the students can reflect upon their study abroad experience, find the appropriate literature to make sense of what they learned, search for answers to many questions that came up while in a foreign country, and push the limits of their research further. They need to provide updates in class on a regular basis, where their peers and the professor ask them to clarify their topics, research questions, methodology, sources, and so on. By mid-March, they need to submit the first complete draft for peer review. The review can be anonymous, but most students prefer to give their draft to another student whose area of expertise comes closest, as well as to their closest friends, because they expect to receive better advice. The professor also reads this draft. The reviewers have a week to give it back to the author with comments and suggestions.

There are no reading assignments in the last third of the semester, other than student drafts. Before the end of the semester they have to defend their thesis in front of the class. They prepare a PowerPoint presentation, dress up, and present their work as if they were attending a professional meeting. Many illustrate their presentations with photos or film they took abroad. They show places, buildings, institutions, people, landscapes, cityscapes, shopping centers, and so on. They have a sense of ownership over the topic. Saying "I've been there" gives them confidence and makes them authoritative in the eyes of the other students. After each presentation, there is time for questions. Students evaluate each other on the content and the form of the presentation (this is part of their final grade). They are encouraged to submit as many new drafts as they want. They can turn in a whole draft, or sections of their thesis for review. We also encourage the students to present their work at Beloit College's spring student symposium (this is a requirement for students pursuing honors). Having presented in class, they feel more confident about speaking at the symposium, which is open to the entire college community.

Examples of Successful Undergraduate Research

The theses by the three students discussed in this chapter were among the best in the spring 2008 semester. They were well written, thoroughly researched, and asked probing questions. Interdisciplinary in nature, the theses built their arguments around a problem and borrowed from different fields such as political science, history, public health, and anthropology to find answers. They were built on research conducted abroad and were enlightened by their own personal experiences. In short, the theses embodied all three areas of inquiry the college emphasizes: experiential, interdisciplinary, and international. The students' defenses and public presentations at the student symposium were superb. The students delivered the arguments clearly, they were confident, and they engaged in a very lively discussion with the audience.

Bobby's thesis compared public health policies of Brazil and India to fight the spread of HIV/AIDS. It was based on the paper he wrote as an independent project during the previous semester, in which he reviewed India's approach to HIV/AIDS. He later added a case study on Brazil to give his paper a comparative approach, and investigated the reasons why India's HIV/AIDS policies have been less successful than Brazil's. Bobby affirms that his thesis would not have been as strong had it not been based on his study abroad experience: "My thesis experience justified my time in India. It showed the amount of work that is needed to truly do justice" (B. Harris, personal communication, August 12, 2008).

Lindsey's thesis analyzed how the international community deals with IDPs, comparing two cases, Angola and Liberia. Since learning about IDPs in Uganda, she wrote papers on this topic during the fall semester in which she reviewed several African cases. In the senior seminar she studied the guiding principles adopted by the international community to deal with IDP crises around the world and focused on Angola and Liberia, so that she could compare a case in which the international community was successful and one in which it was not. This allowed her to evaluate the guiding principles and make some recommendations.

> This thirst for finding connections between "theory" and "practice" led me to devote a large chunk of my senior year to writing an International Relations honors thesis on internal displacement in the international system, a topic [with] roots . . . based in my international experience in Uganda and [that] allowed me to take the passion stoked by everyday experiences during international education and channel it toward productive and progressive learning back at Beloit. Study abroad made the process of writing my thesis much easier as I felt that was merely continuing on a path of exploration I had started on in Uganda and expanding my knowledge. When I was feeling lost or discouraged during the thesis process I was able to bring myself back to study abroad and think about the faces of the IDPs whom I had met. Thinking of them and what they had taught

and shared with me gave me an extra boost to continue to explore a difficult, complex, and frustrating subject. (L. Green, personal communication,
August 23, 2008)

Nick's thesis analyzed the origins and importance of the discourse of
democracy and equality in Costa Rica, which he defined as "the Costa Rican
myth." Before going to Costa Rica he became fascinated by the emphasis
placed by Costa Ricans on democracy and equality. This fascination was
reinforced by his interactions with the locals there. His thesis traced the origins of "the myth" to its origins in the 19th century and showed how it
influenced the political development of the country, facilitating the adoption
of free and periodic elections, universal health care, and universal access to
education.

My thesis helped me better understand the people of Costa Rica in retrospect. Aspects of Costa Rican culture, politics, and economy became
clearer for me after I completed my thesis. It also acquainted me with
material (research, writings) produced by Costa Ricans about their own
country that I did not encounter while I was abroad. (N. Stuber, personal
communication, August 12 2008)

Conclusion

This chapter discusses how the international relations program at Beloit College helps students integrate study abroad into their courses and especially
their senior research project. Through good advising and flexible requirements, other disciplines can develop a similar model. From students' perspectives, study abroad becomes a "life-changing" experience when it makes
them think about their own identity in new terms and when it allows them
to feel passionate about a future professional career. The three students mentioned in this chapter decided to spend the first years after college working
in the areas they explored abroad. Bobby decided that he wants to pursue a
career of service by working in the field of humanitarian aid. After graduating from school he worked for four months with a Canadian NGO called
Para el Mundo in Mancora, Peru, creating sustainable development programs in three major areas: education, health, and the environment. In February 2009 he will join the Peace Corps on a public health program in South
Africa. He writes:

I owe all of that to my time in India, and the opportunity my thesis gave me to realize what this world can offer for someone who wants to make a difference and is willing to find and fight for that opportunity. Having that time to sit back and realize what happened smoothed over some rough edges that had needled me since returning home. I was very unsure if my work over there was worth anything, mainly because there was no way to measure something in the present that can only be seen in retrospect. My thesis reinforced an assurance that what we did over there helped people's lives. The thesis was definitely a look into the world of humanitarian aid as a profession. (B. Harris, personal communication, August 12, 2008)

After graduation, Lindsey moved to the Netherlands to attend a seminar organized by Humanity in Action on minority rights and majority responsibility, and in 2009 she will serve in the Peace Corps in Sub-Saharan Africa. She reports:

My thesis definitely gave me a big confidence boost and sense of achievement as I graduated from Beloit. It solidified that I would like to continue to explore and be involved in human rights and humanitarian issues in Africa. Additionally it gave me a renewed sense that I could wrap my mind around difficult international issues in a productive way. Broadly, my study abroad experience has shaped the way I think about who I want to be after college and therefore profoundly affects the choices I make. Furthermore, it has made me much more confident and comfortable in my abilities to dive into a new challenge and adjust to new situations. Therefore as I approach my post-college choices and decisions I am much more adventurous than I would be had I not gone abroad. (L. Green, personal communication, August 23, 2008)

Spending a semester abroad and writing a thesis made Nick think about his future professional career in terms that were very different from what he had anticipated when he went to college. Nick's critical analysis of the discourse of democracy and equality in Costa Rica made him think about democracy and equality in the United States as well. He applied for a position with AmeriCorps and is now working for Iowa's Civil Rights Commission, through AmeriCorps. His longer-term plans involve more international travel and more research. He gives his stay abroad and his thesis credit for this: "Both my thesis and study abroad showed me that I want to continue to research after Beloit and I want to go abroad again, possibly while doing both" (N. Stuber, personal communication, August 12, 2008).

References

Bennett, J. M. (2008). On becoming a global soul: A path to engagement during study abroad. In V. Savicki (Ed.), *Developing intercultural competence and transformation: Theory, research, and application in international education* (pp. 13–31). Sterling, VA: Stylus.

Bollen, M., & Martin, P. (2005, November). Undergraduate research abroad: Challenges and rewards. *Frontiers: The Interdisciplinary Journal of Study Abroad, 12,* 11–16.

Downey, G. (2005). From personal reflection to social investigation: Undergraduate research as an antidote to autobiographical cliché. In L. C. Anderson (Ed.), *Internationalizing undergraduate education: Integrating study abroad into the curriculum* (pp. 117–121). Minneapolis: University of Minnesota.

Edwards, J. (2000, Winter). The "Other Eden": Thoughts on American study abroad in Britain. *Frontiers: The Interdisciplinary Journal of Study Abroad, 6,* 83–98.

Green, L. (2008). *Description of how the international experience contributed to the learning experience.* Unpublished essay. Beloit College, Beloit, WI.

Ingebritsen, C., Cassell, M., Lamy, S., Martin, P., & Mason, D. (2006). *Internationalizing APSA: A report from the working group to ACE.* Retrieved August 11, 2008, from https://www.apsanet.org/imgtest/Internationalizing%20APSA%20Report 4-2-06.pdf.

Macey, D. (2005, November). Intellectual growth and the integration of the study abroad experience. *Frontiers: The Interdisciplinary Journal of Study Abroad, 12,* 55–57.

NAFSA: Association of International Educators. (2003). *Securing America's future: Global education for a global age: Report of the strategic task force on education abroad.* Washington, DC: Author.

NAFSA: Association of International Educators. (2008). *Internationalization at home.* Retrieved July 21, 2008, from http://www.nafsa.org/knowledge_com munity_network.sec/teaching_learning_and/internationalizing_the_3/practice_ resources_24/iah_best_practices.

Olson, C. L., Evans, R., & Shoenberg, R. F. (2007). *At home in the world: Bridging the gap between internationalization and multicultural education. Global Learning for All.* Working Papers on Internationalizing Higher Education, 4. Washington, DC: American Council on Education.

Pusch, M. D., & Merrill, M. (2008). Reflection, reciprocity, responsibility, and committed relativism: Intercultural development through international service-learning. In V. Savicki (Ed.), *Developing intercultural competence and transformation: Theory, research, and application in international education* (pp. 297–321). Sterling, VA: Stylus.

Selby, R. (2008). Designing transformation in international education. In V. Savicki (Ed.), *Developing intercultural competence and transformation: Theory, research, and application in international education* (pp. 1–10). Sterling, VA: Stylus.

CAPACITY BUILDING FOR STUDY ABROAD INTEGRATION

The Institution and the Faculty

Elizabeth Brewer and Kiran Cunningham

A recent monograph titled *The Senior International Officer (SIO) as Change Agent* by John Heyl (2007) discusses the conclusions of a series of publications by the American Council on Education (ACE) on the process of change within the institutional context. The project, sponsored by the W. K. Kellogg Foundation and taking place from 1998 through 2001, identified transformational change as "deep, pervasive, intentional [and] long-term" such that the culture of the institution is changed (Heyl, 2007, p. 9). Further, such institutional change requires coalition building among campus units and individuals and should span the institution to include changes in the academic program (curriculum, learning outcomes), budget, and self-image.

Chapter 1 of this volume discusses campus internationalization as an impetus for institutional capacity building in the area of international education. Indeed, this process is enabling both Beloit College and Kalamazoo College to transform their institutions. Although the two colleges have taken different paths toward their internationalization, they have in common an assessment-driven reexamination of their international education programs leading to further institutional transformation. In the case of Beloit, this assessment began with a series of discussions on the role of international education in the liberal arts during the college's annual fall conferences marking the opening of the academic year. These led to changes in the mandate of both the Office of International Education and the Committee on International Education to support campus internationalization more broadly. Previously, the office had primarily focused on the administration of the study abroad program and supports for international students, whereas the committee mostly convened to review study abroad applications. A subsequent self-study and external review of Beloit College's international education program confirmed that the steps taken thus far had been productive in facilitating greater campus internationalization, and led to further internationalization activities, including the study abroad integration work that is the focus of this volume.

At the same time that Beloit College was moving toward greater campus internationalization, Kalamazoo College similarly had reexamined its own approach to study abroad and international education. Funding from the Andrew W. Mellon Foundation and the McGregor Fund supported a new initiative called "Reclaiming International Studies: Helping the Campus Benefit From International Programs," intended to better integrate study abroad with the campus curriculum. One outcome was the course described by Jan Solberg in chapter 3. The larger outcome, however, was the reexamination by the faculty of the institution's goals for international and intercultural learning, and how these might be facilitated by the curriculum at Kalamazoo College. Although the curriculum in Kalamazoo's study abroad programs also would be affected, the primary focus would be on the day-to-day work of the faculty on the home campus.

A focus on internationalization rather than on discrete international activities allows institutions to engage actors across the institution to set out the goals for their programs of international education and to implement them. Furthermore, such a process allows the institution to deploy its resources strategically to further its internationalization, as well as to solicit external resources. Internationalization thus aligns the academic program with budget and self-image, as in the institutional transformation described by Heyl (2007). In doing so, the institution also makes it possible for faculty members to see that their efforts to internationalize their work, and therefore their students' learning, are consonant with institutional mission and priorities.

Writing in the *Journal of Studies of International Education*, Michael Stohl (2007) asserts that assessing institutional progress toward campus internationalization by counting or tabulating markers (the number of students studying abroad or coming from abroad, the number of courses with international content, the number of countries represented in the curriculum or in collaborations, and so on) will not necessarily lead to the kind of internationalization educational institutions want to achieve. Rather, institutions need to understand how internationalization contributes to learning. "If we think of internationalization as how faculty and students (as well as administrators) learn about, learn from, and learn with others, we suggest that internationalization has value in and of itself" (Stohl, 2007, p. 369). He further argues that because transforming learning requires the transformation of faculty members' scholarship, the faculty members' efforts need to be rewarded and recognized (Stohl, 2007).

This transformation of faculty members can be facilitated through the provision of multiple opportunities for growth and professional development. The following section, therefore, discusses a variety of strategies for engaging faculty members with internationalization generally and study abroad integration more specifically.

Linking Faculty Development to Study Abroad Curriculum Integration

If one were to imagine a continuum of activities to engage faculty in the process of integrating study abroad into the on-campus curriculum, it might begin with exposure to study abroad itself, pass through engagement in the study abroad process, and move on to the transformation of the faculty members' teaching and scholarship. Thus, faculty development opportunities designed to engage faculty in curricular integration need to include activities all along this continuum. Moreover, to be effective, faculty development needs to be based on "faculty ownership, choice, and support," integrated with "other internationalization strategies," and reach an ever-expanding "circle of engaged faculty" (Green & Olson, 2003, p. 78). Both Kalamazoo College and Beloit College have developed an array of faculty development opportunities to further study abroad curricular integration and, through it, campus internationalization. These are presented in the following text so that they can serve as models for other institutions.

Faculty travel overseas is a powerful tool in the internationalization of a college or university and in the delivery of an internationalized curriculum to students. "If faculty play such a critical role in international education, then shouldn't we be talking more about study abroad opportunities for those who teach? Otherwise, if we do succeed in getting greater numbers of our students to study abroad, might we end up with faculty members who are less worldly than their students?" (Peterson, 2000, pp. 3–4). This resonates with Mestenhauser's argument, referred to in chapter 1, that faculty members will be more effective international educators if they allow lessons learned from their students to help shape their teaching (Mestenhauser, 1998).

At Kalamazoo College there are several kinds of opportunities available for faculty to gain international experience generally and visit study abroad sites more specifically. The funding for many of these opportunities comes from a combination of operating funds of the Center for International Programs (CIP) and the Isabel Beeler Fund, an endowed fund administered by the CIP to support faculty and student projects abroad. Over the past seven years, about half of the Kalamazoo College faculty have taken advantage of these opportunities to travel abroad for longer or shorter sojourns.

Faculty members frequently take advantage of available CIP funds to conduct site visits to one of the college's study abroad sites. These visits may be undertaken solely for the purpose of visiting the site or in conjunction with a trip already planned to the region for research purposes or to attend a conference. Often the former take place in lieu of visits that would typically be made by CIP staff. As a result, these trips involve meetings with students and on-site staff. Most important for these visits, however, is the opportunity for faculty to talk with their counterparts at the host institution. These conversations lead to better coordination and articulation of courses, and allow faculty to better describe the academic program offered abroad. Because each of the college's 12 study abroad program locations is normally visited each year, there are many opportunities for faculty visits. Indeed, all of the Kalamazoo College contributors to this volume have made a study abroad site visit and either developed new courses or altered the content of existing courses as a result.

The CIP also offers occasional Faculty/Staff Familiarization Study Tours. Since 2002, two of these tours have taken place: one to Oaxaca, Mexico, and San Jose, Costa Rica; and one to Strasbourg, France, Clermont-Ferrand, France, and Madrid, Spain. Approximately six to eight faculty and staff (both clerical and administrative) participated in each tour and, except for nongroup meals and incidentals, all travel and other costs were covered by Kalamazoo College. Finally, Beeler funds are available to support a one-term leave for faculty members conducting research abroad. Ideally, the research is undertaken in or near one of the college's study abroad sites, but that is not a criterion for receiving the funds. The award covers the cost of course replacements for the faculty member and airfare overseas. On average, these funds are used once every two years.

Grant-funded opportunities are also available from time to time. For example, a Freeman Foundation Grant received by Kalamazoo College enabled several faculty members in Asian studies, including Carol Anderson (chapter 4), to lead 2-week summer study tours to China or Japan. Further, a grant from the Andrew W. Mellon Foundation to support faculty development activities at Kalamazoo College will enable Jennifer Redmann (chapter 5) to further develop her sophomore seminar by supporting a visit to Istanbul while she is on sabbatical.

Whether the nature of the trip is a familiarization visit to a study abroad site, a research term abroad, or leading a study tour, an important goal of these kinds of faculty development activities is that the faculty member experience some of what the students go through on study abroad as they adjust to a new linguistic environment, get to know a new academic context, learn to navigate a new city, meet their daily needs, and attend to their studies without recourse to a familiar paradigm. In addition, it is important to provide opportunities for faculty members to connect with their counterparts in academic departments abroad.

When Kalamazoo faculty members return to campus from their time abroad, regardless of how long, they are asked to share something of their visit with their colleagues either in their department or more broadly at a faculty study group. Just as reflection is important for students as a way of translating experience into learning, it is equally so for faculty. Discussing a recent visit overseas at a departmental meeting or study group is one form of structured reflection and thus one more way to move from experience to learning.

Beloit, too, engages faculty in study abroad in a variety of ways. At the most basic level of informing faculty members about study abroad, it has dedicated Web pages for advisors about study abroad and advising sheets by major about study abroad programs. Membership in the Committee on International Education and service as an advisor for a Beloit or consortium program bring faculty into the study abroad process, and help them understand the opportunities and challenges of study abroad for students and their academic departments. Like Kalamazoo, Beloit also provides opportunities for faculty to travel and study abroad, and has been especially attentive to designing opportunities that maximize the potential of the experience to result in on-campus curricular enhancement. A faculty development program administered by a faculty committee, for example, encouraged international engagement by offering a supplemental award for activities that would further institutional collaborations. This program supported the visit of a small delegation to Beloit's partner in Moscow to explore possible connections with Beloit's dance and theater programs, and, as a result, a group of Beloit dancers traveled to Moscow the following summer to participate in an international dance competition, and several individual students have since studied dance while in Moscow. A Russian choreographer also visited Beloit College following the visit for a short residency.

In addition, a consortial project called Global Partners, involving the member institutions of the Associated Colleges of the Midwest, the Colleges of the South, and the Great Lakes Colleges Association, supported the internationalization of liberal arts colleges through study abroad programs and faculty development activities, among others, and focused on Central Europe, Turkey, and East Africa. Beloit College faculty members both participated in group faculty development visits to these locations and received individual grants for visits to the countries involved, resulting in curricular innovations at the college, the incorporation of the countries into research agendas, and the residencies of two East African faculty members as Fulbright Scholars-in-Residence at the college, leading to curricular developments in the Women's and Gender Studies and the Health and Society programs.

Similar to Kalamazoo's familiarization study tours, Beloit also provides opportunities for group visits to study abroad sites. The most recent such visit was to Beloit's partner in Ecuador, the Universidad San Francisco de Quito (USFQ). Faculty from six different disciplines participated, visiting USFQ's campus in the Cumbaya section of Quito. Five faculty subsequently visited USFQ's Riobamba campus, and the sixth visited its Galapagos campus. Support for the visit came from the Andrew W. Mellon Foundation as part of a larger study abroad integration project at Beloit College. For most of the faculty, the main outcome of the visit was a better understanding of the learning opportunities in Quito for their students. However, two faculty, in International Relations and Spanish, are incorporating more materials about Ecuador into their teaching as a way to encourage more study in Ecuador. Further, PowerPoint presentations and large-format posters created by the faculty using photos from the visit are being used to inform students about study opportunities in Ecuador. Interest among biology and environmental studies students in the Galapagos in particular is increasing. Elizabeth Brewer, Darren Kelly, Nancy Krusko, and Pablo Toral, all contributors to this volume, participated in the Ecuador visit, and the other Beloit authors in this volume each have made site visits to other study abroad sites.

The courses discussed by Daniel Youd in chapter 8 and Nancy Krusko in chapter 9 were developed under another of Beloit's faculty development programs: the Cities in Transition project. Created in response to weak study abroad learning outcomes (underdeveloped language skills and understanding of the host countries and peoples) in some study abroad locations, the project was launched by a grant from a one-time faculty initiative fund. The grant supported a weeklong workshop in Beloit, in which representatives of study abroad partners joined Beloit faculty members to develop learning goals for courses intended to engage students more productively and critically with host environments abroad. As a result, two new courses emerged in Dakar, Senegal, and Quito, Ecuador, while a third in Shanghai, China, was significantly updated. In addition to discussing a variety of readings, workshop participants engaged in the kind of activities they might assign their own students. Two subsequent workshops, one in Moscow (funded by a donor), and another in Beloit (funded by the Mellon study abroad integration project) similarly asked faculty to engage in activities they might assign their students. This allowed them not only to test new pedagogical approaches encouraging experiential and intercultural learning, but also to experience for themselves challenges faced by study abroad students as outsiders in environments where they exercise very little social, cultural, and linguistic control. To a large extent, the workshops were intended to help faculty revise their prior understandings of study abroad environments so that they could better help their students "re-vision" what they know, to borrow from Winston (2001, p. 69). All of the Beloit authors in this volume participated in Cities in Transition seminars.

Finally, with funding from the Freeman Foundation, Beloit has offered faculty members the opportunity to participate in three group seminars focusing on China, Hong Kong, and Japan. Preceded by weekly seminar meetings taking place either over six weeks or one semester, the seminars brought together interdisciplinary teams who planned to use the campus seminars and subsequent site visits for teaching and/or research. The composition of the groups included some Asian experts; however, the majority of participants came from outside the Asian Studies program. The campus seminar meetings were devoted to discussion of readings about aspects of the target country, presentations by the participants about the questions and sites they hoped to explore in-country, and basic language instruction. Then, while in-country, participants visited sites relevant to their individual or shared interests and met together to review the day's activities and connect them to prior readings and discussions. Virtually all of the participants in the seminars subsequently developed course assignments based on their participation, several pursued the study of Chinese or Japanese, and others presented or published papers that emerged from the seminars. Elizabeth Brewer, Nancy Krusko, Pablo Toral, and Daniel Youd each participated in these activities.

Until recently, the kind of programmatic attention to curricular integration that is evident in Beloit's group seminars and Cities in Transition project has been less evident at Kalamazoo. However, Kalamazoo College's recently completed strategic plan, which came on the heels of the internationalization process, calls for the creation of globally focused core seminars that foster the integration of study abroad with the on-campus curriculum. Building upon the college's successful first-year seminar program, the new core seminars will be designed mainly for the sophomore and senior years. To promote the creation of these core seminars, the college awarded strategic planning funds in the form of $2,500 summer stipends to develop new sophomore seminars. In the summer of 2008, 21 faculty members were awarded stipends to create sophomore seminars. In addition, for the next three years, Kalamazoo, thanks to a curriculum grant from the Mellon Foundation, has funding for faculty international travel related to the development of these seminars. Anderson, Solberg, Haeckl, and Redmann are all developing sophomore seminars through this program. Although all of their courses are influenced to some degree by the ACE mini-grant-funded work that led to this volume, Redmann's course, "Reading the City in Today's Europe: Berlin, Vienna, Istanbul" is a particularly direct outcome of the initiative.

As the faculty development opportunities at Beloit and Kalamazoo suggest, even institutions fairly advanced in terms of their internationalization efforts need to develop and continually offer a broad range of activities in recognition of the turnover in faculty, disciplinary and institutional developments, and changes in the political and economic conditions surrounding internationalization efforts. Perhaps most importantly, faculty members, just as is true of students, need opportunities to move beyond the boundaries of what they already know. Chapter 1 in this volume discusses the importance of teaching students to learn experientially and interculturally. Other chapters, and especially chapter 11, provide examples of how courses and advising can also help students connect their experiential and intercultural learning to their disciplinary studies, both while abroad and on the home campus. These courses came about because, for example, faculty development activities allowed faculty members normally at home teaching literary texts to develop and practice experiential learning techniques so that their students engage more effectively with the environments outside the classroom. Similarly, science faculty members became more expert at helping their students navigate new linguistic and cultural environments by doing so themselves.

Faculty development activities thus must continue to inform and engage individual faculty and departments in campus activities and encourage ownership of study abroad programs through site visits. Further, study abroad integration will be advanced if faculty members engage in interdisciplinary inquiries about the nature of international education and study abroad and the relationships of these to their teaching, research, and advising. Finally, as seen in the next section, the home curriculum itself can be transformed to support study abroad integration if faculty members are given opportunities to develop new pedagogical approaches and areas of expertise, through both group project and individual initiatives.

Integration for Transformation

As we strive to build the capacity for greater curricular integration, it is critical that we not lose sight of the reason that this integration is important, namely student learning. This volume began with the assertion in chapter 1 that linking study abroad more closely with the on-campus curriculum will dramatically increase the probability that the kind of transformative learning we hope to see in students who study abroad actually occurs. We argue that for students to experience this kind of learning while abroad, they need to be developmentally ready and equipped with an intercultural toolkit of essential knowledge, attitudes, and skills. Moreover, we claim that equipping students with that toolkit is itself a strategy for helping them achieve developmental readiness and connecting their study abroad to their studies on the home campus. The subsequent chapters in the book provide examples of courses and advising across the curriculum—from the humanities, social sciences, and natural sciences—designed to help students amass key elements of their intercultural toolkit and achieve this readiness as well as integrate their study abroad learning with their ongoing studies upon return from abroad.

Key to the knowledge compartment of the toolkit is place-based knowledge, linguistic knowledge, and knowledge of intercultural theory. The courses described by Redmann (chapter 5), Kelly (chapter 6), and Haeckl and Manwell (chapter 7) all use a focus on cities to help students become familiar with their study abroad site, while at the same time developing language skills (Redmann) or experiential-learning skills (Haeckl and Manwell, Kelly) essential to the navigation of the cities in which students will live. Kelly (chapter 6), Youd (chapter 8), Krusko (chapter 9), and Fass and Fraser (chapter 10) also focus on place-based knowledge, providing students with the tools to understand the ecological and public health contexts of their study abroad sites. In addition, they discuss strategies for helping returned students process the knowledge they learned while abroad and integrate it back into their biology major (Fass and Fraser) or other studies (Krusko). Working with returning students to more fully process and build upon the knowledge gained on study abroad is also the focus of Toral (chapter 11). He describes strategies for connecting their learning with future career possibilities, thus using the senior thesis as a vehicle for truly capturing the transformative potential of study abroad.

Providing students with a knowledge of intercultural theory is a key element of the courses described by Brewer and Solberg (chapter 3). Not only do students become familiar with important theory about intercultural dynamics in these courses, but they learn about how it will play out in their own experiences abroad, providing them with important tools for understanding the cognitive and emotional ups and downs they will experience. Also essential to the knowledge toolkit is knowledge of self, or positionality; this is addressed by Brewer and Solberg and by Anderson and Cunningham.

Providing students with the tools to unpack and understand their own cultural assumptions is a key dimension of the course described by Anderson and Cunningham (chapter 4). They use theory, fieldwork, and structured reflection to help students learn how to bracket and then examine their own cultural assumptions and positionality vis-à-vis the cultural group with whom they are interacting through their fieldwork. The chapters by both Brewer and Solberg and Anderson and Cunningham also address key components of the attitudes compartment of the intercultural toolkit, particularly those connected with suspending judgment and embracing ambiguity.

The skills compartment of the toolkit is composed of various tools associated with effective experiential learning: observing, listening, describing, interpreting, verifying, explaining, and reflecting. Several courses described in this volume use experiential learning very explicitly as a strategy for helping students develop these tools: Kelly (chapters 2 and 6), Brewer and Solberg (chapter 3), Anderson and Cunningham (chapter 4), Haeckl and Manwell (chapter 7), Youd (chapter 8), Krusko (chapter 9), and Fass and Fraser (chapter 10). These authors, grounded in perspectives as diverse as science and literary criticism, all discuss the importance of helping students learn how to closely observe and carefully describe their observations without interpretation or explanation.

Several chapters also discuss the importance of working with students to develop the skills and habits of reflection. Krusko (chapter 9), Brewer and Solberg (chapter 3), Anderson and Cunningham (chapter 4), Kelly (chapter 6), and Haeckl and Manwell (chapter 7) all discuss reflection as critical not only to understanding who and what one is studying, but also to understanding who and what one is becoming. In addition to describing strategies for and, in some cases, the outcomes of this reflection, these authors connect the learning about how to engage in structured reflection with the development of other intercultural knowledge, attitudes, and skills such as positionality, suspending judgment, curiosity and openness to learning, and distinguishing among description, interpretation, and explanation.

The chapters in this volume also offer a variety of strategies for structurally connecting learning on campus with learning off campus. For example, Krusko describes a course in which a trip to Nicaragua is embedded into an "on-campus" course; Youd describes a course taught mainly from Beloit College to students studying in China; Redmann argues for embedding a more comprehensive preparation for study abroad into the language curriculum;

one of the courses described by Brewer and Solberg spans the time before, during, and after study abroad; Toral as well as Fass and Fraser describe strategies for connecting study abroad directly to the major, advising structures, and senior capstone experiences; and several authors (e.g., Anderson and Cunningham, Haeckl and Manwell, and Krusko) describe various strategies for connecting service- and community-based learning with study abroad.

Conclusion

The courses discussed in these chapters provide an extensive repertoire of pedagogical strategies for equipping students with an intercultural toolkit and a level of developmental readiness that will allow them to take full advantage of the transformative potential of their study abroad experience. As these courses attest, there are multiple materials, structures, and pedagogies that can be used as vehicles for providing this readiness for transformative learning. Moreover, no one discipline or set of disciplines can claim to own the key to study abroad integration. Indeed, through the wise and creative use of faculty development activities, faculty across the institution can be encouraged to incorporate pedagogical strategies such as these into their courses.

Reflecting on the processes that led to the creation of the courses presented in this volume, we are struck by the ways in which the process of developing, teaching, and revising the courses functioned as a form of faculty development in itself. The process put the authors into situations similar to those their students experience and forced them to make the same kind of connections between out-of-classroom learning and classroom learning that they want for their students. They were greatly aided in the process by dialogue and discussion within disciplines, across disciplines, and across institutions, which enabled them to advance their understandings of study abroad's potential and its implications for their work. Thus, the project and process of integrating study abroad into the curriculum are at once a vehicle for transforming faculty members, students, and educational institutions, *and* for teaching and learning abroad and at home. It is just this kind of transformation that is hoped for when colleges and universities, international higher-education associations, government agencies, and foundations and private donors take up the call for the continued internationalization of higher education and the expansion and improvement of study abroad.

References

Green, M. F. & Olson, C. (2003). *Internationalizing the campus: A user's guide.* American Council on Education: Center for Institutional and International Initiatives.

Heyl, J. D. (2007). *The senior international officer (SIO) as change agent.* [Monograph]. Durham, NC: Association of International Education Administrators.

Mestenhauser, J. A. (1998). Portraits of an international curriculum: An uncommon multidimensional perspective. In J. A. Mestenhauser & B. S. Ellingboe (Eds.), *Reforming the higher education curriculum: Internationalizing the campus* (pp. 3–39). Phoenix, AZ: American Council on Education and Oryx Press.

Peterson, P. (2000). The worthy goal of a worldly faculty. *Peer Review, 3*(1), 3–7.

Stohl, M. (2007, Fall/Winter). We have met the enemy and he is us: The role of the faculty in the internationalization of higher education in the coming decade. *Journal of Studies in International Education, 11*(3/4), 359–372.

Winston, R. P. (2001, Fall). Discipline and interdiscipline: Approaches to study abroad. *Frontiers: The Interdisciplinary Journal of Study Abroad, 6,* 61–93.

Carol S. Anderson is professor of religion and women's studies at Kalamazoo College. She is the author of *Pain and Its Ending: A Study of the Four Noble Truths in Theravāda Buddhism* (Curzon, 1999), and co-editor of *Embedded Languages: Studies in Religion, Culture, and History of Sri Lanka* (Godage, 2009). She has also published articles on women in Hinduism, lay Buddhism in the 19th century, and feminism and South Asian studies in religion. Her research and teaching focuses on religion in South Asia, and feminist and post-colonial approaches to the study of religion.

Elizabeth Brewer is Director of International Education at Beloit College. Her experience includes work in international education at Boston University and the University of Massachusetts at Amherst and graduate student affairs at the New School for Social Research, as well as service as a Peace Corps volunteer in Slovakia prior to coming to Beloit College. The latter has influenced her work with students and faculty to encourage productive and critical engagement with local environments. Since arriving at Beloit, her work has also focused on the integration of study abroad with the curriculum. She has presented on international education topics at a number of conferences and published on community development and international education topics. Her Ph.D. is in German literature.

Kiran Cunningham is the Kurt D. Kaufman Professor of Anthropology at Kalamazoo College. At the core of her teaching, scholarship, and service is using action research to catalyze social change. As an action researcher, she works with communities and organizations desiring change and uses participatory research methods to bring a broad range of community members into the change process. This work has led to publications in several fields including community mental health, higher education reform, and community transformation. She led Kalamazoo College's comprehensive internationalization planning process, and is currently working on designing a developmental approach to embedding transformative learning in the undergraduate curriculum.

Marion Field Fass is professor of biology at Beloit College, where she has taught since 1991. She is one of the co-creators, with Nancy A. Krusko, of Beloit's interdisciplinary health and society major. Marion initiated a course on AIDS in the World in 1991, and realized quickly that she would need to travel more widely to be able to teach her students about the complexities of HIV and public health. Since then she has traveled to South Africa, Kenya, Tanzania, and Senegal, to learn and to teach about HIV/AIDS. Marion is active in biology education reform efforts through the BioQUEST Curriculum Consortium and the SENCER (Science Education for New Civic Engagements and Responsibilities) project. She co-edited a book of educational activities in microbiology called "Microbes Count!"(ASM Press, 2002) and is completing "Case Investigations in Human Biology and Global Health," which is scheduled for publication in 2010.

Ann M. Fraser received her B.S. in biology from Acadia University in Canada and her Ph.D. in biology from Harvard University. She is an associate professor of biology at Kalamazoo College, where she teaches classes in evolution, animal behavior, entomology, and organism diversity. Her research addresses questions related to the ecology and evolution of species interactions and biological diversity. She has conducted field research in Costa Rica, Australia, and the United States.

Anne E. Haeckl is a Roman archaeologist and art historian (B.A. in Classical Greek from the College of Wooster; M.A. and ABD for the Ph.D. in Classical Art and Archaeology from the University of Michigan) who since 1998 has been an instructor in the Classics Department at Kalamazoo College. Her scholarship centers on archaeological fieldwork in the Roman provinces (the Dermech site, Roman circus, and Yasmina Necropolis in Carthage, Tunisia; the Roman legionary fortress at El-Lejjun and Hauran town of Umm el-Jimal in Jordan; the Red Sea ports of Berenike and Marsa Nakari in Egypt), although her most recent project (2003–2006) took her to Rome as Co-Director of the Kalamazoo College/University of Colorado Excavations at the Villa of Maxentius on the Via Appia. Most of her excavations have included on-site archaeological field schools where college students gain experiential, international education in the discipline.

Darren Kelly has lectured on comparative literature, post-colonial Irish literature, theory, modernism, travel writing, film, and drama at St. Patrick's

College, Dublin City University, Ireland and has written and directed several plays. He teaches Communal Irish Identity for IES Dublin, an interdisciplinary course specifically created for American study abroad students, and has designed and taught summer courses for Temple University and the University of Notre Dame. A Fulbright Scholar-in-Residence at Beloit College, 2007–2008, he earned an interdisciplinary Ph.D. in Geography, for which he studied the socioeconomic, cultural, and political forces contributing to the segregation of non-Irish nationals in Dublin and contemporary Irish identity. His current research focuses on American study abroad students' use of the Internet, the impacts of this use on their study abroad experiences, and how Internet use might be subverted to strengthen the study abroad experience.

Nancy Krusko is professor and chair of the Anthropology Department at Beloit College. She teaches courses in biological anthropology, human osteology, primate behavioral ecology, medical anthropology, interdisciplinary studies, and women's health. Nancy received her B.A., M.A., and Ph.D. in anthropology from the University of California, Berkeley. Her current research focuses on community health assessment in Rock County Wisconsin and studying the relationship between biology and culture on health related issues. Her most recent work examines the hygiene hypothesis and its relationship to the increase of allergy and asthma in developed areas of the world.

Elizabeth A. Manwell is the Sally Appleton Kirkpatrick Assistant Professor of Classical Studies at Kalamazoo College in Kalamazoo, Michigan. She has written on Latin lyric and epic poetry, Greek elegy and tragedy, the reception of classical texts in contemporary America, and is currently at work on a book about bodily functions and fantasies in the poetry of Catullus, a Roman poet of the first century BCE. She teaches courses in Ancient Greek and Latin language, as well as an array of courses on the ancient world and continues to experiment with ways to pair experiential learning and the study of the antiquity.

Jennifer Redmann is associate professor of German at Kalamazoo College. She received her Ph.D. in German literature at the University of Wisconsin-Madison with a dissertation on an early 20th-century German-Jewish poet,

Else Lasker-Schüler. She has published articles on German-Jewish literature and culture, women's literature, children's and youth literature, and autobiography, as well as foreign language pedagogy and curricular reform. She is currently working on a comparative study of series literature for adolescent girls published in the United States and Germany between 1850 and 1950, and she is co-author (with Pennylyn Dykstra-Pruim) of a forthcoming German textbook for developing writing skills (*Schreib mal wieder! A Writing Guide for Students of German*, Yale University Press, 2010).

Janet Solberg is professor of Romance Languages and Literature at Kalamazoo College. She received her Ph.D. in French from the University of Minnesota in 1988. Her main areas of interest are 16th century French short narrative, francophone literature (especially the literatures of sub-Saharan Africa and Asia), intercultural communication, and second language acquisition. In addition to teaching French language and literature courses, she teaches "Cross-Cultural Understanding and Intercultural Communication," a course designed specifically for students studying abroad. Her publications include *Controverses*, a French textbook.

Pablo Toral is associate professor of international relations at Beloit College. He teaches courses in international political economy, environmental politics, development, international governance, international relations of Latin America and Europe and peace studies. Pablo received his Ph.D. in international relations from Florida International University in 2003. He also holds a B.A. in journalism and an M.A. in international studies. His main research interests include political economy of the environment, multinational enterprises, development, social theory, and pedagogy. His publications include *Multinational Enterprises in Latin America* (New York: Palgrave, forthcoming 2010), *Latin America's Quest for Globalization: The Role of Spanish Firms* (edited with Felix E. Martin) (London: Ashgate, 2005) and *The Reconquest of the New World. Multinational Enterprises and Spain's Direct Investment in Latin America* (London: Ashgate, 2001).

Daniel Youd is associate professor of Chinese language and literature at Beloit College and chair of the Department of Modern Languages and Literatures. He received his Ph.D. in East Asian Studies from Princeton University. Both his teaching and research interests center on Ming and Qing dynasty vernacular fiction, comparative literature, and translation studies.